C000218834

HUMAN RIGHTS OF, BY, ⎰
FOR THE PEOPLE

Together, the US Constitution and the Bill of Rights comprise the constitutional foundation of the United States. These—the oldest governing documents still in use in the world—urgently need an update, just as the constitutions of other countries have been updated and revised. *Human Rights Of, By, and For the People* brings together lawyers and sociologists to show how globalization and climate change offer an opportunity to revisit the founding documents. Each proposes specific changes that would more closely align US law with international law. The chapters also illustrate how constitutions are embedded in society and shaped by culture. The constitution itself sets up contentious relationships among the three branches of government and between the federal government and each state government, while the Bill of Rights and subsequent amendments begrudgingly recognize the civil and political rights of citizens. These rights are described by legal scholars as "negative rights," specifically as freedoms from infringements rather than as positive rights that affirm personhood and human dignity. The contributors to this volume offer "positive rights" instead. The Universal Declaration of Human Rights (UDHR), written in the middle of the last century, inspires these updates. Nearly every other constitution in the world has adopted language from the UDHR.

The contributors use intersectionality, critical race theory, and contemporary critiques of runaway economic inequality to ground their interventions in sociological argument.

Keri E. Iyall Smith is Associate Professor of Sociology at Suffolk University in Boston, Massachusetts and is author of *The State and Indigenous Movements* (Routledge).

Louis Edgar Esparza is Assistant Professor of Sociology and Latin American Studies at California State University at Los Angeles.

Judith R. Blau is Professor Emerita at the University of North Carolina–Chapel Hill, retiring in 2014 after a teaching career that spanned forty-five years.

HUMAN RIGHTS OF, BY, AND FOR THE PEOPLE

How to Critique and Change the US Constitution

Edited by Keri E. Iyall Smith, Louis Edgar Esparza, and Judith R. Blau

Routledge
Taylor & Francis Group

NEW YORK AND LONDON

First published 2017
by Routledge
711 Third Avenue, New York, NY 10017

and by Routledge
2 Park Square, Milton Park, Abingdon, Oxon, OX14 4RN

Routledge is an imprint of the Taylor & Francis Group, an informa business

© 2017 Taylor & Francis

The right of the editors to be identified as the authors of the editorial material, and of the authors for their individual chapters, has been asserted in accordance with sections 77 and 78 of the Copyright, Designs and Patents Act 1988.

All rights reserved. No part of this book may be reprinted or reproduced or utilized in any form or by any electronic, mechanical, or other means, now known or hereafter invented, including photocopying and recording, or in any information storage or retrieval system, without permission in writing from the publishers.

Trademark notice: Product or corporate names may be trademarks or registered trademarks, and are used only for identification and explanation without intent to infringe.

Every effort has been made to contact copyright-holders. Please advise the publisher of any errors or omissions, and these will be corrected in subsequent editions.

Library of Congress Cataloging in Publication Data
Names: Iyall Smith, Keri E., 1973– editor. | Esparza, Louis Edgar, editor. |
Blau, Judith R., 1942– editor.
Title: Human rights of, by, and for the people: how to
critique and change the US Constitution / edited by Keri E. Iyall Smith,
Louis Edgar Esparza, and Judith R. Blau.
Description: New York, NY: Routledge is
an imprint of the Taylor & Francis Group, an Informa Business, [2017]
Identifiers: LCCN 2016036313 | ISBN 9781138204164 (hbk) |
ISBN 9781138204188 (pbk) | ISBN 9781315470016 (ebk)
Subjects: LCSH: Human rights—United States. | Constitutional amendments—United States. |
Constitutional law—United States. | United States. Constitution.
Classification: LCC KF4749 .H75 2017 | DDC 342.7308/5—dc23
LC record available at https://lccn.loc.gov/2016036313

ISBN: 978-1-138-20416-4 (hbk)
ISBN: 978-1-138-20418-8 (pbk)
ISBN: 978-1-315-47001-6 (ebk)

Typeset in Bembo
by Out of House Publishing

To Change!

CONTENTS

ILLUSTRATIONS

Figures

Tables

Boxes

CONTRIBUTORS

Kathleen B. Basile is a graduate student in Sociology at East Carolina University and holds a B.S. in Sociology from the same university. She is the recipient of several academic awards and values her membership in the Alpha Kappa Delta and Phi Kappa Phi honor societies, as well as the National Society of Leadership and Success. Katie is planning to teach Sociology courses at the post-secondary level upon earning her M.A. and is excited about the prospect of introducing students to a broad range of social issues and concerns. Her hope is to inspire the next generation to seek social justice and equality for all those who cannot speak for themselves. Katie's contribution concerning Women's Rights, co-authored with Dr. Susan Pearce, is her first publication.

Judith R. Blau is retired from the University of North Carolina and lives on Cape Cod. She has published books and articles on human rights, architecture, and art. See https://en.wikipedia.org/wiki/Judith_Blau.

Rodney D. Coates was born in East St. Louis, Ill., received his B.A. from Southern Illinois University, an M.A. in sociology and anthropology from the University of Illinois, and a second M.A. and Ph.D. in sociology from the University of Chicago. He holds the rank of professor in the Department of Global and Intercultural Studies at Miami University. Dr. Coates specializes in the study of race and ethnic relations, inequality, critical race theory, and social justice. He has published dozens of articles; several edited books, and frequently writes on issues of race and ethnicity, education and public policy, civil rights, and social justice. His 2004 edited book *Race and Ethnicity: Across time, space and discipline* won the Choice award from the American Library Association. In 2007, he received the Joseph Himes Career Award in Scholarship and Activism from the Association of Black Sociologists. In

2010–2011 he received the Edward Said Award for Public Sociology & Poetry, Sociologists without Borders. In 2014, he received the Founders Award from ASA's Section on Race and Ethnic Minorities. Dr. Coates is an associate editor for *Critical Sociology* and is on the editorial board for *Social Problems*. He has served on the Ford Foundation Dissertation and Post-Dissertation Sociological Panel for multiple years. He is currently finalizing a co-authored volume on *The Social Construction of Race* under contract with SAGE.

Leah Edwards is a recent graduate of Denison University with a double major in International Studies and Spanish. She studied abroad in Ecuador and began a research focus on environmental and human rights specifically as it relates to the oil spills on indigenous lands. As such, Leah's senior thesis focused on the power of the transnational advocacy network in protecting human rights, specifically with regards to transnational corporate power.

Zachary Elkins is Associate Professor in the Department of Government at the University of Texas at Austin. His research focuses on issues of democracy, institutional reform, research methods, and national identity, with an emphasis on cases in Latin America. He co-directs the Comparative Constitutions Project and the web resource, Constitute. He earned his B.A. from Yale University, his M.A. from the University of Texas at Austin, and his Ph.D. from the University of California, Berkeley.

Steven L. Foy is an Assistant Professor of Sociology at the University of Texas Rio Grande Valley. His work is situated at the intersection of medical sociology, social psychology, and the sociology of race and ethnicity and primarily focuses on stigma, mental health, and racial construction and attribution.

Mark Frezzo is Associate Professor of Sociology, University of Mississippi. He has published a number of articles and books in the areas of human rights, social movements, development, and globalization. His book, *The Sociology of Human Rights* (Polity 2014), establishes a theoretical and conceptual framework for the sociological analysis of debates on and struggles over human rights. He serves as Secretary-Treasurer of the Thematic Group on Human Rights and Global Justice in the International Sociological Association.

Tom Ginsburg is the Deputy Dean and Leo Spitz Professor of International Law at the University of Chicago, where he also holds an appointment in the Political Science Department. He holds B.A., J.D., and Ph.D. degrees from the University of California at Berkeley.

Keri E. Iyall Smith is Associate Professor of Sociology at Suffolk University in Boston, Massachusetts. She is the author of *The State and Indigenous Movements*, and several articles on indigenous peoples. With David L. Brunsma and Brian K. Gran, she is co-editor of *The Handbook of Sociology and Human Rights*, which received an Honorable Mention for the 2014 Hirabayashi Book Award from the American Sociological Association's Section on Human Rights.

Ben Manski is President of the Liberty Tree Foundation, Director of Special Initiatives with the Next System Project, and an Associate Fellow with the Institute for Policy Studies. Manski is pursuing a doctorate in sociology at the University of California, Santa Barbara; he has a J.D. from the University of Wisconsin (2005), and practiced public interest, non-profit, and cooperative law for eight years in Wisconsin. His recent academic publications include *The Democratic Turn of the Century: Learning from the US democracy movement* (*Socialism and Democracy*) and *Seattle WTO Uprising Still a Force in World Events, 15 Years Later* (*Berkeley Journal of Sociology*). Manski has contributed to six books and published many articles for popular audiences on topics ranging from home rule, to higher education, corporatization, democracy, and national security. See www.BenManski.com.

Autumn McClellan is a Sociology Ph.D. student at the University of North Carolina–Chapel Hill. She has served as the Administrative Manager for Sociologists without Borders–US for many years, where she coordinated communications and web hosting for the member-driven "Constitutional Convention" classroom project in the Spring of 2015. This collaborative effort quickly coalesced into this publication, for which Autumn served as a communications liaison and provided proofreading and copyediting for the chapters. Her dissertation evaluates traditional pathways to social movement participation in an online context using experimental data. Her career goals include teaching and mentoring low-income and first-generation college students.

James Melton most recently served as Senior Lecturer in Comparative Politics in the Department of Political Science at University College London, UK, from 2012–2015. Before joining UCL, he was an Assistant Professor at the IMT Institute for Advanced Studies in Lucca, Italy. He holds a B.A. from Illinois Wesleyan University, and M.A. and Ph.D. degrees from the University of Illinois, Urbana-Champaign. His research focuses on how the design of formal institutions contributes to economic, political, and social development. He recently published an edited volume that analyzes the historic and contemporary influence of Magna Carta entitled *Magna Carta and Its Modern Legacy* (with Robert Hazell).

Steven Panageotou is a Ph.D. candidate at the University of Tennessee–Knoxville. His dissertation addresses the political role of corporations in US democracy by offering a theory of how corporate political power is constituted. He has published on political sociology, the connection between critical theory and democratic theory, and the Greek financial crisis.

Susan C. Pearce is Associate Professor of Sociology at East Carolina University, in North Carolina. She would like to acknowledge the Sociology Department of East Carolina University for its support of this curricular experiment. See www.ecu.edu/cs-cas/soci/Susan-Pearce.cfm.

K. Russell Shekha is an Assistant Professor of Sociology in the Department of Anthropology & Sociology at Denison University. In the spirit of the liberal arts college mission, he works across disciplinary boundaries collaborating with the Environmental Studies Program, the International Studies Program, advising student-led research projects across these departments, and is the faculty adviser for the Denison Student/Farmworker Alliance. He publishes on the intersections of human rights and the welfare state in Latin American countries and on the determinants of human rights attitudes, beliefs, and commitments, as well as teaching classes on human rights, social and global justice, and research methods. He is also active in the American Sociological Association's Section on Human Rights serving as the Secretary-Treasurer from 2014–2016 and is the current section Newsletter Editor. He is a Research Scholar for the Binzagr Institute for Sustainable Prosperity. Finally, he is a member and Secretary of the Board of Trustees for the Welsh Hills School in Granville, Ohio.

Davita Silfen Glasberg is College of Liberal Arts and Sciences Associate Dean of Social Sciences at the University of Connecticut, and a Professor of Sociology. Her co-edited book (with William T. Armaline and Bandana Purkayastha), *Human Rights in Our Own Back Yard: Injustice and resistance in the United States* (University of Pennsylvania Press), received the Hirabayashi Book Award for Best Book from the American Sociological Association's Human Rights Section in 2012. Other recent books include *The Human Rights Enterprise: The state, resistance, and human rights* (with William T. Armaline and Bandana Purkayastha) (Polity Press) and *Political Sociology: Oppression, resistance, and the state* (with Deric Shannon) (Sage/Pine Forge Press).

ACKNOWLEDGMENTS

Together we thank Autumn McClellan for her tireless efforts as we worked on this book. Without her, the book and our group would have been the lesser.

Keri E. Iyall Smith would like to thank the Suffolk University College of Arts and Sciences, which granted her sabbatical leave to complete this project. She also thanks Clarence and True for their support and encouragement.

Judith R. Blau would like to thank the Wellfleet Library for inviting her to lead a seminar on revising the constitution, which led to her teaching a course at the Cape Cod Community College.

1

CONSTITUTING HUMAN RIGHTS IN THE US

Keri E. Iyall Smith

What if we really did learn everything we needed to know in kindergarten? I recall summer days with fingers stained purple by Bing cherries. A cherry tree grew in my neighbor's yard and when they were ripe you could find all of the neighborhood children under that tree. We were a cooperative bunch. First we would pick cherries together, gathering the harvest in a hammock. Smaller children picked from the branches they could reach, taller ones reached high or bent branches down for the little ones. Adventurous children climbed high and handed the cherries down to others who would transport the fruit to a grow- ing pile. Once we had picked all of the ripe cherries we could find—leaving the less ripe ones for later in the week and dropping the bird pecked ones for the birds to finish—we would gather in the shade. One of the older kids would create piles of cherries for each of us. It was not a precise accounting, but an eyeball estimate. Younger children would choose their lot first and the person who made the piles received the last allotment. Then we would all enjoy our bounty together. As children we knew and valued what the US Constitution does not acknowledge: cooperation, collaboration, dignity, equality, honor, and trust are best enjoyed together—of, by, and for *the people*.

Societies, it turns out, can create moral systems that promote human rights. Friesen's (2014) study of moral systems and human nature uncovers scientific studies of many species that are intolerant of gross inequality, need social engage- ment, and protect others within the group. The US—as it currently stands—is not one of these societies and yet it is made up of people who may indeed be born to protect the human rights of themselves and others. Our humanness, Friesen (2014) points out, makes us only more vulnerable and in greater need of human rights. For instance, we lack fur and we require a long period of socialization and development as young people, among other things. Living as humans together in society means that we can reject Darwin's survival of the fittest. Rather, humans create societies for the good of all and perpetuate these societies through norms and values, socialization, and regulation.

For countries the root of regulation is the constitution. Most countries have embraced human rights, which is to say that their constitutions encompass the broad spectrum of rights that are proclaimed in the Universal Declaration of Human Rights (UDHR) (Beck, Drori, and Meyer 2012). These include economic, social, cultural, political, and civil rights. The 1791 Bill of Rights and its few amendments[1] (most notably to end slavery and enfranchise blacks and women) comprise civil and political rights, not positive rights that most constitutions embrace. Indeed, in the twenty-first century many countries, in recognition of climate change, have further amended their constitutions to include environmental rights. Others have formally changed their constitutions to recognize the rights of LGBT people, and a few, including Greece, recognize that access to the internet is a human right. In other words, the conception of constitutions can be dynamic while resting on the bedrock principles of human dignity and equality. Whether a constitution is dead or alive should not be the primary issue, rather what is the best constitution?

What is the Best Constitution?

The US Constitution is one of the world's oldest, garnering deep respect and pride. Examining attitudes of respondents to questions about the understanding of the constitution as utilized in the work of the Supreme Court, conservatives overwhelmingly support the understanding of its meaning as it was originally written: 88 percent of steadfast conservatives and 74 percent of business conservatives (Pew Research Center 2014). Nearly half of the general population (46%) agrees. Yet, 49 percent of the general population believes the Supreme Court should apply an understanding of the constitution's meaning in current times. This is reflected in the beliefs of solid liberals (84%), faith and family left (53%), and the next generation left (68%). To assert that the constitution is a living document *or* a dead document is a polarizing statement (Balkin 2010; Dorf 2012; Strauss 2010; and Strauss 2012).

In this reverence Dunbar-Ortiz (2014) sees a nod to the perception that the US Constitution is a covenant with more than political meaning but something akin to being sacred. The US Constitution, written in 1789 and last updated in 1992, represents the interests of its authors: elite, landholding, white males. Even with the changes found in the Bill of Rights and beyond, which offer modest expansions of freedoms and protections, the US Constitution is not representative of the US population as a whole—either in 1789 or 2016.

Elsewhere we find examples of new constitutions: The United States has been an ardent supporter of Afghanistan's new constitution, pressing for changes to protect human rights. The resulting document offers special protections for women, families, the elderly, children, disabled persons, and more. Article 32 states that "Debt shall not curtail or deprive the freedom of the individual." Might a college student's debt burden be unconstitutional in Afghanistan? Might the current US elections system, which results in a congress consisting of 80 percent men and 20 percent women, be unconstitutional in Afghanistan, which requires female representation from each province?

Yet the United States turns a blind eye to actions within its states that violate the constitution or threaten the human rights and dignity of its citizens. Thirty-one states and the federal government practice the death penalty—a violation of the UDHR. US citizens experience increasingly precarious privacy, as revealed by Snowden, questions surrounding the San Bernardino shooter's phone, and via the widespread use of body scanning devices or enhanced pat down in airports. Within the United States human rights are in competition rather than in harmony: one person's right to wellbeing conflicts with another person's right to hold private property, one person's right to free speech through campaign donations threatens another person's right to participate in electoral politics (Bonds 2014). A country of immigrants denies the rights of citizen children to family if their parents did not enter the country legally or have overstayed their visas. We could write a book about this—in fact we have and you are holding it in your hands.

Modern constitutions recognize the emergence of human rights, cultural rights, economic rights, political rights, the importance of gender equality, the environment, and so much more. The US Constitution, last updated in 1992 and never rewritten, does not acknowledge these rights. Even the Bill of Rights (ratified in 1791), offers an expansion of the rights of US citizens, yet this pales in comparison to human rights doctrine. Inspired by constitutions from around the world and human rights instruments (especially the Universal Declaration of Human Rights, the International Covenant on Economic, Social, and Cultural Rights, and the International Covenant on Civil and Political Rights, plus more recent UN Declarations), a team of sociologists, activists, and lawyers are examining what it would mean to produce a US Constitution that is of the people, by the people, for the people.

In an era of Edward Snowden, threats to voting rights, corporate personhood and speech, a choice between oil or water within the US and beyond our borders, expanding capitalism, climate change, and critical reviews of the US human rights record, it is time for a book like *Human Rights Of, By, and For the People*. Seeing the dated US Constitution as an opportunity, authors of this volume shared in a teaching project that quickly expanded to encompass our research and writing. An important new resource is the Constitute Project, which includes all state (country) constitutions, with useful search and compare functions. Constituteproject. org is a way to empower citizens as new constitutions are written around the world—including citizens in the US. In spring 2015 all of the authors who contributed to this volume taught classes designed to revise the Bill of Rights and the students used the Constitute Project webpage to research how other constitutions framed human rights. Two principle investigators of Constitute Project—Zachary Elkins and Tom Ginsburg—are the authors of Chapter 14 in this volume.

A Path to Change

This book is divided into three parts, offering a journey to expanded rights through constitutional change. To familiarize you with the current state of the US Constitution, procedures for change, and the role of history in attitudes towards the constitution and its protections (or lack thereof), we start by examining what is going on in the US. How does our constitution compare to those of other countries? Blau reveals in Chapter 2 that our peers and even those in less-developed countries enjoy greater rights as enshrined within their constitutions. Manski offers an explanation of how the constitution can be changed through legal pathways in Chapter 3 and Coates (Chapter 4) gives a narrative revealing how the US arrived at this point both in our society and our history.

With some knowledge of the current constitution, we move on to chapters that assert the importance of integrating human rights into the US Constitution. Pearce and Basile (Chapter 5) examine the ways that the US Constitution fails to address the rights of women and LGBTQI people. Blau examines the rights of vulnerable populations in her chapter on equality (Chapter 6). Economic security is examined, looking at basic income (Panageotou, Chapter 7) and basic needs such as housing, food, and health care (Foy, Chapter 8). To better understand the importance of including the environment in the US Constitution, Shekha and Edwards (Chapter 9) look at constitutions in the Americas. There they explore how different kinds of human rights are in fact interconnected. Blau (Chapter 10) then identifies the particular vulnerabilities that may unfold as the effects of climate change are felt. In these six chapters we find ways to imagine a new society if changes to the US Constitution are indeed achieved.

Finally, we need to explore how to achieve change through social action in the US. This section begins with an examination of the role of sociological study and teaching in human rights (Frezzo, Chapter 11). Silfen Glasberg (Chapter 12) presents one model for studying the US Constitution in the sociological classroom. To assist your thinking about what a new US Constitution might look like, Iyall Smith (Chapter 13) makes the case for a decolonized constitution that is informed by the laws and norms of indigenous nations. Elkins, Ginsburg, and Melton (Chapter 14) examine other constitutions informed by the Universal Declaration of Human Rights and underscore the fact that the US remains an outlier—being one of the few constitutions around the world without human rights protections. Blau (Chapter 15) concludes the volume, calling for a modern US Constitution that embraces human rights for all.

CVS

By its very nature, *Human Rights Of, By, and For the People* is a revolutionary project seeking to rewrite the way that United Statesians live and experience their freedoms and duties as citizens. It is timely for a new constitution to emerge: people are increasingly interconnected, which expands our awareness of how our country upholds human rights; human rights are expanding in international governance which presents a growing contrast with the Bill of Rights, climate change, the US Government is violating the Bill of Rights; and the US just completed its second Universal Periodic Review within the United Nations system. The result: it is increasingly clear that our citizenship rights within the United States pale in comparison to the citizenship rights of others around the world—even some of the least-developed countries. This is happening at the same time that both globally and locally, we are more vulnerable and precariously positioned, thus we have a greater need of protections as citizens.

But how do we start? Most of your friends and family have probably not read the US Constitution since high school (unless they are lawyers). Take a little time to read the constitution and you will find a document that is only a little easier to grasp than Hobbes. Students sometimes confess to looking for a "Constitution for Dummies" website to help them wade through it and glean some basic understanding. Others may believe that the US Constitution does not matter because rights kept within the document are already threatened or lost—maybe in the name of airport security, due to corporate interests, or because the government didn't think we would notice. Not to mention rewriting the constitution seems like a pretty huge undertaking itself. On the other hand, these might be precisely the reasons *to* begin anew.

The constitution was born out of a revolution—do we need another to remake it? Maybe. Thankfully there are models for how we can move through the process of rewriting the constitution together. An excellent model to try might by CVS, or Consciousness, Vision, and Strategy, created by Project South (Katz-Fishman, Brewer, and Albrect 2007). Through Consciousness, you and your communities become aware of our current society—what does it value, what does it devalue, and how does it operate? With this knowledge, you are then ready to create a vision of what your community would prefer to see— what do you value, devalue, and how do you wish to operate? With your Vision in mind, it is then possible to Strategize for change—social change, structural change, personal change, constitutional change. In the pages that follow, you will find materials to assist you through the steps of CVS. This book will present you with information that helps you to reach a deeper level of knowledge and consciousness about life in the US under the constitution. Thinking about how the US compares to other constitutions and the UDHR, along with the ideas presented by our authors, will assist you in imagining a new constitution. We invite you to envision a new US Constitution that joins the constitutions of our peers as one that embraces human rights language and practices, in the hope that together we may enjoy human rights enshrined in a constitution that is of, by, and for the people.

Note

1 The dates of subsequent amendments are listed in Appendix 1.

References

Balkin, Jack M. 2010. *Living Originalism*. Cambridge, MA: The Belknap Press of Harvard University Press.

Beck, Colin J., Gili S. Drori, and John W. Meyer. 2012. "World Influences on Human Rights Language in Constitutions." *International Sociology* 27(4): 483–501.

Bonds, Eric. 2014. *Social Problems: A Human Rights Perspective*. New York: Routledge.

Dorf, Michael C. 2012. "The Undead Constitution: A Review of Two Recent Books on Living Constitutionalism." *Harvard Law Review* 125(8): 2011–2055.

Dunbar-Ortiz, Roxanne. 2014. *An Indigenous Peoples' History of the United States*. Boston: Beacon Press.

Friesen, Bruce. 2014. *Moral Systems and the Evolution of Human Rights*. Dordrecht: Springer.

Katz-Fishman, Walda, Rose Brewer, and Lisa Albrect. 2007. *The Critical Classroom: Education for Liberation and Movement Building*. Atlanta, GA: Project South.

Pew Research Center. 2014. "Supreme Court's Rulings Should Be Based on..." www.people-press.org/2014/06/26/typology-comparison/supreme-court-interpretation/ (last accessed July 5, 2016).

Strauss, David A. 2010. *The Living Constitution*. New York: Oxford University Press.

Strauss, David A. 2012. "Legitimacy, 'Constitutional Patriotism,' and the Common Law Constitution." *Harvard Law Review* 125(8): 50–55.

PART I

What's Going On?

.

2

WHY REVISE?

Judith R. Blau

Most constitutions embrace human rights as both societal norms and legal standards. Yet the US lags far, far behind, and Americans are only minimally assured of rights because our constitution only includes provisions for civil and political rights, namely those spelled out in the 1791 Bill of Rights and a few subsequent amendments. While it is true that human rights, as understood in the world today, do include civil and political rights, they encompass much, much more than that. Besides, the founders framed the Bill of Rights (and additional amendments) as negative rights, which juxtapose what each person would like to enjoy with what the government is willing to cede. Most constitutions spell out rights as positive and unconditional. In the complicated world in which we live today, it's important for Americans to understand what rights we do and do not have and—even better—to enjoy the rights that other people have.

A subtle but highly deleterious aspect of the US Constitution and Bill of Rights is that the constitution was interpreted until 1865 to mean that African slaves were property. True enough, the 13th Amendment of 1865 abolished slavery, but it did so in a singular way, without addressing its economic, social or cultural aspects. Very specifically the United States was founded on the principle that slaves were property. As clearly put in the 1788 Federalist Paper #54, "Slaves are considered as property, not as persons. They ought therefore to be comprehended in estimates of taxation which are founded on property, and to be excluded from representation which is regulated by a census of persons."[1] This opinion acquired constitutional certainty with the 1825 Supreme Court Decision *Antelope* that explicitly states that slaves were property.[2] While it is of course true that the 13th Amendment abolished slavery, other parts of the constitution were not rewritten to underscore this disassociation. This typically happens when a country wishes to repudiate and transcend a humiliating and catastrophic past; notable illustrations are the constitutions of Spain (after Franco), South Africa (after apartheid), Germany (after Hitler), Argentina (after Perón), and post-war Japan. It did not happen in the case of the eighteenth-century US Constitution.

There is another difficulty. Eighteenth century prose may have worked in the eighteenth century, but nowadays these statutes are interpretable only within an esoteric legal context and tradition. Besides, some of them are vague and impre-cise. Americans must go to lawyers to clarify what their rights are; they must then go to court, accompanied by their lawyers, to defend them.

Human rights have evolved from individual rights within particular nation-states to universal rights that are globally recognized. To highlight this, consider the following: (1) that people, everywhere, contend with economic uncertainty and, often, exploitation as well; (2) some of us are threatened by war and conflict; (3) some of us suffer at the hands of a corrupt government; (4) all of us need food, housing, work and an education; and (5) all of us will cope with the inevitability of global warming, which will continue to take an increasingly huge and unpredictable toll on crops, climate, health and much else. The Framers could not have imagined living in a world like ours, with international air travel, Skype conferences, the internet, and women physi-cians. Moreover, they could not have imagined that there would be interna-tional standards for the rights of *everyone on the planet*, which is exactly what we aspire to today.

The Framers of the 1788 US Constitution and the 1791 Bill of Rights[3] con-ceived of rights as being secured precariously (even entrepreneurially) from a reluctant state. Consider the 1st Amendment: "Congress shall make no law…" And, not all had even negative rights. At the time of the first Presidential election in 1789, only 6 percent of the population—white, male property owners—were eligible to vote.[4] That is, not all people in America were recognized as citizens (or perhaps as fully human in 1789). (Note: The Bill of Rights and subsequent amendments are—in part—reproduced in Appendix 1 and usefully compared with the Universal Declaration of Human Rights in Appendix 2.)

Yet, I suggest that there is an alternative tradition in the US, cherished by Americans but nonetheless "subversive" of the official tradition, one that is rooted in eighteenth-century political doctrine. I trace this alternative tradition and describe it as one that promises positive human rights and unrelentingly insists on equality and an inclusive society. This alternative tradition is also consciously "self-referencing" as phrases and themes repeat themselves over and over again, which I shall show. It is illustrated in the writings and speeches of Thomas Jefferson, Abraham Lincoln, Eleanor Roosevelt, Franklin Delano Roosevelt, Malcolm X, and Martin Luther King Jr. Although this tradition has no formal or legal status in the US, it is one that I believe Americans cherish, and is potentially compatible with international human rights.

What are Human Rights?

Human rights have been progressively elaborated, first as civil and political rights in the late eighteenth century, then significantly so as economic, social and cultural rights at the end of World War II (in 1948), and now again as global interdependencies have increased. Human rights are often described in terms of generations, so that although the US was initially a leader in the eighteenth century, protecting civil and political rights, it remains stuck while most of the world's peoples have moved ahead, sharing a conception of human rights that is entirely different from that held by Americans, based on eighteenth century political thought.

Generations of Rights

Civil and political rights—"first-generation rights"—refer to individual rights, such as the right to stand trial, to speak freely, and to profess religious beliefs. These rights were first introduced in the 1789 French Declaration of the Rights of Man and of the Citizen and in the 1791 US Bill of Rights, and by now, all country constitutions have clauses that at least profess to protect their citizens' individual rights. In the US Constitution, rights are claimed by the person against the state, or as the 1st Amendment states, "Congress shall make no law…" Therefore, legal scholars refer to the "negative rights" spelled out in the US Constitution. Because the US Bill of Rights has never been updated to be compatible with prevailing international norms, it still conveys the eighteenth-century notion that government officials (like monarchs) aspire to holding absolute power and must be restrained from trampling on the rights of individual citizens. Of course it is true that there are US *laws* that provide protections for Americans. These include, for example, federal and state minimum wage laws, the 1935 legislation act that established social security, and the many codes and regulations that help to ensure that the buildings in which we live are habitable and safe. Yet, laws can be quashed by Congress, overturned by the Supreme Court, or just simply ignored by authorities.

Economic, social and cultural rights—"second-generation rights"—are enshrined in the 1948 Universal Declaration of Human Rights (UDHR) which was widely embraced by countries at the end of World War II. The majority of constitutions include at least some of these rights—with the US being an exception and, indeed, a notable exception—among developed countries. They include, for example, protections for children and disabled people; guarantees for women's rights, and protection of minorities against discrimination; the right to education; the right to security—notably rights including food, housing, healthcare, and decent work—as well as the rights of migrants, asylum seekers and refugees; and the right to culture and an identity. In contrast with first-generation rights, second-generation rights are positive rights.

"Third-generation rights" are collective rights that are realized through global cooperation and solidarity. They now take on special urgency, not only because of the dangers posed by global warming, but also because of the staggering levels of global economic inequality and the inordinate power of multinationals. One conundrum is whether or not these can be tackled internationally. This would require an unprecedented level of international cooperation. The most hopeful approach to such global cooperation is through the Sustainable Development Goals (SDGs), which promise to pave the way for further clarification of universally recognized human rights, especially as we together face the perils of climate warming, devastating crop failures, and erratic weather patterns. The question is whether rich countries will be generous and pay for development in the Global South, create opportunities for refugees and migrants, and pay for infrastructure that poor countries cannot pay for on their own. These are perilous times, and global interdependencies require robust cooperation and generosity.

Struggle for Human Rights in the US

The Founding Fathers thought of human rights as derivatives of property rights. James Madison, who wrote the Bill of Rights, maintained in the 10th Federalist that: "The protection of these faculties [that is, property] is the first object of government. From the protection of different and unequal faculties of acquiring property, the possession of different degrees and kinds of property immediately results; and from the influence of these on the sentiments and views of the respective proprietors, ensues a division of the society into different interests and parties."[5] More specifically, he later wrote, "The first object of government is the diversity in the faculties of men, from which the rights of property originate."[6] Along these lines, Ayn Rand and many contemporary libertarians consider all rights to be derivatives of property rights.[7]

The conflict between the Federalists and the Jeffersonian Democrats was a conflict between those who feared anarchy and sought a strong government (the Federalists), and those who feared tyranny and sought a weak one (Jeffersonian Democrats). There were also religious differences. Many Federalists, unlike Jeffersonian Democrats, were Calvinists. There also were economic differences between them. Federalists, representing financial and propertied interests, preferred a strong national government, whereas the Jeffersonian Democrats, representing landholders and agrarian interests, favored more diffuse and decentralized political power.[8]

Civil and Political Rights

Laid out in the 1791 Bill of Rights and subsequent amendments are Americans' civil and political rights. They are summarized in Appendix 1 at the back of the book. Below is a list of those that are being violated, at least according to any literal interpretation:

- 1st Amendment. In clear and unambiguous language, speech is protected under the 1st Amendment, and yet the 2011 Patriot Act provided secret cover for the National Security Agency (NSA) to routinely collect data about the phone numbers that we call and how often, our personal library habits, emails, internet usage, and our medical records.[9] It expired on June 1, 2015, but the Freedom Act that was enacted on June 2 restores in modified form important provisions of the Patriot Act, and further authorizes telecommunications companies to collect and store private communications on Americans.[10]

- The 4th Amendment reinforces the 1st Amendment by reassuring the US that we are secure "against unreasonable searches and seizures." However, under the Patriot Act, and now the Freedom Act, the government can secretly (electronically) collect personal data on US citizens.[11]

- The 8th Amendment states that "cruel and unusual punishments [shall not be] inflicted." The Senate Intelligence Committee Report on Torture provides ample evidence that the CIA and military contractors tortured prisoners at Abu Ghraib and black sites throughout the world.[12] Likewise, torture by police is also a violation of the 8th Amendment, but it is not rare.[13]

- The 14th Amendment states that the State cannot deprive "any person of life, liberty, or property without due process of law…" The key phrases are "any person" and "due process." Clearly, the phrase "any person" applies to everyone, yet migrants (including children) are imprisoned in the US who are not charged with a crime, making migrant prisons comparable to US internment camps for the Japanese during World War II.[14] Additionally, the National Defense Authorization Act gives the President the power to apprehend and detain Americans indefinitely on no more authority than a suspicion of their complicity with enemies in the "War on Terror."[15]

- The 15th, 19th, 24th, and 26th Amendments appear to progressively strengthen voting rights. Not so. It should be noted that it was not until 1850 that voting restrictions on white men who didn't own property were dropped.[16] The 15th Amendment (promising assured voting rights) was added later, in 1870, but blacks were often disenfranchised by the poll tax. In 1920 women were granted voting rights under the 19th Amendment; in 1962 the 24th Amendment eliminated the discriminatory poll tax, and the 1965 Voting Rights Act provided federal oversight for states that had a pattern of discriminatory voting practices. On June 25, 2013, the Supreme Court ruled in *Shelby County v. Holder* that states with a history of discriminatory voting would no longer have to submit their redistricting plans for clearance from the federal government. As a consequence, many African Americans in Southern states are disenfranchised.[17] As noted, today blacks cannot assuredly vote in some southern states, and some states banned indigenous Americans from voting until 1962.[18]

- Finally, there is the question as to what constitutes a person. Since 1819 (and in cases in 1886, 2011, and 2014), the Supreme Court has ruled that private corporations are inviolable and have personhood rights. This provides them with protections under the following Amendments: 1st, 4th, 5th, and 6th.[19]

Checks and Balances? Or Watch your Back?

At the country's founding there were deep divisions in the country—between North and South; between city dwellers, farmers, and plantation owners; between those who held property and those who did not; and between various Protestant sects. To be sure, whites feared and distrusted black slaves as well as indigenous Americans. They might have had good reason since the English and then the Americans were responsible for both the displacement and the genocide of indigenous Americans as well as the brutal enslavement of black Africans. Neither indigenous peoples nor blacks are mentioned in the constitution or the Bill of Rights.

Even Benjamin Franklin, probably the most egalitarian of the constitutional theorists, stated that to allow landless Americans to vote would be "an impropriety."[20] Besides, it wasn't until 1856 that white people in America who didn't own property could assuredly vote. In other words, the United States started as a plutocracy and remained that way for nearly sixty-five years.[21]

Most would say that the adoption of the constitution in 1788 was the beginning of the New Republic, but it is useful to briefly point out that the Preamble is considered by historians to be anomalous.[22] It is uncharacteristically upbeat, affirmative, and inclusive. Instead the constitution itself pits one branch of government against the other and the individual amendments of the Bill of Rights are snarly and negativistic. Although the heyday of Calvinism was much earlier and there is no evidence that the Framers were adherent Calvinists—say, who believed in predestination, advocated burning witches at the stake, or extreme frugality—there is evidence to suggest that many of the Federalists, responsible for writing the constitution, tended to be Calvinists; even those who were not were strongly influenced by Calvinism.[23] Max Weber describes early Calvinists as especially distrustful, contentious, and interested in pecuniary gains; he further notes, the Calvinist "counsels deep distrust of even one's closest friend," and "exhorts to trust no one and to say nothing compromising to anyone." "Only God should be your confidant."[24] As already noted, the Founding Fathers thought of rights as derivatives of property rights.[25]

James Madison wrote *The Federalist No. 51*, titled: *The Structure of the Government Must Furnish the Proper Checks and Balances between the Different Departments*. It was published on February 6, 1788, under the pseudonym, *Publius*, the name under which all *The Federalist Papers* were published. Extracts from it serve to make my point that Madison's conception was that branches of government were designed to be pugilistic, not complementary.

> In framing a government which is to be administered by men over men, the great difficulty lies in this: you must first enable the government to control the governed; and in the next place oblige it to control itself.

Ambition must be made to counteract ambition. Whilst all authority in [the federal republic of the United States] will be derived from and dependent on the society, the society itself will be broken into so many parts, interests, and classes of citizens, that the rights of individuals, or of the minority, will be in little danger from interested combinations of the majority.

It is of great importance in a republic not only to guard the society against the oppression of its rulers, but to guard one part of the society against the other part.[26]

Not only were the Federalists preoccupied with contentiousness, power struggles, and fear of the masses, they also provided political legitimacy for nascent capitalism, seeking a close alliance between the political system and property owners. From very early on, the Supreme Court tended to favor legislation that promoted trade, economic contracts, and property rights. Although Jefferson became president in 1800, he, along with other Jeffersonian Democrats were not very effective in countering Federalist views until 1828, when Andrew Jackson became president, who more popularly embraced democratic ideals.

Subversive Tradition

We will discover in this volume that many, if not most, countries have constitutions that embrace far more protections and rights for their citizens and residents than the US Constitution does. Yet we have not entirely turned our back on these protections and rights. Box 2.1 captures key speeches and documents that exemplify this subversive (if quiet) tradition. Indeed, it may as well have been a subversive tradition since it never has been allowed to fully bloom. In this Box key terms are highlighted. It is as if advocates of this tradition are footnoting their predecessors.

BOX 2.1 KEY WORDS AND PHRASES IN THE QUIET (SUBVERSIVE?) AMERICAN TRADITION

Thomas Jefferson, Declaration of Independence (July 4, 1776)[i]

We hold these truths to be *self-evident*, that all men are **created equal**, that they are endowed by their Creator with certain *unalienable rights* that among these are *life, liberty and the pursuit of happiness*. That to secure these rights, governments are instituted among men, deriving their just powers from the consent of the governed. That whenever any form of government becomes destructive of these ends, it is the *right of the people to alter or to abolish it*, and to institute new government, laying its foundation on such principles and organizing its powers in such form, as to them shall seem most likely to effect their safety and *happiness.*

Abraham Lincoln, Gettysburg Address (November 19, 1863)[ii]

Four score and seven years ago [i.e. 1776] our fathers brought forth on this continent a new nation, conceived in Liberty, and dedicated to the proposition that all men are *created equal.*

It is rather for US to be dedicated to the great task remaining before US–that from these honored dead we take increased devotion to that cause for which they gave the last full measure of devotion–that we here highly resolve that these dead shall not have died in vain–that this nation, under God, shall have a new birth of freedom–and that *government of the people, by the people, for the people.*

Franklin D. Roosevelt, State of the Union Message to Congress (January 11, 1944)[iii]

We have come to a clear realization of the fact that true individual freedom cannot exist without *economic security* and independence. "Necessitous men are not free men." People who are hungry and out of a job are the stuff of which dictatorships are made.

In our day these economic truths have become accepted as **self-evident**. We have accepted, so to speak, a second Bill of Rights under which a new basis of security and prosperity can be established for all regardless of station, race, or creed.

Among these are:

The *right* to a useful and remunerative job in the industries or shops or farms or mines of the Nation;

The *right* to earn enough to provide adequate food and clothing and recreation;

The *right* of every farmer to raise and sell his products at a return which will give him and his family a decent living;

The *right* of every businessman, large and small, to trade in an atmosphere of freedom from unfair competition and domination by monopolies at home or abroad;

The *right* of every family to a decent home;

The *right* to adequate medical care and the opportunity to achieve and enjoy good health;

The *right* to adequate protection from the economic fears of old age, sickness, accident, and unemployment;

The *right* to a good education.

All of these rights spell *security*. And after this war is won we must be prepared to move forward, in the implementation of these rights, to new goals of human *happiness* and well-being.

Malcolm X, Interview by A.B. Spellman (March 19, 1964)[iv]

Now, as a *civil rights movement*, it remains within the confines of American domestic policy and no African independent nations can open up their mouths on American domestic affairs, whereas if they expanded the civil rights movement to a *human rights movement* then they would be eligible to take the case of the Negro to the United Nations the same as the case of the Angolans is in the UN and the case of the South Africans is in the UN.

Martin Luther King, Jr., Confidential Letter to the President, Congress and the Supreme Court, Bill of Economic and Social Rights (February 6, 1968)[v]

The Bill of Economic and Social Rights should proclaim:

The *right* to a decent job
The *right* of every citizen to a minimum income
The *right* to a house and free choice of neighborhood
The *right* to an adequate education
The *right* to participate in the decision making process
The *rights* to the full benefits of science in modern health care

Without these rights, neither the black and white poor, and even some who are not poor, can really possess the *inalienable rights* to liberty and the pursuit of *happiness*.

i See www.archives.gov/exhibits/charters/declaration_transcript.html
ii See www.abrahamlincolnonline.org/lincoln/speeches/gettysburg.htm
iii See www.fdrlibrary.marist.edu/archives/address_text.html
iv See monthlyreview.org/2005/02/01/interview-with-malcolm-x/
v See www.thekingcenter.org/archive/document/economic-and-social-bill-rights#

Let's start with Jefferson's 1776 Declaration of Independence. Its basic premise sharply contrasts with those of the 1781 Bill of Rights, notably by stressing that it is "self-evident" that all people are "created equal" and that governments are created for the good of people. In fact, more than that; people have the right to change or abolish their government. The Declaration advances the proposition that government is created by people to best serve their unalienable rights— notably, life, liberty, and the "pursuit of happiness."

Much later—87 years later, "four score and seven years" later—at the Soldiers' Memorial Cemetery in Gettysburg, Pennsylvania, Abraham Lincoln refers to the birth of the nation dedicated to the proposition that all people are "created equal," and he also added, "a government of the people, by the people, and for the people," which, at least to a contemporary audience, captures the thought behind the Declaration, but not its wording.

For the first time in 1944 an American leader advocated for fundamental human rights. Franklin Delano Roosevelt contended in his State of the Union address that Americans should have basic security—including employment, food, clothing, recreation, a decent living, a decent home, good health and medical care, and education. In the tradition of Jefferson, Franklin Delano Roosevelt said this was "self-evident," and advanced the goal of "happiness." He sent it to a congressional committee to be marked up as a bill. FDR died in 1945 and his proposal never made it out of committee, but Eleanor Roosevelt played a key role in drafting the Universal Declaration of Human Rights, which includes FDR's list in Articles 23, 24, 25, and 26.

In 1964, an American Muslim, el-Hajj Malik el-Shabazz (Malcolm X) may have been the first prominent American to have distinguished between civil rights and human rights, suggesting that the former are parochial and confined to America whereas the latter are international. It is possible, too, that he was also being critical of Martin Luther King, who had not, at least publicly, used the term "human rights."

In February 1968, two months before he was assassinated, King drafted a confidential letter to the president (Johnson), members of Congress, and the Supreme Court. In it he proposed a "Bill of Economic and Social Rights" that would provide basic human rights, including a decent job, minimum income, healthcare (by the highest standards of science), education, and housing. This was underscored with an emphasis on democracy and empowerment; people would be free to choose where they lived and they had the right to participate in democratic decision making. With his choice of words—"inalienable rights" and "happiness"—King affirmed the tradition that began in 1776 with the Declaration of Independence.

Thus, it would not be too far-fetched to conclude that there is a tradition in the United States that affirms basic and inalienable human rights, yet this has been so muted that we refer to it as the subversive tradition. Why has it been muted? Is it because only a small minority upholds it? This is unlikely because it has been upheld for so long and by such prominent Americans. Moreover, of what is it so subservient? Of the dominant political discourse? Of capitalism? Of social hierarchies? Of political hierarchies? Perhaps it is subversive of all of these, but its tenacity is striking.

Capitalism, of course, has been the dominant economic tradition in America; it may have flourished precisely because it was so compatible with America's earliest political tradition, namely one based on distrust, fractionalization, and competition. Again, the philosophical foundation of the constitution is based on the Federalist's idea that society must be "broken into so many of parts, interests, and classes of citizens…" and to "guard one part of the society against the other part."[27] Neither the US Constitution nor the Bill of Rights even suggests that there is a shared or collective interest. In fact, the Bill of Rights is based on the premise that people—as individuals—struggle to wrench their rights from a reluctant state. So too do capitalists struggle, entrepreneurially and competitively, to wrench money from reluctant buyers. In contrast, the "quiet, subversive tradition" is based on the premise that there is a shared, or collective, interest in promoting the common welfare.

Why? Here I can be more explicit. First, there are some components to that common welfare that cannot be enjoyed by any single individual alone, and that are indivisible, such as peace or a healthy environment. Second, there are some components to the common welfare that solely depend on diverse voices that accompany large numbers—indeed, everyone's voices—such as democracy. Third, there are components of that common welfare that depend on interaction among people who are different from one another, which is the basis of trust and empathy. Fourth, the common welfare can, by definition, only be debated and advanced by everyone with equal rights.

Human Rights

In the United States, the term or concept of human rights does not have the same overarching significance that it does in most other countries, because historically the term "rights" refers only to civil and political rights and confounds the rights of persons with the rights of property and the rights of corporations. It is true that Eleanor Roosevelt played a major role in the drafting of the 1948 Universal Declaration of Human Rights (the UDHR) and Franklin Delano Roosevelt, as we have seen, advocated in 1944 that all Americans have rights that would enhance their economic security. His speech may have played a role in the drafting of the UDHR, but the UDHR itself has had no subsequent influence in American political life just as the international human rights treaties are not binding and have no legal consequence.

For a definition of human rights, we can turn to the UN Office of the High Commissioner for Human Rights.

> Human rights are rights that are inherent to all human beings, whatever our nationality, place of residence, sex, national or ethnic origin, color, religion, language, or any other status. We are all equally entitled to our human rights without discrimination. These rights are all interrelated, interdependent, and indivisible.

All human rights are indivisible, whether they are civil and political rights, such as the right to life, equality before the law and freedom of expression; economic, social and cultural rights, such as the rights to work, social security and education, or collective rights, such as the rights to development and self-determination, are indivisible, interrelated and interdependent. The improvement of one right facilitates advancement of the others. Likewise, the deprivation of one right adversely affects the others.

Non-discrimination is a cross-cutting principle in international human rights law. The principle is present in all the major human rights treaties.

Human rights entail both rights and obligations. States assume obligations and duties under international law to respect, to protect and to fulfill human rights. ... States must refrain from interfering with or curtailing the enjoyment of human rights. ... States must take positive action to facilitate the enjoyment of basic human rights. At the individual level, while we are entitled our human rights, we should also respect the human rights of others.[28]

These principles were enshrined in the 1948 Universal Declaration of Human Rights (UDHR), which is the bedrock foundation for subsequent international human rights law. Its provisions and philosophical premises greatly influenced the drafting of new constitutions in countries that were liberated from colonial powers in the later decades of the twentieth century and also were incorporated into older constitutions through revision. It would not be too far-fetched to say that nearly all national constitutions, with the exception of the US Constitution, include provisions from the UDHR. Another indication of its extraordinary appeal and influence is that it has been translated into 444 different languages; regional bodies, such as the Inter-American Commission of Human Rights and the African Commission on Human and Peoples' Rights, incorporate much of the language and many of its provisions into their treaties.

The UDHR is not a treaty, but provides the foundation for subsequent human rights treaties and, more generally, international human rights law. There are ten treaties altogether (nine treaties plus the optional protocol to the convention against torture), and additional optional protocols, which unless otherwise stated, establish review mechanisms for compliance with the particular treaty. It is important to note that the US has not unconditionally ratified a single treaty, at least in such a way as to ensure that it applies domestically.[29]

The Universal Periodic Review was established in 2006 to advance human rights in every country and ensure the steady advance of adherence to human rights norms around the world. Every country participates. Its objectives are: (1) Promote the universality, interdependence, indivisibility and interrelatedness of all human rights; (2) Ensure universal coverage and equal treatment of all

BOX 2.2 UNITED NATIONS HUMAN RIGHTS TREATY SYSTEM (TREATIES AND OPTIONAL PROTOCOLS), YEAR OF GENERAL ASSEMBLY APPROVAL; NUMBER OF RATIFYING STATE PARTIES OUT OF 193; US LIMITATIONS (UPDATED TO FEBRUARY 1, 2015)

International Convention on the Elimination of All Forms of Racial Discrimination (ICERD), 1965
  177 parties, US is a party with exempting qualifications (*)
International Covenant on Economic, Social and Cultural Rights (ICESCR), 1966
  163 parties; US is not a party
Optional Protocol to the International Covenant on Economic, Social and Cultural Rights (OP-ICESCR), 2008
  17 parties; US is not a party
International Covenant on Civil and Political Rights (ICCPR), 1966
  168 parties; US is a party with exempting qualifications (*)
Optional Protocol to the International Covenant on Civil and Political Rights (ICCPR-OP1) (implements Treaty), 1966
  115 parties; US is not a party
Second Optional Protocol to the International Covenant on Civil and Political Rights, aiming at the abolition of the death penalty (ICCPR-OP2), 1989
  81 parties; US is not a party
Convention on the Elimination of All Forms of Discrimination against Women (CEDAW), 1979
  188 parties; US is not a party
Optional Protocol to the Convention on the Elimination of All Forms of Discrimination against Women (OP-CEDAW) (implements Treaty), 1999
  105 parties; US is not a party
Convention against Torture and Other Cruel, Inhuman or Degrading Treatment or Punishment (CAT), 1984
  156 parties; US is a party with exempting qualifications (*)
Optional Protocol to the Convention against Torture and Other Cruel, Inhuman or Degrading Treatment or Punishment (implements Treaty), (OP-CAT), 2002
  76 parties; US is not a party
Convention on the Rights of the Child (CRC), 1989
  194 parties; US is not a party
Optional Protocol to the Convention on the Rights of the Child on the involvement of children in armed conflict (OP-CRC-AC), 2000
  159 parties; US is a party with exempting qualifications (*)

Optional Protocol to the Convention on the Rights of the Child on the sale of children, child prostitution and child pornography (OP-CRC-SC), 2000
    169 parties; US is a party with exempting qualifications (*)
Optional Protocol to the Convention on the Rights of the Child on a communications procedure (OP-CRC-CP), 2011
    14 parties; US is not a party
International Convention on the Protection of the Rights of All Migrant Workers and Members of their Families (ICRMW), 1990
    47 parties; US is not a party
Convention on the Rights of Persons with Disabilities (CRPD), 2006
    151 parties (**); US is not a party
Optional Protocol to the Convention on the Rights of Persons with Disabilities (implements Treaty), (OP-CRPD), 2006
    85 parties; US is not a party
International Convention for the Protection of all Persons from Enforced Disappearance (CPED), 2006
    44 parties; US is not a party

Source: United Nations Treaty Collection: http://treaties.un.org/Pages/Treaties. aspx?id=4&subid=A&lang=en
    Based on summary prepared quarterly for ACLU-North Carolina by Slater Newman.
    (*) The United States has attached reservations, understandings and/or declarations to each of the three treaties and two protocols that it has ratified, thus making them "not self-executing."
    (**) For this treaty only, the number of State Parties (151) includes the European Union.

States; (3) Be an intergovernmental process; (4) UN Member-driven and action oriented; (5) Fully involve the country under review, conducted in an objective, transparent, non-selective, constructive, non-confrontational and non-politicized manner; (6) Fully integrate a gender perspective; (7) Take into account the level of development and specificities of countries; (8) Ensure the participation of all relevant stakeholders, including non-governmental organizations (NGOs).[30]

All countries are reviewed every four years for compliance with international human rights standards. In May 2015, the US was up for its second review. All documents related to the review are compiled by the Office of the High Commissioner of Human Rights.[31] This time over 117 State Parties participated in the review[32] and 91 NGOs prepared reports. It is a comprehensive and methodical process, carried out according to a schedule with full transparency.

The review of the US in 2015 for its compliance with international human rights standards was highly negative or, as Jamil Dakwar, Director of ACLU's Human Rights Program, put it, was a "scathing assessment of the US's human rights record."[33] Box 2.3 summarizes the points made by State Parties. For each topic we include the number of State Parties that commented on that particular topic. For example, 71 States urged the United States to ratify the Human Rights treaties, while 1 and 3, respectively, urged the US to ratify the Arms Trade Treaty and the Rome Statute. As evident here, many of the concerns are about the US's responsibilities in the international community while there are also many concerns about the US's responsibilities to its own citizens and residents. For example, poverty is a violation of international human rights norms, and that makes it, ipso facto, a violation of domestic human rights norms.

BOX 2.3 HUMAN RIGHTS COUNCIL. DRAFT REPORT OF THE WORKING GROUP ON THE UNIVERSAL PERIODIC REVIEW. UNITED STATES OF AMERICA. GENEVA MAY 4– 15, 2015 A/HRC/WG.6/22L.10

Number in parentheses is the number of State Parties that highlighted that particular topic in their review.

Note: 117 State Parties participated in the review of the US

International Obligations

Ratify human rights instruments (71)

Ratify Arms Trade Treaty (1)

Ratify Rome Statute of the ICC (13)

Ratify ILO Conventions (1)

Ratify Inter-American human rights instruments (1)

Implement the Declaration on the Rights of indigenous peoples (1)

End military presence in foreign territories (2)

Ensure that foreign assistance enables safe abortion for women and girls who have been raped in conflict situation (2)

Raise the level of Official Development Assistance (ODA) to achieve the UN target of .7 percent of GDP (1)

Repeal the unilateral coercive measures imposed on sovereign countries (5)

End human trafficking (5)

Respect the rights and privacy of individuals outside of the US (2)

Desist from extrajudicial killings such as drone strikes (3)

Close Guantanamo (13)

Safeguards against torture in any detention facility anywhere in the world (17)

Take further steps to implement recommendations accepted during the 1st UPR (2)

National plans for climate change (5)

Surveillance

Protect right to privacy (2)

Ensure surveillance is consistent with international human rights law (11)

Advance Inter-Group Justice/End Discrimination/Comply with International Law for Migrants

Human rights education programs for law enforcement and immigration officers (2)

Address racial profiling (11)

End discrimination against Muslims and Arabs (4)

Combat racial discrimination (4)

End discrimination against indigenous Americans (1)

Improve police-community relations (4)

Counter hate crimes (4)

Counter crimes against religious minorities (3)

Counter discrimination against migrants (1)

Investigate causes of deaths of migrants (6)

Due process for migrants and to protect the human rights of migrant persons (17)

Continue progress protecting rights of LGBTI people (1)

Halt detention of immigrant families and children (6)

End violence against indigenous women (1)

Consult with indigenous people on matters of interest to their communities (5)

Promote Gender Equality and Children's Rights

Have paid maternity leave (2)

Nationwide legal and safe abortion (2)

Ensure women are paid equally as men for the same work (2)

Develop plans to deal with sexual violence (2)

Provide for safe abortion (3)

End child labor on farms (2)

Prohibit corporal punishment of children (3)

Ensure that youths in conflict with law are handled by a juvenile justice system (3)

Increase minimum age from 17 to 18 for eligibility to go into military (1)

Inequality and Poverty

End discrimination against poor people (6)
End various form of inequality (1)
Reduce poverty (1)
End criminalization of homeless (1)
Provide adequate housing, food, health, and education (9)
Guarantee right to water and sanitation (1)

End/Reduce Violence and Prison Reforms

Abolish the death penalty (23)
Reduce gun violence (5)
Improve conditions of prisons (2)
Devise national plan for re-insertion of former detainees into jobs (1)
Prosecute those responsible for torturing prisoners (1)
Investigate torture (7)
Measures against excessive use of force by police (15)

Create a Climate to Promote Human Rights

Create national human rights institution/commission (19)
Establish a mechanism to ensure compliance with international human rights
 at the federal, state and local levels (7)

Source: www.ohchr.org/EN/HRBodies/UPR/Pages/USSession22.aspx

Conclusion

The American Dream—like the American work ethic and like American entre-preneurship—is all about the individual. This way, at the very beginning—as we shook off the British, the nobility, the imperial tradition—we could pat ourselves on the backs and say it's not the inheritance of title that is important, but rather whether we—as individuals—were successful in, say, acquiring property or acquiring wealth. That was the beginning of American capitalism and the American nation. Of course, we were white and of course, we were male. That is not to deny that America was the land of opportunity for millions and millions of immigrants, and we led the world in competitive entrepreneurship for much of the nineteenth and twentieth centuries.

Let's jump to 2050 with this possibility: the temperatures are soaring, all of the Arctic ice has melted; Small Island States have disappeared; California has to import all of its water; the Atlantic Ocean has claimed New York and other East Coast cities. Because of domestic policies, very many people who did not inherit wealth are working two full-time jobs. Healthcare, food, education, and housing are far too expensive for many Americans. Americans are learning that current outcomes are not fair; that is, it is sheer luck—or worse, connections or inheritance—that will determine who is well-off or poor. Now is precisely the historical moment to revise the constitution while there is still time to cultivate habits of cooperation and teamwork.

Notes

1 Federalist 54. Tuesday, February 12, 1788. *The Apportionment of Members among the States from the New York Packet.* (Attributed to either Hamilton or Madison). http://avalon. law.yale.edu/18th_century/fed54.asp (last accessed October 11, 2016).
2 Jonathan M. Bryant. 2015. *Dark Places of the Earth: The Voyage of the Slave Ship Antelope.* New York: Liveright Publishing.
3 James Madison wrote the Bill of Rights. He was influenced by George Madison, who wrote the Virginia Declaration of Rights.
4 US Government Archives: "Expansion of Rights and Liberties." www.archives.gov/ exhibits/charters/charters_of_freedom_13.html (last accessed October 11, 2016).
5 James Madison. 1787. "The Federalist No. 10: The Same Subject Continued (The Union as a Safeguard against Domestic Faction and Insurrection)." http://avalon.law. yale.edu/18th_century/fed10.asp (last accessed October 11, 2016).
6 Quoted in Charles A. Beard. 2004. *An Economic Interpretation of the Constitution of the United States.* Mineola, NY: Dover Publications, p. 156.
7 Jan Narveson. *The Libertarian Idea* (orig. Temple University Press, 1989; republished Broadview, 2001).
8 Alan Pendleton Grimes. 1955. *American Political Thought.* New York: Henry Holt, pp. 119–127.
9 Patriot Act of 2001 stands for "*Uniting and Strengthening America by Providing Appropriate Tools Required to Intercept and Obstruct Terrorism.*" https://epic.org/privacy/terrorism/ hr3162.pdf (last accessed October 11, 2016).
10 The Freedom Act also restores authorization for roving wire traps and tracking "lone wolf terrorists." The title of the act is USA FREEDOM that stands for "*Uniting and Strengthening America by Fulfilling Rights and Ending Eavesdropping, Dragnet-collection and Online Monitoring Act.*" www.congress.gov/bill/113th-congress/hoU.S.e-bill/3361 (last accessed October 11, 2016).
11 In March 2015, Wikimedia sued the National Security Agency for its mass surveillance programs that violate peoples' constitutional rights: www.reuters.com/article/ 2015/03/10/U.S.-U.S.a-nsa-wikipedia-idU.S.KBN0M60YA20150310 (last accessed October 11, 2016).
12 Senate Select Committee on Intelligence. 2014. *The Senate Intelligence Committee Report on Torture.* Brooklyn, NY: Melville House. When interviewed Justice Antonin Scalia said: "The Constitution itself says nothing about torture. The Constitution speaks of punishment. If you condemn someone who has committed a crime to torture, that would be unconstitutional." Matt Ford, Antonin Scalia's Case for Torture, *The Atlantic,* Dec 13, 2014. www.theatlantic.com/politics/archive/2014/12/antonin-scalias-case-for-torture/383730/ http://ccrjU.S.tice.org/home/press-center/press-releases/ french-court-investigating-U.S.-torture-summon-former-gitmo-commander (last accessed October 11, 2016).
13 Wikipedia. List of police torture cases. https://en.wikipedia.org/wiki/List_of_cases_ of_police_brutality_in_the_United_StatesNOLO: Law for LL: www.nolo.com/legal-encyclopedia/police-brutality.html (last accessed October 11, 2016).
14 Satsuki Ina, "I Know an American Internment Camp when I see one." American Civil Liberties Union. www.aclu.org/blog/speak-freely/i-know-american-internment-camp-when-i-see-one (last accessed October 11, 2016). The criminal prosecution

of undocumented entrants has grown exponentially over the past ten years. In 2002, there were 3,000 prosecutions for illegal entry and 8,000 for illegal reentry; a decade later, in 2012, these prosecutions had increased to 48,000 and 37,000, respectively. These cases now outnumber other frequently prosecuted federal offenses such as drug, firearm, and white-collar crimes. By 2011, the proportion of defendants with convictions considered most serious had dropped to 27 percent, while the proportion of defendants with no prior felony convictions had increased to 27 percent. www.pewhispanic.org/2014/03/18/the-rise-of-federal-immigration-crimes/ (last accessed October 11, 2016).

15 On Wednesday, January 2, 2013, President Barack Obama did what constitutionalists and civil libertarians knew he would do: He signed into law the renewal of his power the National Defense Authorization Act that allows him power to apprehend and detain Americans indefinitely on no more authority than his own suspicion of their complicity with enemies in the "War on Terror." www.thenewamerican.com/U.S.news/constitution/item/14120-obama-signs-2013-ndaa-may-still-arrest-detain-citizens-without-charge (last accessed October 11, 2016).

16 Alexander Keyssar. 2009. *The Right to Vote: The Contested History of Democracy in the United States*, 2nd ed. Philadelphia: Basic Books of Perseus Books Group.

17 Leadership Conference. "Voting Rights Act." www.civilrights.org/voting-rights/vra/ (last accessed October 11, 2016).

18 Library of Congress. "Voters." www.loc.gov/teachers/classroommaterials/presentationsandactivities/presentations/elections/voters9.htm (last accessed October 11, 2016).

19 https://supreme.justia.com/cases/federal/U.S./17/518 (last accessed October 11, 2016); https://supreme.justia.com/cases/federal/U.S./118/394/ (last accessed October 11, 2016); https://supreme.justia.com/cases/federal/U.S./573/13–354(last accessed October 11, 2016); https://supreme.justica.com/cases/federal/uw/558/08-205/(last accessed October 11, 2016); Brandon L. Garrett. 2014, December. "The Constitutional Standing of Corporations." *University of Pennsylvania Law Review* 163(1): 95–164. www.pennlawreview.com/print/?id=457(last accessed October 11, 2016).

20 Micheline R. Ishay. 2004. *The History of Human Rights: From Ancient Times to the Globalization Era*. Berkeley: University of California Press, p. 96; Alan Pendleton Grimes. 1955. *American Political Thought*. New York: Henry Holt, p. 148.

21 Voting rights timeline. www.kqed.org/assets/pdf/education/digitalmedia/U.S.-voting-rights-timeline.pdf (last accessed October 11, 2016).

22 Gouverneur Morris wrote the Preamble. http://iipdigital.U.S.embassy.gov/st/english/article/2006/04/20060403182030pssnikwad0.6276056.html#axzz3ijRzMmuR(last accessed October 11, 2016).

23 Stuart D. B. Picken. 2011. *Historical Dictionary of Calvinism*. Lanham, MD: Scarecrow Press, p. 69.

24 Perry Miller. 1953. *The New England Mind: From Colony to Province*. Cambridge, Mass.: Belknap Press; Max Weber. 1905. *The Protestant Ethic and the Spirit of Capitalism*. London: Routledge, p. 62. www.d.umn.edu/cla/faculty/jhamlin/1095/The%20Protestant%20Ethic%20and%20the%20Spirit%20of%20Capitalism.pdf (last accessed October 11, 2016).

25 See the Foundation for Economic Education. http://fee.org/freeman/private-property-and-government-under-the-constitution/ (last accessed October 11, 2016).

26 (Hamilton or Madison). Friday, February 8, 1788. "Federalist Paper No. 51: The Structure of the Government must Furnish the Proper Checks and Balances between the Different Departments." *New York Packet*. http://avalon.law.yale.edu/18th_century/fed51.asp(last accessed October 11, 2016).

27 James Madison. Wednesday, February 6, 1788. "The Federalist No. 51: The Structure of the Government must Furnish the Proper Checks and Balances between the Different Departments." *Independent Journal*. www.constitution.org/fed/federa51.htm(last accessed October 11, 2016).

28 UN, "What are Human Rights?" www.ohchr.org/EN/Issues/Pages/WhatareHuman Rights.aspx (last accessed October 11, 2016).
29 The U.S. declares that the human rights treaty is "not self-executing" until domestic laws are changed. This never happens. The UN Treaty pages for human rights provides this information. https://treaties.un.org/pages/Treaties.aspx?id=4&subid=A&lang=en(last accessed October 11, 2016).
30 See www.ohchr.org/EN/HRBodies/UPR/Pages/BasicFacts.aspx(last accessed October 11, 2016).
31 See http://daccess-dds-ny.un.org/doc/UNDOC/GEN/G15/039/92/PDF/G1503992. pdf?OpenElement (last accessed October 11, 2016).
32 See www.U.S.hrnetwork.org/sites/U.S.hrnetwork.org/files/final_U.S._upr_report_adopted_hrc_wg.6_22_l.10_5_15_15.pdf (last accessed October 11, 2016).
33 See www.huffingtonpost.com/jamil-dakwar/un-issues-scathing-assess_b_7294792.html (last accessed October 11, 2016).

References

Beard, Charles A. 2004. *An Economic Interpretation of the Constitution of the United States.* Mineola, NY: Dover Publications.
Bryant, Jonathan M. 2015. *Dark Places of the Earth: The Voyage of the Slave Ship Antelope.* New York: Liveright Publishing.
Dakwar, Jamiil. 2016. "UN Issues Scathing Assessment of US Human Rights Record." *Huffington Post.* www.huffingtonpost.com/jamil-dakwar/un-issues-scathing-assess_b_7294792.html (last accessed May 15, 2016).
Ford, Matt. 2014. "Antonin Scalia's Case for Torture." *The Atlantic.* www.theatlantic.com/politics/archive/2014/12/antonin-scalias-case-for-torture/383730/ (last accessed December 13, 2014).
Garrett, Brandon L. 2014. "The Constitutional Standing of Corporations." *University of Pennsylvania Law Review* 163(1): 95–164. www.pennlawreview.com/print/?id=457 (last accessed October 11, 2016).
Grimes, Alan Pendleton. 1955. *American Political Thought.* New York: Henry Holt.
Ina, Satsuki. 2015. "I Know an American Internment Camp When I See One." *American Civil Liberties Union.* www.aclu.org/blog/speak-freely/i-know-american-internment-camp-when-i-see-one (last accessed October 11, 2016).
Ishay, Micheline R. 2004. *The History of Human Rights: From Ancient Times to the Globalization Era.* Berkeley: University of California Press.
Keyssar, Alexander. 2009. *The Right to Vote: The Contested History of Democracy in the United States,* 2nd ed. Philadelphia: Basic Books of Perseus Books Group.
King, Martin Luther King, Jr. 1968. "To the President, Congress and the Supreme Court." www.thekingcenter.org/archive/document/economic-and-social-bill-rights# (last accessed October 11, 2016).
Lincoln, Abraham. 1863. "Gettysburg Address." www.abrahamlincolnonline.org/lincoln/speeches/gettysburg.htm (last accessed October 11, 2016).
Madison, James. 1788. "The Federalist No. 51: The Structure of the Government must Furnish the Proper Checks and Balances between the Different Departments." *Independent Journal.* www.constitution.org/fed/federa51.htm (last accessed October 11, 2016).
Miller, Perry. 1953. *The New England Mind: From Colony to Province.* Cambridge, MA: Belknap Press of Harvard University Press.

Narveson, Jan. 2001. *The Libertarian Idea*. Peterborough, ON: Broadview.

Picken, Stuart D. B. 2011. *Historical Dictionary of Calvinism*. Lanham, MD: Scarecrow Press.

Roosevelt, Franklin D. 1944. "State of the Union Address." www.fdrlibrary.marist.edu/ archives/address_text.html (last accessed October 11, 2016).

Senate Select Committee on Intelligence. 2014. *The Senate Intelligence Committee Report on Torture*. Brooklyn, NY: Melville House.

Spellman, A. B. 1964. "Interview with Malcolm X." http://monthlyreview.org/2005/02/ 01/interview-with-malcolm-x/ (last accessed October 11, 2016).

United Nations. "Basic Facts about the UPR." www.ohchr.org/EN/HRBodies/UPR/ Pages/BasicFacts.aspx (last accessed October 11, 2016).

United Nations. "Multilateral Treaties Deposited with the Secretary-General." https://trea-ties.un.org/pages/Treaties.aspx?id=4&subid=A&lang=en: IV (last accessed October 11, 2016).

United Nations. "Universal Periodic Review Second Cycle – United States of America." www.ohchr.org/EN/HRBodies/UPR/Pages/USSession22.aspx (last accessed October 11, 2016).

United Nations. "What are Human Rights?" www.ohchr.org/EN/Issues/Pages/ WhatareHumanRights.aspx (last accessed October 11, 2016).

United States. 1776. "Declaration of Independence." www.archives.gov/exhibits/charters/ declaration_transcript.html (last accessed October 11, 2016).

Weber, Max. 1905. *The Protestant Ethic and the Spirit of Capitalism*. London: Routledge. www.d.umn.edu/cla/faculty/jhamlin/1095/The%20Protestant%20Ethic%20and%20 the%20Spirit%20of%20Capitalism.pdf (last accessed October 11, 2016).

3

BEGINNING THE WORLD AGAIN

Social Movements and the Challenge of Constitutional Change

Ben Manski

The Clamor for Constitutional Change

In the six years since the Supreme Court ruling in *Citizens United v. FEC*, more than 700 local governments and sixteen state legislatures have adopted resolutions in support of the provisions of the "We the People Amendment," which states that "The rights protected by the Constitution of the United States are the rights of natural persons only," and that "The judiciary shall not construe the spending of money to influence elections to be speech under the First Amendment." Over 300 of these resolutions, including those in major cities like Los Angeles, San Francisco, Chicago, and Milwaukee as well at the state level in Colorado and Montana, won adoption by a popular vote (Move to Amend 2014). Altogether, these resolutions cover more than one-third of the population of the United States.

The movement to overturn *Citizens United* is significant but it is not the only large-scale constitutional reform effort in the United States today. The proposed Balanced Budget Amendment has won majority support in both houses of Congress in recent years. A renewed campaign for ratification of the Equal Rights Amendment (ERA) is moving forward in the fifteen states which have not yet ratified the ERA. In the years since the Supreme Court ruling in *Bush v. Gore*, voting rights and election reform advocates have united behind the proposed Right to Vote Amendment. Both at the state level and nationally a series of constitutional struggles have emerged over marriage, immigration, war powers, treaty rights, federalism, the rights of future generations, and much else (Manski 2015).

Popular constitutionalism has returned to the politics of the United States. In response to a widespread perception that some of our society's problems are in part structural in origin, many Americans are increasingly looking for constitutional solutions. That some of these constitutional reformers espouse clashing political views only strengthens the impression of a generalized democratization of constitutionalism. The energies and resources already invested toward achieving these new social movement goals suggest a belief that constitutional change is not only possible, but also, fruitful.

Constitution Making 101 for Human Rights Advocates

The *amendment* process is the most familiar procedure for constitutional reform. Article V of the US Constitution provides for not one but two formal paths toward amendment. The first of these is amendment initiated by Congress. Here the process begins when one or more members of Congress propose an amendment resolution. For ratification, the amendment must first win a vote of two-thirds of the members in each chamber of Congress. Then it must secure the support of the legislatures of three-quarters of the states.

Every change to date to the text of the federal constitution has been the direct result of amendment by this familiar process. Yet some important amendments have actually occurred in response to the probability of implementation of the second constitutional amendment process, that of the constitutional convention initiated by the states.[1] Here a state legislature begins the process by adopting a resolution calling for a national *constitutional convention* and specifying the purpose and scope of that convention. Once two-thirds of the states have adopted such a resolution, Congress is charged with convening a convention. Any amendments to the constitution proposed by that convention must then, again, secure the ratification of three-quarters of the states.

Constitutional review is the less formal and much more commonplace set of procedures through which various political actors have changed the federal constitution. In the process of constitutional review, the text of the constitution remains unchanged, yet the meaning of that text is reinterpreted by the federal courts, Congress, the president, or the people of the United States. This is deeply problematic, for as we shall see, the practice of constitutional review is dominated by elites concerned more with enlarging the role of the state than with the protection of human rights.

When the federal courts engage in constitutional interpretation, this is called *judicial review*. The Supreme Court of the United States and its lower courts have engaged in so much judicial review that much of what Americans believe themselves to understand about their constitution has actually been the product of court decisions. When the constitution said that Black people were, "so far inferior that they had no rights which the white man was bound to respect," that was the Supreme Court of *Dred Scott*, not the text of the constitution, speaking. And when forty years later the constitution said that "separate but equal" was consistent with the principles of equal protection—and then again sixty years later still, when the constitution changed its mind and said that "separate" was "inherently unequal"—in each case it was the Supreme Court that was speaking.

Americans have become so accustomed to hearing the voice of the constitution come from the robes of the Court that the process of constitutional review has become subsumed within the doctrine of *judicial supremacy*. But judicial review and judicial supremacy are not the same thing; the former was contested and the latter was anathema for much of US history (Kramer 2004). In his first inaugural address in 1861, Abraham Lincoln spoke for a dominant, republican critique of the notion of judicial supremacy:

> The candid citizen must confess that if the policy of the Government upon vital questions affecting the whole people is to be irrevocably fixed by decisions of the Supreme Court, the people will have ceased to be their own rulers, having to that extent practically resigned their Government into the hands of that eminent tribunal (Kramer 2004: 212).

Lincoln's criticism of judicial supremacy remains a vital force in debates over constitutional review to this day. Political scientists and legal scholars have long debated what Alexander Bickel termed the *counter-majoritarian difficulty* and what Jamin Raskin more recently described as "reading democracy out of the Constitution" (Raskin 2005; Martens 2007). The Supreme Court of the United States, an elite body if ever there was one, has more often discovered rights and protections for the wealthy and powerful as opposed to the poor and disenfranchised (Jung, et al. 2011; Cobb 2007; Coleridge, et al. 2000; Coleridge 2014; Morris 2008; Kairys 2006).

Yet if not the Supreme Court, who should decide what the US Constitution means? Originally, it was held that Congress and "the People" themselves were to serve as the final arbiters of constitutional review. In practice, *congressional review* has proven limited. When the Supreme Court issues a determination on a constitutional question, it does so with a clear voice and following a formal, visible procedure. Congress, however, rarely speaks with one voice. To the extent that Congress has engaged in constitutional review, it has done so most effectively through its role in the confirmation and rejection of federal judges. Efforts to settle constitutional questions through resolutions of Congress have been undermined by the federal courts as well as by Congress' own inability to function as a disciplined institution (Bryant and Simeone 2001).

Complicating matters has been the expansion of the powers of the presidency to shape the meaning and practice of constitutional rights, powers and duties. The idea that the executive branch would ever attain something akin to *executive review* was considered and flatly rejected by the first generations of US citizens. Yet today the president exercises review powers all the time through claims of executive privilege, the use of signing statements, and the issuance of uncontested executive orders (Berger 1974).

This last practice has very serious consequences in questions of war and peace. Article I, Section 8 of the Constitution makes clear the primary role of Congress as the branch responsible for overseeing the US military and deciding on the use of military force. Yet in the twentieth and twenty-first centuries, successive presidents have ignored Congress' primary authority over war powers and engaged in unauthorized warfare across the globe. And Congress and the federal courts have let them. The text of the constitution says one thing, but the practice of all three branches of the federal government says another (Irons 2005; Constitution Project 2005; Scarry 2011a; Scarry 2011b). The American people are left without any direct say on war powers, so their opposition to empire building, war, human rights violations, and the expanded security state takes form beyond the Washington D.C. beltway.

Washington today does not show much respect much for the institution of the sovereign power, that branch of government which the revolutionaries of 1776 called "The People." Yet the role of the people in deciding constitutional questions has never been a matter left to Washington to decide on its own. Popular sovereignty is a matter of practice, not simply of normative law; the power of the people earns respect when it is exercised, not in its absence. Popular movements have repeatedly decided for themselves what the constitution does say and what it should say. This practice of *popular review* predates the Constitution of 1787 and has played a significant and largely progressive role throughout US history (Kramer 2004).

The procedures of popular review are sometimes quite formal, involving public meetings, testimony, and popular votes. Formal popular review can be seen in constitutional amendment processes as well as in efforts to counterpose local, state, and global governmental institutions against federal power. In other cases, popular review is less formal and less direct, manifesting in mass mobilizations for or against a particular interpretation of the constitution (Irons 2006).

Where does all of this leave the advocate of a human rights constitution? Most of what we think of today as constitutional law is the product of some form of constitutional review. Yet constitutional review is dominated by the judiciary and the executive, the least democratic and least accessible federal branches. Popular constitutional review is commonly practiced, but when its practice is informal its impact is usually indirect. Formal popular participation in the shape of efforts to amend the constitution is more directly effective. Yet social movements seeking formal constitutional change face such significant challenges that it is often said that they are unworkable … or are they?

A History of Amending America

Much of the history of social change in America is a history of popular movements engaged in constitutional struggles. The same revolutionaries who destroyed $2 million dollars' worth of British East India Company tea in Boston Harbor weren't just saboteurs, they were also constitutionalists. They engaged in popular lawmaking as a matter of course, drafting and adopting hundreds of local resolutions of independence and statements of principles that prefigured the US Declaration of Independence and the Constitution (Maeier 1997; Raphael 2002; Young 2006; Beaumont 2014).

The abolitionists who voted in the years immediately following the Revolution to end slavery in northern states and sought to nullify the various Fugitive Slave Acts, grounded their actions in what they sometimes called the "Liberty Constitution." This was an interpretation of the constitution that drew on the Declaration of Independence and earlier revolutionary documents to conclude that in disputes between liberty (for slaves) versus property (in slaves), the constitution favored liberty (Goodell 1845). Radical constitutionalism had more than a small role in the two most significant revolutionary movements of the first century of US history (Manski 2006).

A journey through American constitutional history is tempting. But our purpose here is limited. It is enough to recognize that the constitution has been changed many times, and that social movements have been the primary agents of those constitutional changes that enlarged human rights and deepened democracy, the two great riverways of progressive constitutionalism.

The many struggles to expand governmental human rights protections are today celebrated in official histories. This may be because so many of them proved ultimately successful. As should be well known, when the Constitution of 1787 was first drafted, the vast majority of human beings living within the borders of the United States did not enjoy the "blessings of liberty" promised by the Preamble. Women, men who didn't own significant property, non-whites, slaves, indentured servants, and non-Christians were denied fundamental rights in most states and across the United States (Lobel 1988; Ollman and Birnbaum 1990; Dahl n.d.; Levinson 2006). Social movements changed all that. Since the 1800s, liberation movements have secured constitutional reforms that brought the majority of Americans within the protections of the constitution.

At least eight constitutional amendments following the adoption of the Bill of Rights constitutionalized the liberation of particular populations. The post-Civil War Reconstruction Amendments—the 13th, 14th and 15th Amendments—respectively abolished slavery (1865), greatly expanded equal protection and due process rights (1868), and guaranteed equal voting rights to non-whites and former slaves (1871). Women secured their part of the vote with the 19th Amendment in 1920. Those who wished to drink alcohol certainly felt liberated by the abolition of Prohibition with the 21st Amendment in 1933. The 23rd Amendment gave the voters of Washington D.C. representation in the Electoral College (1961). The use of the Poll Tax and other taxes to deny poor people the right to vote was abolished with the 24th Amendment in 1964. Eighteen, nineteen and twenty-year-olds gained access to the vote with the 26th Amendment in 1971.[2]

Social movements sought each and every one of these amendments, and more. For instance, the early nineteenth-century extension of the right to vote to non-propertied white males was the result of constitutional struggle at the level of the states. In 1848, one-hundred women's rights delegates at the Seneca Falls Convention engaged in archetypal popular constitutionalism with their signatures on the Declaration of Rights and Sentiments. In the decades following, working at the state level, women won liberation from *coverture*, the old system of property law in which children and married women were the possessions of the male head of the household. Constitutional amendment campaigns like the Child Labor Amendment (1924) and the Equal Rights Amendment (1974) remain unratified, yet they have recognizably affected American law and culture by framing public debates over child labor and the status of women.[3] Even where constitutional debates have been initiated by the opponents of human rights, the resulting public deliberation has often produced the opposite from the intended effect. Over the past twenty years, as the state-by-state conflict over same-sex marriage has gone on, the debate altered social norms, eventually leading to the Supreme Court's 2015 recognition of equal marriage rights.[4]

As we have seen, campaigns to secure human rights protections in the constitution have profoundly changed our society. Yet that is only half the picture. Struggles for human rights and collective liberation have nearly always been associated with struggles for political and economic democracy. The logic of this is simple. Democratic processes are often thought to be more likely than elite-driven processes to generate human rights protections. Human rights protections that are the result of democratic deliberation are thought to be more resilient than those handed down from on high (Kramer 2004; Raskin 2005).

The history of efforts to democratize the constitution is less recognized than the history of campaigns to expand constitutional rights. This may be in part because only one amendment to date—the 17th Amendment, which mandates the direct election of US Senators (1913)—is commonly thought of as having democratized the structure of the federal government. But American democracy movements have played a much more powerful role in the history of constitution making than the textual residue of a single amendment suggests.

Consider the most celebrated provisions of the US Constitution, the Bill of Rights. These first ten amendments not only provide negative rights against state action. They are also designed to strengthen the capacity of "the People" to act as the sovereign (Ollman and Birnbaum 1990). The 1st Amendment constitutionalized the critical role of popular assemblies, public debate, citizen petitions, and the popular press as institutions of self-government. The 2nd Amendment, together with the constitution's War Powers and Militia clauses, was largely intended to protect against the development of a standing army (Buhle, et al. 2010). The 5th, 6th, and 7th Amendments enshrine that democratic bane of many a judge, prosecutor, and corporate attorney—the jury. The 9th and 10th Amendments reserve powers to the people and the states not expressly delegated to the federal government. We should remember, as well, that the Bill of Rights was forced upon the Framers, anti-democrats that most of them were. Democratic uprisings compelled a second (in this case, progressive) crucial compromise, without which the new republic might not have survived (Ollman and Birnbaum 1990).

This dynamic was to repeat in later years. Suffrage for unpropertied white males followed widespread popular constitutionalism such as that famously practiced with Rhode Island's People's Convention and the Dorr Rebellion. The US Civil War, Abolition, and Reconstruction had at least a little something to do with a man named John Brown who, together with forty-five others, convened a convention in Chatham, Canada to draft the *Provisional Constitution and Ordinances for the People of the United States.* The idea was that, after arming slaves with weapons from the armory at Harpers Ferry,Virginia, insurrectionary forces would need a constitutional framework for the administration of territories under their control (Tsai 2010).

Brown's guerrillas were not alone among abolitionists in this. In 1859, Wisconsin's legislature, dominated by radical abolitionists engaged in determined resistance to enforcement of the Fugitive Slave Act of 1850, began secession proceedings (Manski 2006). Two years later, with the Confederacy threatening to defeat Union forces, a conference of western governors gathered in Cleveland and warned President Lincoln that if the federal government proved too incompetent to win the war, the abolitionist states "will act for themselves."[5] Some to this day deride the radical constitutionalism of the abolitionist movement as unrealistic. They should remember that that movement *did* realize its primary goals.

Popular constitutionalism has also taken less confrontational forms. The populist, progressive, and socialist movements of the late nineteenth and early twentieth centuries succeeded in bringing democratic reforms such as municipal home rule and direct legislation to the constitutions of states across the country. Both of these critical initiatives originated in popular frustration at the inability of the state and national legislatures to achieve desired human rights and good government policies. Both democratic reforms have proven useful to human rights campaigners to this day (Manski and Dolan 2009).

The intended lesson here is that a powerful mutualism can form between liberation movements and democracy movements (Flacks 1988). Movement demands for human rights and collective liberation challenge the legitimacy of the existing order, and strengthen the case for democratization. Movement demands for democratization challenge the authority of the existing order, causing the establishment to consider giving in on specific human rights questions rather than risk losing state power. Similarly, human rights amendments expand the circle of standing and personhood, and thereby democratize the polity. Democracy amendments strengthen the capacity of the people to safeguard their own rights.

Amending Society by Amending the Constitution

Constitutional reform movements in the United States face serious challenges. Nevertheless, popular constitutionalism sometimes succeeds. When it does, we find that it is not merely the written constitutional text that has been amended, it is society itself. The process of overcoming the structural, cultural, and strategic obstacles to constitutional reform is deliberative, participatory, and usually transformative.[6] In reconstituting law, constitutional reform movements play a role in the reconstitution of existing social relations (Teubner 2012; Anderson 2013; Anderson 2002; Buechler 2000; Eyerman and Jamison 1991).

The procedural obstacles to reform posed by the anti-democratic Burkean provisions of the constitution can be turned to advantage. The need to secure the support of at least thirty-eight states creates a long-range terrain of struggle composed of many intermediate campaigns that each of them have clear, definable goals. This, in turn, necessitates serious organizing, outreach, and public debate. Length by length, stoked along the way by the incremental availability of winnable victories, constitutional reform movements build up their resource mobilization capacity. Thus, the political opportunity structure of constitutional change may actually be advantageous to the very kind of long-term movement building required to amend the constitution.[7]

The collective identity problems faced by constitutional reform efforts similarly invoke broad deliberation. The notion of an inviolate Sacral Constitution often falls aside when confronted with the living constitutionalism inherent in popular participation. In the case of *Citizens United v. FEC*, for instance, concerns about constitutional tampering have given way in the face of broad popular support for constitutional amendment.

Fears of the other often prove less tractable. The construction of a majoritarian constitutional reform block in a society that is evermore plural involves significant engagement across class, racial, gender, geographic, age, ideological, and other boundaries. In the process, individuals and groups will take sides, recognizing common interests and defining differences. Constitutional debate acts as a focal lens through which momentous social questions emerge with clarity. From Reconstruction to the Equal Rights Amendment, popular constitutionalism has a demonstrable history of generating new collective identities and antagonisms—both of which are essential elements in the process of social change.

Individuals considering whether to become involved in a constitutional reform effort will often weigh these and other factors, including alternative uses of their time and energies. They will look not only at the success rate for past amendment campaigns, they will also consider the success rate of alternatives. In some cases, as with women's suffrage, they may decide that they cannot secure the social changes they seek without amending the constitution. And always they will find their evaluation of their strategic alternatives shaped by how they feel about the present constitutional situation; what is merely a disagreeable nuisance to some may prove intolerable for others (Aminzade and McAdam 2002; Taylor 2002; Taylor 2010).

The world of the twenty-first century bears some resemblance to those of the eighteenth, nineteenth and twentieth centuries, but only some. Revolutions against aristocracy, slavery, and colonialism produced constitutions consecrating particular conceptions of human rights and democracy. Those constitutions do not encompass modern conceptions and therefore do not mandate the kind of participatory and socially just society that growing numbers of people around the world have come to expect (Blau and Moncada 2006; Wark 2013). Furthermore, the old conceptions of representative democracy and individual liberties are under a constant assault by the institutions of global capitalism (Robinson 2014). Constitutional reform in one country—even a country as powerful as the United States—may not be, on its own, enough (Gannaway 2012; Wiener, et al. 2012; Müller 2010).

In the challenge of constitutional reform, we are presented with a singular opportunity to reconstitute not only our basic law, but our society. We have, as Paine promised us, the "power to begin the world over again," and to do so in a deliberative, democratic, and non-violent manner. If we are serious about constitutionalizing human rights and democracy, we should decide whether the path forward involves a series of amendments or a constitutional convention, as per the procedures of the US Constitution. Maybe the path involves an entirely new constitutional process, a democratic revolution, or popular engagement in global constitutionalism. Perhaps there are multiple paths forward. Decisions about constitutional strategy should be informed not only by an analysis of law and the state, but by an understanding of the kind of social movements necessary for the radical reconstitution of society. Constitutionalism is a social movement form. Constitutionalization is a social change process. The history of American progress is a history of amending America.

Notes

1 For instance, the 17th Amendment, providing for the Direct Election of Senators, was adopted by Congress in order to avoid a probable constitutional convention.
2 I write "access to the vote" as opposed to the "right to vote" because the Supreme Court of the United States has ruled that, "the individual citizen has no federal constitutional right to vote for electors for the President of the United States ..." as per *Bush v. Gore*, 531 U.S. 98 (2000). One response to that ruling has come in the form of the national campaign for a Right to Vote Amendment.
3 President Franklin D. Roosevelt's proposal for an Economic Bill of Rights has played a similar role as a North Star for employment, wage, health, housing, welfare, and other critical economic rights (Blau and Moncada 2006).
4 A review of *Obergefell v. Hodges*, 576 U.S. ___ (2015) will show that both the majority and the dissents claimed popular grounding, with the majority pointing to a marked shift in public opinion in the course of the marriage debate, and the minority claiming that a plebiscite would be required to find equal protection rights for same-sex couples.
5 "I must *be permitted to say it, because it is a fact*, there is a spirit evoked by this rebellion among the liberty-loving people of the country, that is driving them to action and if the Government *will not permit them to act for it, they will act for themselves*. It is better for the Government to direct this current than to let it run wild. So far as possible we have attempted to allay this excess of spirit, but there is a moral element and a reasoning element in this uprising, that cannot be met in the ordinary way. There is a conviction

of great wrongs to be redressed, and that the Government is to be preserved by them. The Government must provide an outlet for this feeling, or it will find one for itself." Alexander Randall to Abraham Lincoln, "Letter on Behalf of the Western Conference of Governors," Reprinted in Quiner 1866: 64.

6 There is an emerging discussion on the question of whether and how constitutional reform processes produce democratization. In a cross-national longitudinal study of 244 countries over 68 years, I found strong evidence of a positive democracy effect from constitutional amendment processes. Devra Moehler makes the case that constitution making in Uganda produced "distrusting democrats" who were better equipped to participate in politics, but less inclined to do so at the national level. Abrak Saati analyzes twenty cases of transitional processes in less stable societies involving constitution making and concludes that the idea that participation produces democratic effects is a myth (Manski 2016; Moehler 2008; Saati 2015).

7 A contemporary example of this approach is to be found with the Move to Amend (MTA) coalition's very deliberate, bottom-up strategy involving a series of escalating campaigns. First, an MTA affiliate is asked to collect signatures to place a resolution supporting the "We the People" Amendment on a local municipal or county ballot. Once a sufficient number of communities in a state have adopted amendment resolutions (generally once 50 percent of the population is represented by such resolutions), the campaign moves to the state level to secure state legislative support or, where possible, to place an amendment resolution on the statewide ballot. In following these steps, prior to serious engagement with Congress, "Move to Amend's" leadership is building up the resource capacity, leadership networks, and social consensus necessary to secure constitutional change.

References

Aminzade, Ron and Doug McAdam. 2002. "Emotions and Contentious Politics." *Mobilization* 7(2): 107–216.

Anderson, Gavin. 2002. "Unthinking Constitutional Law—Towards a Legal Pluralist Theory of Constitutionalism." SJD Thesis, University of Toronto.

Anderson, Gavin. 2013. "Societal Constitutionalism, Social Movements, and Constitutionalism from Below." *Indiana Journal of Global Legal Studies* 20(2): 81–906.

Beaumont, Elizabeth. 2014. *The Civic Constitution: Civic Visions and Struggles in the Path toward Constitutional Democracy*. Oxford, England: Oxford University Press.

Berger, Raoul. 1974. *Executive Privilege: A Constitutional Myth, Studies in Legal History*. Cambridge, MA: Harvard University Press.

Blau, Judith and Alberto Moncada. 2006. *Justice in the United States: Human Rights and the U.S. Constitution*. Lanham, MD: Rowman & Littlefield Publishers, Inc.

Bryant, A. Christopher and Timothy J. Simeone. 2001. "Remanding to Congress: The Supreme Court's New 'On the Record' Constitutional Review of Federal Statutes." *Cornell Law Review* 86(1): 328–396.

Buechler, Steven. 2000. *Social Movements in Advanced Capitalism: The Political Economy and Cultural Construction of Social Activism*. New York, NY: Oxford University Press.

Buhle, Paul, George D. O'Neill, Jr., Bill Kauffman, and Kevin Zeese (eds). 2010. *Come Home America. US*. Lake Wales, FL: Titan Publishing.

Cobb, David. 2007. "The Case against Judicial Review." *By What Authority* 9(2): 1–3.

Coleridge, Greg. 2014. "Supreme Authority: The Growing Power of the US Supreme Court and Democratic Alternatives." *By What Authority* October: 1–4.

Coleridge, Greg, Richard Grossman, and Mary Zepernick. 2000. "Rumors of USA Democracy Discovered to Be Counterfeit." *By What Authority* 3(1): 3–6.

Constitution Project (Georgetown Public Policy Institute). 2005. "Deciding to Use Force Abroad: War Powers in a System of Checks and Balances." Washington, D.C.: The Constitution Project. www.constitutionproject.org/wp/WarPowers_final.pdf (last accessed October 9, 2016).

Dahl, Robert. n.d. *How Democratic Is the American Constitution?* 2nd ed. New Haven, CT: Yale University Press.

Elkin, Stephen L. and Karol Edward Soltan (eds). 1993. *A New Constitutionalism: Designing Political Institutions for a Good Society.* Chicago: University of Chicago Press.

Eyerman, Ron and Andrew Jamison. 1991. *Social Movements: A Cognitive Approach.* University Park, PA: The Pennsylvania State University Press.

Flacks, Richard. 1988. *Making History: The American Left and the American Mind.* New York: Columbia University Press.

Gannaway, Adam. 2012. "Cosmopolitan Constitutionalism: Democratic Legitimacy and the International Order." PhD Dissertation, The New School.

Goodell, William. 1845. *Views of American Constitutional Law, In Its Bearing on American Slavery,* 2nd ed. Utica, NY: Lawson & Chaplin.

Greenberg, Douglas, et al. (eds). 1993. *Constitutionalism & Democracy: Transitions in the Contemporary World.* New York: Oxford University Press.

Irons, Peter. 2005. *War Powers: How the Imperial Presidency Hijacked the Constitution, American Empire Project.* New York: Metropolitan Books.

Irons, Peter. 2006. *A People's History of the Supreme Court: The Men and Women Whose Cases and Decisions Have Shaped Our Constitution.* New York: Penguin Books.

Jung, Moon-Kie, João H. Costa Vargas, and Eduardo Bonilla-Silva (eds). 2011. *The State of White Supremacy.* Stanford, CA: Stanford University Press.

Kairys, David. 2006. "A Brief History of Race and the Supreme Court." *Temple Law Review* 79: 751.

Kramer, Larry D. 2004. *The People Themselves: Popular Constitutionalism and Judicial Review.* New York: Oxford University Press.

Lummis, D. Douglas. 1996. *Radical Democracy.* Ithaca, NY: Cornell University Press.

Maeier, Pauline. 1997. *American Scripture: Making the Declaration of Independence.* New York: Alfred A. Knopf.

Manski, Ben. 2006. "State Power Against the Slave Power: How Wisconsin Warred on Slavery, and Won." *Liberty Tree Journal* 1(3).

Manski, Ben. 2015. "The Democratic Turn of the Century: Learning from the US Democracy Movement." *Socialism and Democracy* 29(1): 2–16.

Manski, Ben. 2016. "Constitutional Change, Deliberation, and Democratization." West Coast Law & Society Retreat, UC Irvine.

Manski, Ben and Karen Dolan. 2009. "Unleash Democracy: Policies for a New Federalism," in *Mandate for Change,* Chester W. Hartman (ed.): 315–326. Lanham, MD: Lexington Books.

Martens, Allison M. 2007. "Reconsidering Judicial Supremacy: From the Counter-Majoritarian Difficulty to Constitutional Transformations." *Perspectives on Politics* 5(3): 447.

Moehler, Davra C. 2008. *Distrusting Democrats: Outcomes of Participatory Constitution Making.* Ann Arbor, MI: University of Michigan Press.

Morris, Jane Anne. 2008. *Gaveling Down the Rabble: How "Free Trade" Is Stealing Our Democracy.* New York: Apex Press.

Move to Amend Coalition. June 10, 2014. "Move to Amend," *MTA Coalition*. https://movetoamend.org/about-us. (last accessed October 11, 2016).

Müller, Jan-Werner. 2010. "Three Constitutionalist Responses to Globalization." in *The Limits of Constitutional Democracy*, Stephen Macedo and Jeffrey Tullis (eds): 239–255. Princeton, NJ: Princeton University Press.

Ollman, Bertell and Jonathan Birnbaum (eds). 1990. *The United States Constitution: 200 Years of Anti-Federalist, Abolitionist, Feminist, Muckraking, Progressive, and Especially Socialist Criticism*. New York: New York University Press.

Quiner, Edwin B. 1866. *The Military History of Wisconsin: A Record of the Civil and Military Patriotism of the State in the War for the Union*. Chicago: Clarke & Co, Publishers.

Raphael, Ray. 2002. *The First American Revolution: Before Lexington and Concord*. New York: The New Press.

Raskin, Jamin B. 2005. *Overruling Democracy: The Supreme Court vs. The American People*. New York: Routledge.

Robinson, William I. 2014. *Global Capitalism and the Crisis of Humanity*. New York: Cambridge University Press.

Saati, Abrak. 2015. *The Participation Myth Outcomes of Participatory Constitution Building Processes on Democracy*. Umeå: Statsvetenskapliga institutionen, Umeå universitet. http://urn.kb.se/resolve?urn=urn:nbn:se:umu:diva-102719 (last accessed October 11, 2016).

Scarry, Elaine. 2011a. "Who Defended the Country?" in *New Democracy Forum*, Joel Rogers and Joshua Cohen (eds). Boston: Beacon Press.

Scarry, Elaine. 2011b. *Thinking in an Emergency*. New York: W.W. Norton & Co.

Taylor, Verta. 2002. "Passionate Politics: Emotions and Social Movements." *Social Movement Studies* 1(2): 199–200.

Taylor, Verta. 2010. "John D. Mccarthy Lifetime Achievement Award: Culture, Identity, and Emotions: Studying Social Movements as If People Really Matter." *Mobilization: An International Journal* 15(2): 113–134.

Teubner, Gunther. 2012. "The New Constitutional Question." Conference on Transnational Societal Constitutionalism, Collegio Carlo Alberto, Torino, Italia.

Tsai, Robert L. 2010. "John Brown's Constitution." *Boston College Law Review* 51: 9–35.

Wark, Julie. 2013. The Human Rights Manifesto. Washington D.C.: Zero Books.

Wiener, Antje, Anthony F. Lang, James Tully, Miguel Poiares Maduro, and Mattias Kumm. 2012. "Global Constitutionalism: Human Rights, Democracy and the Rule of Law." *Global Constitutionalism* 1(1): 1–15.

Young, Alfred F. 2006. *Liberty Tree: Ordinary People and the American Revolution*. New York: New York University Press.

4

A PLACE CALLED LIBERTY[1]

Rodney D. Coates

Emma Lazarus' poem which graces the Statue of Liberty proclaims:

Give me your tired, your poor,
Your huddled masses yearning to breathe free,
The wretched refuse of your teeming shore.
Send these, the homeless, tempest-tost to me,
I lift my lamp beside the golden door!

I live coincidentally in a place called "Liberty," just north of Cincinnati, to some in the middle of nowhere. I live in what my dear friend Elijah Anderson ubiquitously refers to as the "cosmopolitan canopy" where a more civilized, relaxed, and laissez-faire attitude regarding race, difference, and identity prevails. Under this canopy, I experience myself and others as equals, mutually enjoying what I elsewhere (Coates 2008) refer to as the "illusion of inclusion." Here, under the bubble, I greet my neighbors, we frequently engage in convivial conversations about the weather, politics, our children, and the like. To my left is a quiet couple from Ghana. He owns his own shipping/container business and she works in retail. Both are republicans, Catholic, and have three kids. To the right, a nice couple, another republican, he is a police officer and she an educator. In back of me is an equally conservative couple. Again, the husband works as a US Marshall and the wife is a stay-at-home mom. And just up the street, there is also a Deputy County Sherriff. I have often remarked that I have never felt so safe, surrounded by all these guns and those sworn to serve and protect. Yes, I do have democratic neighbors—several families who live on the other side the street in fact. These families also boast a couple of teachers, an account representative, and a dentist. For almost ten years our kids have played and discovered the neighborhood together. Within the canopy of illusion, it is easy to ignore the realities of those living elsewhere. For here, the water is pure, the air is fresh, the birds sing, and the life's prospects appear to be full of both promise and hope. Here, all is well in this place called liberty.

My regular excursions to work, shopping, and church are all within corridors that link one canopy to another, therefore the illusion is preserved—just as long as I stay within the pre-set boundaries. It would therefore be easy to maintain the illusion, to continue to live in this wonderful '*land of Oz*' where all is well, all is pure, and all is as it should be. Would that this was so, or would that it would be this way for the rest of America. For, you see, the rest of America, well at least the majority of America lives not under the canopy but in the real world. In this real world, the harsh reality of racial animus, class distinctions, gender discrimination, and homophobia are all too real. In this real world, the water is not so pure, the air is not so fresh, and the prospects for promise and hope seem dim, fragile, and hard to achieve. In this other America we ask not only if "black lives matter" but if life in general matters. In this other America, liberty appears more of an illusion, despair more keenly experienced, and failure more likely the outcome regardless of effort. In this other America, the canopy is a haven that few get to experience. Together, these two realities—one within the canopy of illusion and the other in the pit of despair—coexist, battle against each other for dominance, and give the appearance of permanence, legitimacy, and normality. How do we reconcile these two realities? How do we come to this place of opposing viewpoints? How can we all experience "a place called liberty"? These are the questions we will explore in this space. For those who still question the importance of this conversation, I would suggest that one need only consider the "Black Lives Matter" protests to demonstrate their relevance.

Across the country—from Baltimore to Oakland, from Ferguson to Cincinnati, from New York to New Orleans—one can hear the refrain "Black Lives Matter." Of course, you say, yes we concur. It's almost trivial to assert the value, dignity, and significance of any lives, not to mention those who are black.

But as we listen to the chants, and the attention being directed at police, as yet another young black male dies—we cannot but wonder why we need to have this conversation. It's obvious—isn't it? Maybe not. Maybe we are so caught up in a world of selfies and narcissism that we fail to see past our last post, text, or groupie.

If, however black lives do matter, then it is not because they are black but that they are lives. Our very humanity requires that we recognize this. And in so doing, we should be clear that the issue should not have to wait to be resolved at the end of a police revolver, nor should it have to wait for the press, the protests, or the collective guilt to reach us that we recognize that the problem is neither black, nor is it necessarily one of policing. Rather, it is one that strikes at the very root of our existence—and it has a name—self-worth. We just might conclude that not only black, but red, and brown lives also mattered.

If black, red, tan, and brown lives mattered, then we might just conclude that they should matter enough that we demand that the abysmal dropout rates affecting persons of color in our schools, both locally and nationally, should matter.

If these lives mattered we would hold our schools accountable and in the process hold teachers, parents accountable, and hold communities accountable. We would recognize that absent education and training, these youths are essentially dead on arrival. We would insist that for our kids, our future, that failure is just not an option. That is if indeed they mattered.

If these lives mattered, we would condemn our thirty-year war on drugs which systematically singled out blacks, Native Americans, and Hispanics, particularly males for differential surveillance, criminalization, and incarceration.

If these lives mattered we would reopen the cases, release those thousands that were inappropriately sentenced under our archaic drug laws, paid restitutions, and readmitted within society.

If these lives mattered, we would look at the neonatal and postnatal condition in which black, Hispanic, and Indigenous infants who are more likely to die prior to term, die during delivery, or not survive past their second birthday. If these lives mattered, we might challenge the almost 50 percent chance of some teens and young adults being unemployed or underemployed.

In so doing, we might conclude these problems are systemically linked—that from the cradle to the grave—black, red, and brown lives are dismissed, marginalized, and delegitimized. If they mattered, maybe, just maybe, we would systematically—from cradle to grave—dismantle the structures that account for the death and demise of all too many of our fellow humans. That is if indeed we believed that they mattered. And then, maybe we will not have to discover that these lives matter as another young life is cut short. As we proceed, we should understand that we did not get here either by accident or by fate; our America with its bifurcated dreams, truncated opportunities, and frustrated aspirations was negotiated, deliberated, and contentious. Let us explore this path to an imperfect union.

Toward an Imperfect Union

The path toward an imperfect union began thousands of miles away, hundreds of years back into our history. This path involved the then greater powers of land and sea, along with what some mistakenly presume as the lesser powers of people and places. This path for one group has been described as a discovery and for the other group an encounter. Unfortunately, even our language about this time is fraught with both illusion and mistaken identities. For example, neither of these groups experiences any unity or unifying themes; as groups, they were as disparate as they were desperate, they were as likely to be enemies as allies, and their visions were never holistic or monolithic. The fact is that as we look back to this period of 1492 we discover that what we have come to call America was a series of misadventures, mistakes, and misfortunes. America, as we know it, was never meant to be, and continues to be what we never intended it to be. For we, living in this space at this time, understand that there are many "Americas." Some occupy a space called the United States, others occupy a much larger space including both North and South America, still others are spaces within spaces, occupied by those who are essentially stateless, placeless, and experience life on the borders of our consciousness, within an ever illusive frontier(s). It should be noted that our use of these categories are not intended to either reflect an historical sequence or a categorical distinction. In fact, they have typically existed and interacted simultaneously, competitively and/or synergistically. Time and space limitations mean that we concentrate on the Americas that occupy the space called the United States. In the process, we shall try to highlight how the other spaces have and continue to have importance to our identity as a country.

Americas—Encounters and Discoveries

The first groups to traverse the paths to the Americas involved ancient peoples that settled these spaces long before Columbus stumbled across the islands in the Caribbean now known as the Bahamas. He never actually landed in North America, and spent all of his time exploring the Central and South American coasts. The original inhabitants that dominated these Americas represented nations, ethnic and tribal groups, bands, and tribes.

Rather than seeking freedom, the first settlers to these Americas from Europe were seeking gold, dominion, and profits. Christopher, having been rejected by King John II of Portugal, finally was able to convince Ferdinand and Isabella of Spain to finance his scheme to locate a westward route to Asia by sea. For their investment, to equip three ships, Spain was to be able to claim "all and every kind of merchandise, whether pearls, precious stones, gold, silver, spices, and other objects and merchandise whatsoever, of whatever kind, name and sort, which may be bought, bartered, discovered, acquired and obtained ... ," Christopher, now Don Columbus, Admiral, and Governor (and his heirs) would receive 10 percent of all profits (after expenses) in perpetuity throughout all time.[2] Columbus' diary is replete with his struggle to find and secure his fortune. Even after he was disabused of the fact that he was nowhere near India, he nevertheless sought to secure his plunder.

Even as Columbus was yet looking for the gold and other riches, other European powers were scrambling to get into the queue. Portugal, claiming that their rights had been violated, appealed to the Pope who responded by issuing a proclamation assigning all lands west of Cape Verde Island to Spain and all lands east of this line to Jon of Portugal. Strangely, no Native Americans were invited to this discussion as their lands were divvied up by Church and State. This omission would be compounded with Columbus' second trip to the New Espanola. He, with more than 1,200 men and seventeen ships enslaved and killed hundreds of Native Americans in search of gold. Columbus, using extreme brutality (ranging from castration to beheading) was forced to work the gold mines until they were exhausted.

The reality was that limited actual gold was available, but this did not stop Columbus. In fact, he became even more fervent in his quest and in his cruelty. Failing to find the gold, Columbus turned to more extreme measures. Forcing some into slavery, while others were raped, murdered, and brutalized, the Native Americans, Arawaks, choosing to fight back, mounted a resistance army. This army, ill-equipped with bows and arrows, faced cavalry armed with muskets and swords. In the first two years of fighting close to 125,000 Haitians were murdered, mutilated or committed suicide. And still, Columbus had no gold. The solution—large landed estates—were carved out of the wilderness for Spanish investors, with slaves to work the plantations. And thus begins our tortured history of the Americas. The other "great powers" of Europe would soon follow with even more insidious, cruel, and insane schemes to make profits on the ignoble path toward "a place called liberty."

Frontiers

One of the staples of US entertainment is the plethora of movies that go under the genre of "Cowboys and Indians," in fact we have even taken the basic themes into outer space with such movies as Star Wars, Star Trek, and of course Avatar. In these futuristic frontiers, we have the good guys (mostly white) confronting the bad guys (mostly evil, lawless, and all-too-often persons of color). Coincidentally, these places are often replete with precious minerals such as "unobtanium." We know that these spaces, where "we boldly go where no *man* has ever gone before," are considered "lawless," until we bring the law to point out the illusive essence of frontiers.

Within the US context, frontiers were contested spaces where European imperialists vied for control. Absent such control, they were considered lawless, wastelands inhabited by savages. The strange thing about these "savages" is that just before they were discovered to occupy the newly identified frontiers, they were typically described as peaceful, unassuming peoples. What turned them into savages, we might ask?

The answer is quite simple—they became defined as savages as imperial powers targeted them, the land, and resources for absorption, control, or acquisition. The Europeans understood that they had neither the military power nor the resources to subdue and control such a vast land mass, peopled by so many competent warriors. What they did have, as Jared Diamond (1997) informs us, were "guns, germs and steel." The volatility of the "frontier" was also heightened as European powers, determined to expand their control offered both guns and steel weaponry to the indigenous populations. Several examples can be identified to illustrate this process. One of the most vicious examples occurred during the French and Indian Wars (1754–1763) in which the British and French fought to expand their control over much of the Ohio valley, up through and including current-day New York, Pennsylvania, and Pittsburgh. The French, with about 60,000

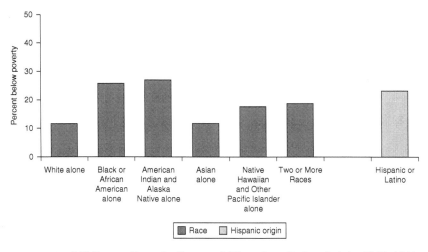

FIGURE 4.1 US Poverty Rates by Race and Hispanic or Latino Origin: 2007–2011

settlers compared to an estimated 2 million British, quickly allied themselves with Ohio Valley federations such as the Delawares and Shawnees. This strategy might have been effective, had the British not utilized an even more effective weapon.

The most effective weapon accounting for European conquest in the Americas was neither guns nor steel, but miniscule, almost invisible germs. Crowd germs such as smallpox, measles and flu ravaged the semi-urban populations, killing an estimated 90 percent of the indigenous populations (Diamond 1997). One of the most infamous, if not first, use of germ warfare took place close to the end of the French and Indian wars (1754–1763) when Lord Jeffery Amherst, commanding general of British forces in North America, sent smallpox-infested blankets and handkerchiefs to the indigenous warring tribes. The results were so devastating, one must wonder who the real savages were. One need not wonder, however, why indigenous peoples did not want to be in proximity with these strange, disease-carrying peoples. Unfortunately, no matter how far the indigenous peoples wandered, the Europeans followed. The result was an ever-expanding frontier, where lawlessness, destruction, and devastation prevailed.

Borders

Borders are those spaces that separate canopies from frontiers. While such borders may be more or less permeable depending upon the needs of the economic, political, and social system; their primary role is to preserve the illusion of permanence. Borders consequently require various mechanisms, processes, and/or structures to accomplish their purposes.

Looking at Figure 4.1, one might be tempted to conclude that poverty, just coincidentally, is associated with being an Indigenous, Black or Hispanic person.

Looking at almost any other set of tables might also lead you to conclude that unemployment, crime and punishment, illness, and ignorance are also, and again coincidentally, associated with these same folks. When one considers the longevity of these problems, which are continuously associated with these same communities and people, you might conclude that they are the problem. Such a conclusion, however, would be devoid of any historical, political or social contexts. They would have to ignore the very real, and ever-present racial reservations that have shaped the life experiences of these peoples.

Several different types of racial reservations have originated within the United States. Native American has historically been associated with these racial reservations where, under the guise of tribal sovereignty, Indigenous peoples have been segregated, victimized, and discriminated against. They constitute the largest percentage (27.0) of our nation's poor, Blacks come in as a close second (25.8) and Hispanics (range from a high 26.3 among Dominicans and 16.2 for Cubans) (Macartney, Bishaw, and Fontenot 2013).

Black racial reservations originated in the United States with the rise of Black Belts after the civil war, the remnants of which became the "dark ghettos" (Clark 1965), that currently the "truly disadvantaged" (Wilson 1987) call home. These reservations reflect the dilapidated racial zones situated in older, urban cores. The racial reservation is culturally heterogeneous, both in terms of class and race, where both space and persons are stigmatized, ostracized, and marginalized. These are the places where work, along with hope, dreams, and opportunities, have all disappeared.

We should also demystify the illusion of whiteness by identifying white racial reservations. These racial reservations—sometimes referred to as white ghettos—include much of Appalachia, and the rural south and southwest. Its residents are typically referred to as "rednecks," "poor white trash," or "trailer park trash." As one reporter remarked, if the residents living in Appalachia "weren't 98.5 percent white, we'd call it a reservation" (Williamson 2014). Here, too, we find the last remnants of the Scots-Irish working class that took the place of African slaves when slavery was abolished. They worked in the mines, farms, and forests providing many of the raw materials that fuel the modern American economy. Illicit drug sales and production, historically ranging from moonshine to today's meth, color a past riddled with family feuds, whiskey stills, hotrods, and pervasive poverty, crime, and illness. As with the other racial reservations, we note the absence of sufficient investment capital, educational shortfalls, and occupational opportunities. We also find stigmatization, social dislocation and isolation, marginalization, and despair.

Racial reservations are maintained by both effective and sustained borders. Such borders are typically maintained by a series of enforcement tactics and personnel. First a definition: racial borders are essentially mechanisms, practices, and structures that serve to restrict capital and persons from leaving the designated area. The use of both police and other para/extra and actual military to control populations within the racial reservations is well documented within our various histories and will be taken up shortly. The not-so-obvious use of legal and extra-legal mechanisms to curtail population and capital into these areas is, to a lesser degree, acknowledged. The reality that racial reservations must be preserved suggests that such mechanisms must be constantly employed and deployed. Let's take a look at some of them.

Several systemic and systematic ways to control racial reservations can be identified as including limiting access to fiscal, educational, political, and other resources. This is indeed the case for all the various racial reservations that we have identified. The long history of federal, state, and corporate interference in Indigenous people's communities is well documented. The very reason, past the official rhetoric, of the creation of "reservations" was not only to justify the stealing of Native American land and other resources, but also to better control, "Americanize," and keep dependent these said peoples. In 1831, when Chief Justice John Marshal declared that Indigenous Peoples on reservations were "domestic dependent nations" he essentially made them wards of the state. As wards, or is that children, the federal government took control of all assets. This forced dependency has meant that they are among the poorest communities in the United States. From the outset, with the allotment policies of the nineteenth century, rights both for individual and collectives were distorted, if not destroyed. Now, almost 80 years since the Wheeler-Howard Act formally ended the process, the basic fragmentation of land holding continues. Thus, while on paper the Indigenous peoples of the United States have the illusion of sovereignty, in reality their prospects, economic well-being, and future are intricately and paternalistically linked to the Bureau of Indian Affairs.

All developments (economic or communal) must first be reviewed and authorized by the federal government. The process, with as many as four agencies and forty-nine separate steps, not only thwarts any real progress, but guarantees that these poor stay poor. Those on racial reservations are also likely to be victimized.

Since crime is under the jurisdiction of the Justice Department, indigenous people cannot effectively use social, judicial, or police control to reduce rates of victimization. For example, federal data reveals that the Justice Department routinely refuses to file charges on about half of murder investigations and nearly two-thirds of sexual assault cases (Williams 2012). While federal prosecutors claim that they have to dismiss these cases because of lack of admissible evidence, indigenous people believe that it demonstrates that they are subjected to a second-class criminal justice system that actually encourages criminal behavior.

On other racial reservations, the flaws in the criminal justice system are just as real, if not as apparent. Of late, racial reservations such as those in Ferguson, Missouri have documented that while the civilian population is more than two-thirds black, they constitute less than 11 percent of the police force. Why might this be a problem? Well, if data from New York is applicable across the country, it appears that Black and Hispanic police are more than 70 percent likely to live in the cities in which they police. White police officers are less than half as likely (Silver 2014). If we look across 75 of the cities with the largest police forces, a full 60 percent of its police officers live outside of the city limits. In these cities, 49 percent of the black and 47 percent of the Hispanic officers live within the city limits. Comparatively, 35 percent of white officers live within the city that they work. Granted we are talking about averages (with the observation that some cities have more and others less), but these tendencies are troubling. While more diversity and more police living in neighborhoods that they serve, can lead to better police—community relations, it may not minimize either police misconduct or high crime rates.

The very presence of racial reservations lies at the heart of racial animus between police and community residents (Rothstein 2015). Part of the problem is that police serve as border guards whose very mission is to keep the lid on the barrel. We should ask a question regarding the frequently cited mission of to "serve and protect," often associated with the police—who is being served and who protected? It is clear—from the rash of police misconducts, the whole slew of "law and order" arguments, and the politics of crime and punishment—that the principal community(ies) that the police are charged with serving and protecting are those outside of the "racial reservation." I am arguing, and I believe that the record will show, that the primary function of police is to protect corporate and personal property. If we recognize that residents of racial reservations are least likely to own either, then it follows that the primary role of the police is to protect said property against the actions of the poor. Even more, if we recognize that racial reservations are bereft of good jobs or the training and education required to secure them, then their existence in these "concrete jungles" becomes even more desperate. The secondary role, therefore, of police is to control such desperation and the anger that it breeds. For this reason, during times of economic downturn, more aggressive policing is ordered. Not, by the way, in anticipation of greater criminality, but in anticipation of higher levels of frustration and anger. Thus, the border is preserved by these officers sworn to "preserve and protect." Lastly, the tendency to put the worst and most troubled cops in these communities does little to defuse these already-tense situations.

As remarked by Steve Biko: "The most potent weapon in the hands of the oppressor is the mind of the oppressed." All too often, history has documented that one way to keep folks on the reservation is to control their education. As a consequence, it should not come as a surprise that often we tend to find the worst, not the best, teachers serving racial reservations. The story of math educator Jamie Escalante is quite telling. Escalante, immortalized in the 1988 film *Stand and Deliver*, became famous for teaching the unteachable troubled Puerto Ricans and black kids in Los Angeles calculus and math. He believed that if the students could have the drive, they could thrive in these subjects. This unconventional teacher, who disdained meetings, pomp, and formality, operated in a rundown school known for violence and drugs, not academic excellence.

Starting an advanced math program with a small group of students, within six years, he had students not only taking but passing the advanced placement test in calculus. The testing service that designed the test charged Escalante and his students with cheating, and invalidated their test scores. Several months later, many of these students retook the exam and again excelled thus proving not only that the company was wrong, but that those who had dismissed them and their lives were also wrong. You would think, after receiving major national and state awards, that the program and its teacher would become the model for not only the district, but for educators across the country. Nothing could be further from the truth: opening minds and pathways out of the racial reservation is often not rewarded. In fact, often much like pieceworkers, such individuals are considered to be "rate-busters" who strive to produce to the utmost of their ability despite opposition from peers. Petty jealousies, disdain, and ridicule hounded Escalante almost to his death in 2010.

The reality of racial reservations is that they can operate without intentionality. Therefore, when we look into school funding, we note that, while on the surface, the processes and mechanisms appear to be unbiased, their actual operations and outcomes are decidedly biased. Such outcomes have been repeatedly observed by courts. For example, in my home state, over eighteen years ago the Ohio Supreme Court ruled that the state's method of funding schools was unconstitutional. Justice Francis E. Sweeney, writing for the majority in 1997 wrote: "by our decision today, we send a clear message to lawmakers: The time has come to fix the system. Let there be no misunderstanding. Ohio's public school-financing system must undergo a complete systematic overhaul" (Siegel and Vardon 2012). There have been three such rulings, yet the system remains in place. The result is that more affluent, typically white suburban schools receive more monies, while poorer, more diverse schools receive less. This is due primarily because of the state's funding formula which overly relies upon local taxes. What this translates to is that those schools in more affluent districts have more monies available to fund their schools then others. When we add the reality that this state, along with most across the US, has cut spending by close to $515 million annually, the poorer schools, which serve the racial reservations, are hardest hit. Just how widespread is this problem? A 2011 US Department of Education study reveals that more than 40 percent of low-income schools do not get their fair share of either state or local funds. These high-poverty schools consequently have markedly fewer educational resources than their peers in wealthier districts. The problem is only compounded when we realize that these schools are also more likely to be older, with their infrastructure in more severe stages of dilapidation. Next, if we understand that the schools are within areas already under stress in terms of crime, violence, and drugs, we would conclude that more not less monies are needed. Finally, these schools serving disadvantaged pupils also are more likely to have less-experienced teachers who are paid less to teach more. Ultimately, as these schools are more likely to be situated on racial reservations, the problems and the gaps associated with inadequate educational funding continues to produce students who are ill-prepared to maximize their opportunities.

Home ownership for both Blacks and Hispanics demonstrates the reality of living on racial reservations. Such disparities range from racial biases with the 1934 National Housing Act which systematically denied home loans to black homeowners, even when their "credit worthiness" was equivalent with whites. This redlining, singlehandedly accounts for the declining home values, higher poverty rates, and disinvestment in black neighborhoods. More recently, the mortgage scandal of the past few years documents how major lenders such as Wells Fargo Bank consistently steered thousands of Black and Hispanic borrowers to subprime mortgages, while sending whites with similar credit profiles to prime lenders (Sullivan, et al. 2015). If we add the overabundance of payday lenders, pawn shops, rent to own, and other predatory lending enterprises within these same communities, the continued capital disinvestment and exploitation of racial reservations accounts for their continued poverty status.

There are those that will suggest that the notion of racial reservations deny agency, and that such agency must be taken into any consideration if we are to understand the plight of those trapped in cycles of poverty, crime, and living on the margins of our collective national consciousness. If such individuals, the argument goes, would just pull themselves up by their bootstraps then they can make a difference in their lives and those of their families. Look, they might point, at the many (me being one) successful folks that have navigated themselves out of the centers of pathology, past the borders of despair, and now have prominent status within the canopy. I would argue that such myths are indeed an illusion, for even though some of us have made it out of the racial reservation, the few success stories (much like lotteries) demonstrate that these are indeed the exception and not the rule. The continual presence of such tokens of success should cause one to wonder about the fairness of the system. But, much like the lotteries, and other forms of gambling—when the lights go off, and the winners have been declared, we lose sight of the countless thousands that did not win. Past this, life should not be a lottery; it should not depend upon being lucky. Rather it should be based upon your effort. Our conclusion is that the problem is not with the people, but with the system. Thus our efforts should be less about fixing, remediating, and enabling the people, but with fixing, remediating and enabling the system. This leads us to the following principle:

A New Bill of Rights

We hold these truths to be self-evident, that for twenty-six score and fifteen years this Nation, conceived in imperialism and dedicated to profits, has consistently avoided human rights, decency, and morality. Moreover, it has consistently practiced genocide, slavery, racism, sexism, homophobia, and has been destructive to both the environment and in general the world we live in and on. We, being the inhabitants of this nation, do thusly believe that a more just and morally sound nation is possible. Toward that end we ascribe and demand that this nation now dedicates itself to both inclusion and liberty, to equity and morality as set forth by the following bill of rights.

We believe that all:

- Regardless of status, gender, sexual orientation, race/ethnicity, place of birth, residency, etc. should have access to quality education as a basic human right.
- Regardless of status, gender, sexual orientation, race/ethnicity, place of birth, residency, etc. should have access to affordable, quality housing.
- Regardless of status, gender, sexual orientation, race/ethnicity, place of birth, residency, etc. should have access to affordable, quality legal counsel.
- Regardless of status, gender, sexual orientation, race/ethnicity, place of birth, residency, etc. should be able to sit in judgment as jurors in all forms of court proceedings taking place within their communities.
- Regardless of status, gender, sexual orientation, race/ethnicity, place of birth, residency, etc. should comprise the bulk of the police community boards charged with the oversight, assessment, and evaluation of police departments serving within their communities.
- That police departments and its officers, school boards and its teachers should reflect the status, gender, sexual orientation, race/ethnicity of the residents of that community.
- That police officers, teachers, and all other public servants serving specific communities must reside within those respective communities.
- Regardless of status, gender, sexual orientation, race/ethnicity, place of birth, residency, etc. should have access to prime lending and credit markets. Further, that lenders be required to demonstrate annually that its loan portfolios reflect the demographic realities of the communities that they serve. Barring this, the government will/shall become a lender of last resort guaranteeing all equitable access to lending and credit markets.

Notes

1 This is part of a much larger project that I am working on with the same title.
2 See p. 79, www.americanjourneys.org/pdf/AJ-061.pdf (last accessed October 11, 2016).

References

Cazenave, Noel A. 2011. *The Urban Racial State: Managing Race Relations in American Cities.* Lanham, MD: Rowman and Littlefield.

Clark, Kenneth B. 1965. *Dark Ghetto: Dilemmas of Social Power.* New York: Harper Collins Publishers.

Coates, Rodney D. 2008. "Covert Racism in the USA and Globally." *Sociology Compass* 2(1): 208–231.

Diamond, Jared. 1997. *Guns, Germs, and Steel: The Fates of Human Society*. New York: W.W. Norton and Company.

Macartney, Suzanne, Alemayeh Bishaw, and Kayla Fontenot. 2013. "Poverty Rates for Selected Detailed Race and Hispanic Groups by State and Place: 2007–2011." *Census: US Department of Commerce*. www.census.gov/prod/2013pubs/acsbr11-17.pdf (last accessed October 11, 2016).

Rothstein, Richard. 2015. "Widespread Racial Housing Segregation Is a Major Instigator for Protests." *Alternet*. www.alternet.org/news-amp-politics/widespread-racial-housing-segregation-major-instigator-protests (last accessed October 11, 2016).

Siegel, Jim and Joe Vardon. 2012. "15 Years – No School-Funding Fix." *The Columbus Dispatch*. www.dispatch.com/content/stories/local/2012/03/25/15-years--no-school-funding-fix.html (last accessed October 11, 2016).

Silver, Nate. 2014. "Most Police Don't Live in the Cities They Serve." *FiveThirtyEight*. http://fivethirtyeight.com/datalab/most-police-dont-live-in-the-cities-they-serve/ (last accessed October 11, 2016).

Sullivan, Laura, Tatjana Meschede, Lars Dietrich, and Thomas Shapiro. 2015. "The Racial Wealth Gap: Why Policy Matters." *Institute for Assets and Social Policy*, Brandeis University. https://iasp.brandeis.edu/pdfs/2015/RWA.pdf (last accessed October 11, 2016).

US Department of Education. "More than 40% of Low-Income Schools Don't Get a Fair Share of State and Local Funds." *Department of Education*. www.ed.gov/news/press-releases/more-40-low-income-schools-dont-get-fair-share-state-and-local-funds-department-education-research-finds (last accessed October 11, 2016).

Williams, Timothy. 2012. "Higher Crime, Fewer Charges on Indian Land." *The New York Times*. http://law.und.edu/tji/_files/docs/article.pdf (last accessed October 11, 2016).

Williamson, Kevin. 2014. "The White Ghetto." *National Review*. www.nationalreview.com/article/367903/white-ghetto-kevin-d-williamson (last accessed October 11, 2016).

Wilson, William Julius. 1987. *The Truly Disadvantaged: The Inner City, the Underclass and Public Policy*. Chicago, IL: University of Chicago Press.

PART II

Claiming Our Rights

5

WHEREFORE "THE DESPOTISM OF THE PETTICOAT"?

American Women, Gender, and Constitutional Omissions

Susan C. Pearce and Kathleen B. Basile

It has been 240 years since Abigail Adams implored her husband, future US President John Adams, to "remember the ladies" as he co-drafted the Declaration of Independence in 1776. The future First Lady warned that "if particular care and attention is not paid to the Ladies, we are determined to foment a rebellion and will not hold ourselves bound by any laws in which we have no voice, or Representation." John Adams famously wrote in response that women are already in control, and if the current order granting authority to men in the colonies were to dissolve, men would be subject to the "despotism of the petticoat" (Donlan 2008: 4).

What has transpired since this high-profile contentious exchange? This addresses the current state of US constitutional guarantees for women, and absence thereof, based on a history of women's movements, in the context of current international human rights developments, and in comparison with other constitutions. We report on the findings and recommendations by students in a 2015 sociological theory class to revise the US Constitution to include women and gender, building upon strong examples from other countries. Centrally, we confront the need to take an intersectional approach to rights for women, recognizing the plurality of social locations that women occupy, and which help determine their status in society across other social locations. This includes gender rights more broadly, such as sexual orientation, gender identity, and gender expression.

Through the following, we argue that one of the most compelling arguments for updating the US Constitution for the twenty-first century is the gaping absence of specified rights across genders. For a society and a democracy to operate, should not everyone be at the table? Should there be obstacles that keep some from sitting at the table? Are there broken chairs, irregularly sized chairs, insufficient numbers of chairs, or an inadequately sized table? Such a project can be framed as a critical cornerstone for forwarding the "unfinished project of modernity" (d'Entreves and Benhabib 1997). We build this argument on the following bases: (1) the modern project contains the seeds of its own critique regarding the inclusion of women; (2) international treaties and recent constitutions are more aligned with changing gender norms than is the US Constitution; and (3) despite legal progress, women experience continued injustices and inequalities that necessitate broader national, more permanent, guarantees. Across this review, we highlight cultural transformations across many societies—in particular, an embrace of human rights norms and a goal of equality across genders—to argue that the time has come for constitutional revision.

Women and Rights: A History

We begin with the project of "modernity." The following brief historical overview illustrates the collective activism that is responsible for the gains that women have made to date, and recounts the philosophical-political grounding of earlier critical gender discourses that remain relevant today. At the time of Abigail's letter to John, normative questions about gender were in a nascent state in European and colonial public discourse. The commonly accepted legal language in the emerging European constitutions was that of "rights of man." Even if the technical meaning of "man" signified the generic person, early Western Enlightenment-inspired constitutions and declarations clearly inferred "man" to be a gendered class. Philosopher Simone de Beauvoir advanced this critique in her classic feminist tome, *The Second Sex*. She insisted that a political philosophy that advances the idea of equality does so at the expense of women by avoiding sexual difference and presuming that the male is the default human (de Beauvoir 2011). The sidelining of Abigail Adams's attempts illustrates de Beauvoir's observation: our constitutional framers excluded women's voices in their political discourses and silenced their proposals for women's full enfranchisement. Those modern/modernizing political discourses were born in emerging free public spheres where debates on Enlightenment ideas could take place, signifying a shift in European political culture (Habermas 1989). Significantly, however, those public arenas were spaces from which women were largely absent.

Nevertheless, key European women were challenging these gender exclusions from the beginning. French playwright and early feminist Olympe de Gouges responded to her country's 1789 Declaration of the Rights of Man, two years after it was penned, with *A Declaration of the Rights of Woman and the Female Citizen* (de Gouges 1791). De Gouges asserted women's right to free speech and political participation, and argued that women's reproductive role for society entitled them to participate in public life. And one year later, in 1792, English philosopher Mary Wollstonecraft followed suit with *A Vindication of the Rights of Woman* (Wollstonecraft 1999). Wollstonecraft argued that women had the same capacity for reason as men and should be public, democratic subjects; she also insisted that women be fully included in democracies since they reproduced and were responsible for the education of society's democratic citizens. In 1793, Olympe de Gouges met the guillotine for her words; Wollstonecraft escaped this fate. Both of these women's campaigns exemplify the fact that Enlightenment-era revolutionary foundational documents carried the seeds of an imminent critique: by excluding any application to women, those documents contradicted themselves.

Across the Atlantic, despite Abigail Adams's best efforts, the US Constitution would contain no specific language devoted to the rights of women or protection from discrimination. Women were excluded from voting, political voice, and other basic citizenship rights and benefits. By default, these former English colonies had followed English Common Law despite the intent to create a political culture distinct from Europe, in which the law of "coverture" proscribed the rights of married women: the husband was the legal subject of the home, and the wife derived rights from her husband. As British jurist William Blackstone described coverture in 1765: "By marriage, the husband and wife are one person in law: that is, the very being or legal existence of the woman is suspended during the marriage, or at least is incorporated and consolidated into that of the husband; under whose wing, protection, and *cover*, she performs every thing…" (Blackstone 1765: 442–445).

American women could not draw up contracts independently, could not sue, and any income or property they acquired went to their husband. An American-born woman who married a foreign-born non-citizen man, in fact, could lose her citizenship upon marriage. In contrast, in early Louisiana, women had property ownership and divorce rights as well as the right to sole inheritance. Louisiana women benefited from a *plaçage* system, which granted limited rights such as property ownership to women (and their heirs) who were married to or common law wives of male European colonists. These women, called *placées*, included Native American women who were captured as wives and formerly enslaved African women. Entitled to as much as one-third of the white man's property upon his death, some women used these inheritances to become small business owners. More generally, American women may have informally enjoyed some liberties not yet visible in Europe; in his 1831 observations of American democracy, French political writer Alexis de Tocqueville remarked on the comparatively relative freedom that he noticed among American women, especially that of single women walking unaccompanied in public (de Tocqueville 1994).

Across Europe and the emerging United States, however, two social tracks paralleled and conflicted with one another: on the one hand, a gender order that was upheld by custom, law, and everyday interactions, reflecting a patriarchal hierarch of gender relations; on the other, an emerging resistant strand that confronted the contradictions between this gender order and the stated ideals of a democratic republic, penned in lofty, aspirational language.

The Vote: Women's First and Only Constitutional Amendment

Hovering between coverture and the *plaçage*, in fact, was an absence of legally encoded, constitutionally grounded rights for women to vote, own property, hold political office, file for divorce, and a host of other rights. American womens' impatience with this unequal treatment in law and society began to gain visibility in the nineteenth century. By 1848, a consolidated effort began by women and their male allies to write themselves into the US Constitution, and thus, the democracy, during the now-legendary Seneca Falls (New York) Convention. Spearheaded by Lucretia Mott and Elizabeth Cady Stanton, women and their male allies penned a manifesto that, like the imminent critiques of De Gouges and Wollstonecraft, intentionally referenced their society's foundational democratic texts in the title: "Declaration of Sentiments and Resolutions," and with its opening of "We hold these truths to be self-evident: that all men and women are created equal; that they are endowed by their Creator with certain inalienable rights; that among these are life, liberty, and the pursuit of happiness;..." ("Report of the Woman's..." 1997). Initiating what is often called the feminist movement's first "wave," this Convention listed a range of demands to dismantle women's systemic societal disadvantages, but eventually narrowed in on the franchise as the doorway to other rights. A contentious racial history at the center of this struggle has been well-documented and is important to emphasize here; despite African American contributions and leadership to the Convention and the movement (including Ida B. Wells Barnett, Frederick Douglass, and Sojourner Truth), both the strategies and the verbiage of white leadership elevated the rights of (white) women over African American women and stoked racial tensions.

Just as the idea for the Seneca Falls Convention grew out of a transnational movement to end slavery (in which Mott and Stanton were involved), the movement to include women in emerging democracies through the franchise also crossed continents.[1] Yet women's suffrage was won only after decades and several generations had passed. In the United States, it came in 1920, through the 19th Amendment to the constitution, seventy-two years after the campaign began. With the exception of New York and Michigan, none of the states east of the Mississippi River offered suffrage to women prior to 1920; thus, it was not the original thirteen colonies that pioneered women's constitutional rights. (Several northeastern states had extended, but then rescinded, the franchise to women in the eighteenth century.) With suffragist Alice Paul at the helm, a group separated themselves from the National American Woman Suffrage Association to push the 19th Amendment forward and campaign for ratification. Calling themselves the National Woman's Party, they were able to narrowly win the final state needed for ratification: Tennessee. The United States had trailed several European countries in extending the vote to women, as well as Australia, New Zealand, and Canada. Notably, the hard-won victory by American women in 1920 would be the last US constitutional change that named women or gender in its wording.

After the Franchise: The ERA

This closure on constitutional change was not the suffragists' intent, however. Recognizing that women needed more guarantees than the franchise, Alice Paul went on to draft the Equal Rights Amendment in 1923, to expand rights for women and make the constitutional presence of women all-encompassing. That amendment stated, simply:

> Section 1. Equality of rights under the law shall not be denied or abridged by the United States or by any state on account of sex.
> Section 2. The Congress shall have the power to enforce, by appropriate legislation, the provisions of this article.
> Section 3. This amendment shall take effect two years after the date of ratification (Lang 2015).

In her speech announcing the amendment, Paul proclaimed, "We shall not be safe until the principle of equal rights is written into the framework of our government" (Francis n.d.).

The ERA uses the language of negative rights, in the style of other constitutional amendments, but with the clear intent to expand negative and positive rights to all individuals regardless of sex. (Negative rights specify that citizens are protected *from* certain infractions, and positive rights specify that citizens can claim rights *to* certain protections or amenities, including social and economic rights.) It was not until 1972 that the ERA passed Congress, in the midst of the feminist movement's so-called "second wave," a mass cultural shift in which rights for women returned to center stage through protests in public arenas. Alice Paul died in 1977, still hoping that the amendment was on the cusp of final ratification. Ratification ultimately failed by the deadline, in part due to divisive public debates over the consequences of the amendment, such as the fear of military conscription of women, debates over abortion (Mansbridge 1986), and the emergence of a conservative political tide, compounded by a cultural backlash against womens' movements of the 1960s and 1970s. By the deadline, 15 states had not ratified: three states short of the required number.[2] As of 2016, ninety-three years have passed since the ERA was penned.

Twentieth-Century Treaties and Normative Shifts

Despite the ERA's fate and much unfinished business, the twentieth century will be remembered for a tidal wave in normative shifts towards expanded rights and opportunities for women in the United States and beyond. Women's movements pressed international governing bodies to address their rights, needs, and concerns in a panoply of treaties that referenced the political-philosophical foundation of "human rights." While the language of human rights has not been fully embraced across the world or across the political spectrum as a consensual cultural shift, and it continues to draw critiques that it carries a Western bias (privileging liberal individualism) (Elkins, Ginsburg, and Melton, this volume), our focus here is on how an expanding human-rights industry is relevant to the project of a constitutional revision. In fact, these developments toward more global human rights governance—specifically the inclusion of gender issues—further underscore the need for a constitutional update.

We begin with the Universal Declaration of Human Rights (UDHR). This document set the stage for the human rights agendas for the new United Nations and clearly incorporated women into an expanded conception of "human." Further, it specifically named needs and barriers that women face as a class. The UDHR states that:

> Everyone is entitled to all the rights and freedoms set forth in this Declaration, without distinction of any kind, such as race, colour, sex, language, religion, political or other opinion, national or social origin, property, birth or other status ("The Universal Declaration..." 1948).

In contrast to the US Constitution, the UDHR specifies that an individual's sex does not bar her/him from the entire range of rights detailed in the Declaration. Further, the Declaration uses gender neutral language ("human," "all," and "everyone") as well as inclusive language ("men and women"). The Convention so pervasively communicates this gender-inclusive language that the rare use of the pronouns "him" and "his" are clearly being used in a generic, gender-neutral sense. The Declaration emphasizes certain positive rights based on the particular social location of motherhood that many women inhabit: "Motherhood and childhood are entitled to special care and assistance. All children, whether born in or out of wedlock, shall enjoy the same social protection." Although the Declaration was penned by a body physically located in the United States (the United Nations) with an American woman at the helm as a key leader in its drafting (First Lady Eleanor Roosevelt), the United States has not incorporated this broader, gender-inclusive, text into its own constitution.

As new human rights instruments and agendas advanced in the twentieth century, concerns grew among women activists globally that the issues that women face as a collective class were not always acknowledged. A key example of this was the experience of domestic violence. As international light was shed on the abuses of political dictatorships, violence against dissenters, and the fates of political prisoners, little attention was given to the violence that women are more likely to experience: intimate-partner violence and other forms of gender-based violence.

It took decades of feminist activism to expose the narrowness of "human rights" and "development" instruments that assumed that the default rights bearer is male. Conventions have now incorporated gender into core provisions. Further, with the emergence of the International Criminal Court and similar region-specific courts came the first prosecutions of rape as a weapon of war. Arguably, these evolving considerations of women as a collective class partially counter the critique that human rights industries are bounded within the philosophical biases of Western individualism.

Among the instruments that now prohibit discrimination on the basis of sex are the International Covenant on Civil and Political Rights, the International Covenant on Economic, Social, and Cultural Rights, and the American Convention on Human Rights. Table 1 lists other relevant international human rights instruments and new interpretations of existing instruments that are now in the global canon.

Despite this progress internationally, the historic tendency of US leaders not to sign or ratify international treaties leaves women in the United States with less recourse beyond our borders than those in other countries. Ironically, it is countries with shallower histories of democratic governance that now have the opportunity to incorporate these new normative shifts toward gender protections into their own constitutions. From the 1980s forward, the transitions from older to newer regime types in regions such as Central and Eastern Europe and Latin America, as well as South Africa, have written and enacted new national constitutions. In all of these cases, that task was one of democratization, of enshrining rights that had not been enjoyed or exercised in the restrictive regimes of the past (Dobrowolsky and Hart 2003).

Several American feminists, including scholar-activist Ann Snitow, made a point to help women in these emerging democracies achieve something that we had never been able to achieve in the United States: to write themselves into the constitutions. Women's organizations based in those countries, however, played a major role in inserting constitutional language to guarantee gender equality and recognize the specific needs of women. As Alexandra Dobrowolsky and Vivien Hart concluded from their cross-national research:

> many women are sceptical about constitutionalism, conventional political structures, and lofty promises of democracy, representation, accountability and equality. But when windows of reform have opened women have felt compelled to seize these political opportunities and, wherever they can, to shape them. They have done so because constitutions matter and they matter fundamentally (Dobrowoslky and Hart 2003: 2).

Further, many new or updated constitutions make international treaties self-executing, such as Turkey's constitution, meaning that international law specified in those treaties overrides any conflicting domestic law. This is particularly

TABLE 5.1 International Instruments Designating Rights for Women*

Instrument	Sample Text	Date put into force
Declaration on the Protection of Women and Children in Emergency and Armed Conflict	"Women and children belonging to the civilian population and finding themselves in circumstances of emergency and armed conflict in the struggle for peace, self-determination, national liberation and independence, or who live in occupied territories, shall not be deprived of shelter, food, medical aid or other inalienable rights, ..."	1974
International Covenant on Civil and Political Rights	"All persons are equal before the law and are entitled without any discrimination to the equal protection of the law. In this respect, the law shall prohibit any discrimination and guarantee to all persons equal and effective protection against discrimination on any ground such as race, colour, sex, language, religion, political or other opinion, national or social origin, property, birth or other status."	1976
International Covenant on Civil and Political Rights	"The States Parties to the present Covenant undertake to ensure the equal right of men and women to the enjoyment of all civil and political rights set forth in the present Covenant."	1976
International Covenant on Economic, Social and Cultural Rights	"The States Parties to the present Covenant undertake to ensure the equal right of men and women to the enjoyment of all economic, social and cultural rights set forth in the present Covenant."	1976
American Convention On Human Rights	"The States Parties to this Convention undertake to respect the rights and freedoms recognized herein and to ensure to all persons subject to their jurisdiction the free and full exercise of those rights and freedoms, without any discrimination for reasons of race, color, sex, language, religion, political or other opinion, national or social origin, economic status, birth, or any other social condition ... For the purposes of this Convention, 'person' means every human being."	1978
Convention on the Elimination of All Forms of Discrimination against Women (CEDAW)	"States Parties condemn discrimination against women in all its forms, agree to pursue by all appropriate means and without delay a policy of eliminating discrimination against women ..."	1981

Instrument	Sample Text	Date put into force
Declaration on the Elimination of Violence Against Women	"States should condemn violence against women and should not invoke any custom, tradition or religious consideration to avoid their obligations with respect to its elimination."	1993
Universal Declaration on Democracy	"Democracy is founded on the primacy of the law and the exercise of human rights. In a democratic State, no one is above the law and all are equal before the law."	1997

* For full treaty texts, please see www.ipu.org/wmn-e/law.htm and www.ohchr.org/EN/Issues/ Women/WRGS/Pages/WRGSIndex.aspx

meaningful for gender rights, which are more likely to be articulated in the recent conventions. Today, constitutions across continents include explicit provisions guaranteeing gender equality; some specify a range of positive rights including employment, maternity benefits, protections from partner violence, and income security. The US Constitution remains unique among most democratic countries in its silence on women's rights beyond suffrage, in part due, ironically, to the stability of our political order that has not afforded the political opportunity structures which women in transitioning regimes have been afforded. With five exceptions, in fact, the world's 44 Muslim-majority nations explicitly mention rights for women in their constitutions. Despite these gains on paper, and a cultural diffusion of gender-based rights discourses, women worldwide encounter backlashes, particularly when those discourses clash with other cultural ideologies. Some constitutions in Muslim-majority nations, for instance, add cultural exceptions to their constitutions that could temper women's rights.

CEDAW

In 1981, an international "bill of rights" for women (Convention on the Elimination of All Forms of Discrimination against Women, or CEDAW) became a legal and binding document. This feat was accomplished faster than any previous human rights instrument ("Convention on the..." n.d.). In the thirty-five years since it entered into force, the Convention has been ratified by more than 180 nations. These include nations as diverse as Afghanistan, China, Trinidad & Tobago, Canada, the Netherlands, Rwanda, Russia, and Argentina. CEDAW defines discrimination against women as "[…] any distinction, exclusion or restriction made on the basis of sex which has the effect or purpose of impairing or nullifying the recognition, enjoyment or exercise by women, irrespective of their marital status, on a basis of equality of men and women, of human rights and fundamental freedoms in the political, economic, social, cultural, civil or any other field" (Šimonović n.d.).

Many of these countries chose to honor the Convention by modifying their constitutions in unequivocal ways. The Constitution of Malawi, for example, is explicit in its condemnation of the inequality of women with men. Its constitution specifically states it shall "actively promote the welfare and development of the people of Malawi by progressively adopting and implementing policies and legislation" to address the many ways in which women in that country have been subjugated in the past. Furthermore, Malawi's Constitution specifically mentions the societal ills of domestic violence, lack of personal safety, lack of maternity benefits, unequal property rights, and economic exploitation as issues the country will continue to address (Comparative Constitutions Project n.d.). Although twenty-two countries that ratified did so with reservations, many based in Shar'iah law, some have since rescinded those reservations.

The post-apartheid South African Constitution offers one example of the incorporation of CEDAW into wording and legal norms. Legal scholar Valorie Vojdik (2007) has compared this constitution with that of the United States on the question of domestic violence. Conventionally, violence against women is considered a private matter; the US Supreme Court views domestic violence as a crime for individual states to prosecute rather than viewing it as "an issue of gender subordination or equality" (Vojdik 2007: 489). This means that in Supreme Court decisions, victims of domestic violence are not guaranteed remedies under the constitution. In contrast, the South African Constitutional Court views domestic violence as a national matter, as a hindrance to women's full and equal participation in society, with "devastating social and economic costs" (Vojdik 2007: 519). This is consistent with the philosophy of CEDAW, which rejects the private/public divide regarding violence against women. The South African Constitution includes both sex and sexual orientation in its wording: "The state may not unfairly discriminate directly or indirectly against anyone on one or more grounds, including race, gender, sex, pregnancy, marital status, ethnic or social origin, colour, sexual orientation, age, disability, religion, conscience, belief, culture, language and birth" (Vojdik 2007: 513, fn 153). It also guarantees the right to bodily and psychological integrity and, in contrast to the United States, extends positive rights; the State must ensure that these rights are protected. The significance of addressing violence against women at a constitutional level cannot be overstated; sociologists Yanyi Djamba and Sitawa Kimuna wrote in 2015 that "Gender-based violence is perhaps the most pervasive and least recognized human rights violation of our time" (Djamba and Kimuna 2015: xi).

Constitutional Change and the Myth of Advancement

Among the key roadblocks to ratification of CEDAW, the ERA, and perhaps any constitutional change regarding gender, is a "myth of advancement" of women.

Some propose that the United States has moved on from the discrimination of its past, such as that chronicled in the popular retrospective television series "Mad Men." More specifically, critics point to legal codes that protect women such as the Civil Rights Act of 1964 and Title IX passed in 1972, which states that "No person in the United States shall, on the basis of sex, be excluded from participation in, be denied the benefits of, or be subjected to discrimination under any education program or activity receiving Federal financial assistance" ("Protecting Survivors..." 2014). Sexual harassment, rape, and sexual assault all qualify as discrimination on the basis of sex under Title IX and a college or university may be held legally responsible if it receives federal funding and either allows sexual harassment or assault in its programs and activities to stand, or ignores a victim's complaint altogether. Yet only recently has this Act begun to be applied to the problem of sexual assault on college campuses, as a result of student activism and new White House initiatives. An estimated 20 to 25 percent of women on US campuses are reported to have experienced rape or attempted rape, a problem which only emerged into the national limelight in 2015 ("Protecting Survivors..." 2014).

There are a host of measures that illustrate that sexism continues to affect women systemically across society, illustrating the need for deep societal change that a constitution should undergird. In 2014, an American woman earned an average of 79 cents for every dollar earned by a man; African American women earned 59.8 cents on every dollar that white men earned; and Latina women earned 54.6 cents on every dollar that a white man earned (Hegewisch and Hartmann 2015). More than three women are killed in domestic violence assaults daily. Native American women report higher than average rates of sexual assault, with one in three reporting to have been raped during their lives ("Tribal Communities" 2015). Further, women hold only 19.3 percent of the seats in the US Congress, and only thirty-three of these 104 representatives or senators are women of color. Feminists continue to battle for rights either lost, eroded, or never won: individual states have restricted access to abortion, paid maternity leave is rare and not federally subsidized, public breastfeeding draws criticism, and mass incarceration of nonviolent offenders removes women from mothering responsibilities and jeopardizes custody. In 2015, a UN Working Group made a site visit to the United States to investigate issues of discrimination against women, and reported that "In the US, women fall behind international standards as regards their public and political representation, their economic and social rights and their health and safety protections" ("UN Working Group..." 2015). The group's report adamantly chided the United States for not ratifying CEDAW, for ranking 72nd globally in proportion of the legislature consisting of women, for the vulnerabilities that undocumented immigrant domestic workers face, for severe restrictions on reproductive rights, and for the near absence of paid maternity leave, among a list of others ("UN Working Group..." 2015).

One legislative gain for women is the 1994 Violence against Women Act, regularly reauthorized approximately every five years. In 2013, this reauthorization faced controversy and backlash over, among other issues, the expansion to include LGBTQ people and undocumented immigrants, although the reauthorization did succeed. These and similar acts do not rise to the level of constitutional guarantees, however, as legislation can be changed by an act of Congress or tempered by individual state laws. Further, a constitutional amendment would be much more difficult to roll back than an act of Congress.

Because of this concern, a new activist push for the ERA has been revived. Supreme Court Justice Ruth Bader Ginsburg, publicly made the case for the ERA in 2014 with the following statement:

> If I could choose an amendment to add to this Constitution, it would be the Equal Rights Amendment.... It means that women are people equal in stature before the law.... We have achieved that through legislation, but legislation can be repealed. It can be altered... That principle belongs in our Constitution. It is in every constitution written since the Second World War (Lang 2015).

Others speaking out for the amendment included Hollywood actress Meryl Streep, who played British suffragette Emmeline Pankhurst in the 2015 docudrama *Suffragette* and capitalized on the movie's public moment to lobby Congress on behalf of the ERA. A coalition of supporters in North Carolina, a state that nearly ratified it in 1982, organized and lobbied for ratification in 2015, but the bill never made it out of the House Committee; its chair, Leo Daughtry, explained, "I don't think it's critical at this time" because of the gains that women had made in society—echoing this myth of advancement (Madden 2015).

ERA author Alice Paul's work was finally recognized for its significance in April of 2016, when President Obama designated the Sewell-Belmont House in Washington, DC, home of the American Women's Party, as the Belmont-Paul Women's Equality National Monument, through a Presidential Proclamation. As the first US monument to women's equality, the timing of the Proclamation was chosen symbolically for Women's Equality Day, April 12, the day that women's wages across 2015 into 2016 have caught up, on average, with the level of wages that their male equivalents earned within the 2015 calendar year (Obama 2016).

Women's right to bodily integrity regarding reproductive decisions has been upheld by Supreme Court decisions such as *Roe v. Wade* in 1973, based in the due process clauses of the constitution. Since that time, the Court has defended the abortion right as a liberty right as well as an equality right (Siegel and Siegel 2013). This right has been eroded in recent years through individual state-level legislation across a number of states; the jury is out regarding the potential for the ERA to reinstate the full protections intended under *Roe v. Wade*. Feminist legal scholars have been divided over the potential relationship between the ERA and abortion rights, and whether an equality right would apply to a condition based in sexual difference (Butler 2015). Abortion rights proponents do view an important role for the constitution and federal-level action to ensure that such laws are not easily overturned.

In addition to the ERA, CEDAW has returned to American activist agendas. Despite being sent to the US Senate by President Carter in 1980, CEDAW has never moved out of the Senate Committee on Foreign Relations to a vote, and thus has never been ratified. In response to the inaction of our federal government, several national women's organizations, such as the NGO Committee on the Status of Women/New York (NGO/CSW NY), have begun to organize grass-roots campaigns to bring the tenets of CEDAW to the local level. NGO/CSW NY has partnered with the Women's Intercultural Network (WIN) and the San Francisco Department on the Status of Women (DOSW) to recruit 100 cities to become "Cities for CEDAW" by December 2016. This campaign assists women's organizations in petitioning their local governments to implement CEDAW policies and laws. As of this writing, a total of thirty-four cities and three counties (encompassing seventy-one additional municipalities) are in some stage of CEDAW implementation. Efforts include measures ranging from the establishment of focus groups and city coalitions to the commissioning of gender studies and the passage of ordinances, resolutions, and agreements to institute CEDAW principles and doctrine. In cities where CEDAW has already been adopted as local law, women have enjoyed an increased sensitivity to women's issues and the protective factor of mandates that ensure that instances of inequality are addressed ("Cities for CEDAW" n.d.). This speaks to the need to equalize CEDAW benefits across municipalities and regions in the United States, through federal action. If women had a stronger political presence, might there be a cabinet-level or Congressional gender equity committee? Ministries of Women's Affairs currently exist at the national governmental level in countries across all continents, but not in the United States.

Social class, race, and immigration status intersect to compound the disadvantages women face. Scholar-activist Gloria Jean Watkins, better known as "bell hooks," in fact, challenges the "equality" frame of much feminist discourse by asking: "Which *men do* women *want to be equal to?*" hooks emphasizes that the goals of bourgeois, predominantly white, feminists often do not resonate with those of women of color. Stating that "[f]eminism is the struggle to end sexist oppression," (hooks 1984: 3) hooks sidesteps the language of "equality." Constitutional revisions that do not recognize and name the intersecting inequalities that confront women due to their social locations as people of color, foreign-born, differently abled, on limited incomes, or in marginalized positions due to sexual orientation or gender identity/expression, would result in only limited progress.

Gender and Sexuality Inclusions

Although legislation has moved forward, if slowly, toward expanding protections for women, little progress can be marked in the legislative and judicial arenas regarding gender identity and sexual orientation. Individuals who identify as lesbian, gay, bisexual, transgender, queer, or are otherwise gender nonconforming have simultaneously built movements domestically and internationally to contest legal exclusions and homophobic laws, with very recent victories and continued uphill battles. As Michel Foucault has illustrated, the term "homosexual" and the designation of individuals as homosexual are historically recent, resulting in increasing attempts by European religious bodies to control sexuality across the centuries resulted in the codification of anti-sodomy laws. Like the law of coverture, those codes traversed the Atlantic and made their way into American state laws. The US Constitution makes no mention of such laws, but the document does not include stated protections for diversity across sexual orientation, gender identity, and gender expression.

Engaging with a sociological perspective on these questions involves a recognition that norms, political cultures, and social patterns shift over time, especially as a result of social movement activism. Such a shift was visible in the landmark 2015 US Supreme Court decision in the case of *Obergefell v. Hodges*. Based in the 14th Amendment guaranteeing citizens equal protection under the law, the decision widened full access to legal marriage for same-sex couples across all fifty states. The decision remains controversial as of this writing, especially in some local magistrates' refusal to implement. Nevertheless, this decision was hailed by many not only due to this expanded application of a negative right, but as a doorway to positive rights such as partner benefits in insurance, retirement, and tax law. LGBTQ activists, however, also counted this victory as one of many yet to be won to end discrimination, inequalities, and violence against gender and sexual minorities. In 2014, for instance, the FBI documented 1,248 reported hate crimes against people based on sexual orientation, and another 109 based on gender identity, across the United States (United States Department of Justice 2015). The constitutional silence on this issue became clear in 2016, when North Carolina and Mississippi passed state-level legislation forbidding transgender use of public restrooms that corresponded to their preferred gender identity, and other states attempted to pass similar laws. As of this writing, the Department of Justice had filed suit against the State of North Carolina, citing that the bill violated the Civil Rights Act, Title IX, and the Violence against Women Act. President Obama furthered the federal resistance to the law by issuing a directive that public schools must allow students to use the bathroom that corresponds to their gender identity.

Turning to the Universal Declaration of Human Rights (UDHR) for leadership on the question of rights for gender and sexual minorities is less useful

than it is for women; it is silent on sexual orientation and gender noncon-
formity, thus is not a source for proposed verbiage for constitutional revision. The language of the UDHR, in fact, remains within a heteronormative
gender binary, employing the terms "men and women" in the two instances
where it calls out gender explicitly. In the 2010s, however, transnational
human rights instruments and treaties finally began to specify the application
of "human rights" to the needs of LGBTQ individuals. In 2012, the United
Nations Human Rights Council announced that it interprets existing basic
human rights law to include LGBTQ rights across the spectrum (Office of
the United Nations 2012) and in 2016 the body passed a resolution entitled
"Protection against Violence and Discrimination Based on Sexual Orientation
and Gender Identity," establishing an independent expert on this issue ("UN
Women Welcomes ..." 2016). Other transnational governing bodies have followed suit, as well as American federal agencies that work globally; the Obama
administration, for example, issued a directive for LGBTQ-friendly practices
across federal agencies, including embassies and consulates. Therefore, the task
of bringing the US Constitution up to global legal standards means incorporating sexual orientation, gender identity, and gender expression explicitly in
constitutional language. As one of those global standards-setters, the UN needs
to be pushed further on these same questions.

Sociology Students "Re-vision" the US Constitution

Comparing Constitutions

In a Theoretical Perspectives course at East Carolina University (ECU) in North
Carolina during spring semester 2015, undergraduate Sociology students studied theories of human rights and joined other participating university students
in reflecting on the US Bill of Rights. Considerable time was spent discussing
the UDHR, CEDAW, and other international agreements. Students were tasked
with applying what they had learned to their evaluation of constitutions around
the globe; they were then instructed to compare those findings with the content
found in the US Constitution. One of the students' first observations was how
antiquated the US Constitution is in relation to those of other countries. The
majority of nations have either revised their existing constitutions in order to
better meet the needs of modern society, or have completely abandoned their old
constitutions and adopted new and more relevant ones. ECU students realized
that, now over 200 years old, the US Constitution needs a facelift; they concluded that it needs to be a more modern, readable, and practical document. They
observed that the constitution was created to solve the problems of the eighteenth
century, but does not serve the needs of the present population.

Secondly, the students noted the US Constitution's many negative rights, as
opposed to other countries' emphasis on positive rights. Negative rights are the

situations, occurrences, and events from which a government protects its citizens; they are indirect and passive; they detail a specific action a government *cannot* take. Accordingly, the US Constitution places specific limits on governmental power. In contrast, a positive right is pro-active and outlines the benefits, accommodations, and assurances that a government is obligated to provide to its citizens. To illustrate, Article 23(1) of the Canadian Charter of Rights and Freedoms requires that French or English minority students receive instruction in their preferred language if a sufficient number of students are in need of this accommodation.[3]

Most importantly, students were chagrined to realize that the US Constitution, unlike other, more progressive constitutions, dealt primarily with political rights, and by extension, some economic rights only as they pertained to educated, white males. However, the constitution was silent on even the most fundamental of human rights for its citizens: with no mention of environmental, cultural, or social rights, women across racial and socioeconomic backgrounds were essentially left without any representation or protection. It was from these observations that students became convinced that the US Constitution should be updated—at the very least—to reflect genuinely the needs *and rights of all people* residing within US borders.

Students then began researching the 194 constitutions of the world in earnest. They formed research groups and each individual member was responsible for researching a specific human rights issue that he or she wished to address. Many focused on the rights of women, as most felt that sexism and the subjugation of women in American society have long been the rule rather than the exception. Additionally, students found that the US Constitution was dissimilar to many other constitutions in its failure to outline the ways in which women have contributed to society and the ways in which women have been both under-valued and under-appreciated. Further, students noticed that the US Constitution did not address methods to eradicate inequality and discrimination. In other countries, constitutional protections for women abound and cover a vast array of issues. For example:

- The constitutions of Rwanda and Cambodia both state that men and women are equal with respect to marriage rights and obligations. The Japanese Constitution also mentions equality of the sexes and then goes one step further: "With regard to choice of spouse, property rights, inheritance, choice of domicile, divorce and other matters pertaining to *marriage* and the family, laws shall be enacted from the standpoint of individual dignity and the essential equality of the sexes."[4]
- Both the constitutions of Switzerland and Germany specifically reference the necessity for equality in the workplace. Switzerland's Constitution asserts that "Men and women have the right to equal pay for work of equal value."[5]
- Ethiopia and the Democratic People's Republic of Korea both have constitutions that grant women the positive right of maternity leave. The Ethiopian

Constitution reads: "Women have the right to maternity leave with full pay. The duration of maternity leave shall be determined by law taking into account the nature of the work, the health of the mother and the well-being of the child and family."[6]

• Nepal and the Dominican Republic are two of the many countries that condemn violence against women in their constitutions. Nepal's Constitution specifically mentions its commitment to the Universal Declaration of Human Rights as the basis for this. The Dominican Constitution outlines a women's right to safety thusly:

> Every person has the right of respect for their physical, psychic, and moral integrity and to live without violence. They have the protection of the State in the cases of threat, risk or violation thereof. In consequence… Inter-family and gender violence in all its forms is condemned. The State shall guarantee through the law the adoption of the necessary measures to prevent, sanction and eradicate violence against women…[7]

Such examples provided inspiration, and direct language, for their project of updating their own constitution.

Student Proposals

A sample of the Constitutional amendments that students proposed were the following, all of which incorporated positive as well as negative rights:

> Proposal 1. Women, men, people of the LGBTQI community, and ALL other peoples are entitled equally to the same human rights guaranteed in all other rights sections of this constitution such as income, voting rights, etc. provided they are in good standing with the law and not under other restrictions of rights due to imprisonment, parole, etc. They are also entitled to equal treatment in the workplace, in hospital care, and any private or non-private setting. Families are entitled to rights of leave from the workplace in the event of a new child, injury, or other reasonable excuse for absence.
> Women and people that are transgender should have equal rights and equal opportunities, especially in the work force. Women and people that are transgender should have the same opportunities with which men are presented and receive the same pay for the same jobs.
> Proposal 2. All citizens, regardless of birth, sex, gender, sexual orientation, expression, preference, religion, creed, race, ethnicity, culture, tribe, language, national and social origins, status, disability, age, marital status, education level, occupation, pregnancy, shall not be discriminated against and have the right to equally enjoy the protection of the law and enjoy all natural, human, political, economic, social, and cultural rights.

Proposal 3. Article 1: Right to Marry: (1) Men and women of full age, without any limitation due to race, sexual orientation, gender, religion or nationality, have the right to marry and found a family. (2) Marriage shall be entered into only with the free and full consent of the intending spouses. (3) The family is the natural and fundamental group of society and is entitled to protection by society and the state.

Article 2: Right to Employment: (1) Everyone, without discrimination, has the right to work, to free choice of employment, to just and favorable conditions of work and to protection against unemployment. (2) Everyone, without discrimination, has the right to equal pay for equal work.

Article 3: Discrimination: (1) No one shall, without an acceptable reason, be treated differently from other persons on the ground of sex, gender, age, origin, language, religion, conviction, opinion, sexual orientation, health, disability or other reason that concerns his or her person. (2) Equality of the sexes is promoted in societal activity and working life, especially in the determination of pay and the other terms of employment, as provided in more detail by an Act.

Some student proposals gave more specific details, naming particular injustices such as human trafficking, rape, and incest, and offering maternity leave rights and lactation breaks at work. Notably, several students were parents and were struggling to combine coursework, employment, and family, and were already attuned to the barriers that adult women face.

In the fall semester of 2015, East Carolina University sociology students repeated this assignment. The group tasked with incorporating women into the constitution recommended a more general change: that all of the pronouns in the US Bill of Rights change to "they." Across both semesters, students explicitly argued for the need for the ERA and proposed its ratification. It is notable that these students reside in, and largely grew up in, a state partly responsible for the ERA's earlier ratification failure. Overall, this exercise proved to be an effective experiment in learning about and grappling with human rights theory, and working through the complex details of applying theory on the ground. Throughout students' research, writing, and oral presentations of their amendments to the class, they built their own knowledge base of the global human rights arena, and expanded their competencies in understanding the gaps in our law and practice regarding gender.

Building upon the work of these sociology students, the authors of this chapter recommend that: (1) the Bill of Rights be amended to include the ERA; (2) gender-neutral and non-gender-binary language replace the word "man" throughout the Constitution and Bill of Rights; (3) sexual and gender difference be acknowledged explicitly to end discrimination against women and all gender minorities; and (4) positive rights that would ensure women's equality with men be articulated, including wage equality and maternity provisions. The US Constitution should incorporate the most progressive versions of the language in other constitutions and in international human rights instruments to demonstrate its self-identity as a "City on a Hill" of democratic rights, and to acknowledge its full participation in a twenty-first-century global society.

Conclusion

The yet-incomplete revolution in women's roles and options has resulted in a global normative shift on gender, reflected in constitutions across the continents. As illustrated here, however, that normative shift was far from a social evolution, but took the strong will of social movement activism and visionaries. This shift is a key example of why constitutions are in need of revision. As normative and aspirational documents, constitutions are reflections of societies' self-understanding at the time of their construction, as well as the state of politics and those in power at the time. The US Constitution was written with a narrow view of the sex of the citizen in mind. Combined with other intersectional locations of those writers (property owners, white), the result was that a small minority was responsible for scripting a document for an entire population and future generations who did not represent that intersection of social locations. The US Constitution enshrines an unequal status to women and subordinates the rights of women. By incorporating women into a revised constitution, we would move forward toward completion of the original "project of modernity" and elevate 50 percent of the society to equal status in law.

The need for constitutional revision to include both gender and sexual minorities may be among the strongest cases that can be made to bring the US Constitution up to date and into line with other constitutions and international treaties. Such changes would more fully flesh out the meaning of "human" in the term "human rights." Where possible, constitutional language should recognize explicitly the intersection between social locations of gender and those of race, class, nativity, ethnicity, ability, sexuality, and age, and call out the consequences of those intersections for full enjoyment of rights. We conclude with the now 225-year-old admonition by Olympe de Gouges, which continues to resonate as a clarion call: "Woman, wake up; the tocsin (sic) of reason is being heard throughout the whole universe; discover your rights" (de Gouges 1791).

Notes

1 Among the prominent male allies of this struggle was English political philosopher John Stuart Mill, who wrote in 1869: "That the principle which regulates the existing social relations between the two sexes—the legal subordination of one sex to the other—is wrong itself, and now one of the chief hindrances to human improvement; and that it ought to be replaced by a principle of perfect equality, admitting no power or privilege on the one side, nor disability on the other" (Mill 2000).

2 One author of this was involved in advocacy work to ratify the ERA in North Carolina, one of three states potentially on target to ratify. Although the North Carolina House had voted for ratification, the Senate votes fell just slightly short.
3 Constitution of Canada, Article 23(1) University of Alberta: Centre for Constitutional Studies. http://ualawccsprod.srv.ualberta.ca/ccs/index.php/pr/534-positive-and-negative-rights (last accessed January 6, 2016).
4 Constitution of Japan, III, Article 24 (Constitute.org).
5 Constitution of Switzerland, Title 2, 1, Article 3 (Constitute.org).
6 Constitution of Ethiopia, 3, Part 2, Article 355A (Constitute.org).
7 Constitution of the Dominican Republic, Title 2, 1, Section 1, Article 42 (Constitue.org).

References

Blackstone, William. 1765. *Commentaries on the Laws of England, Vol. 1*. Chicago: University of Chicago Press. http://womenshistory.about.com/cs/lives19th/a/blackstone_law.htm (last accessed January 4, 2016).
Bulter, Twiss. 2015. "Law Professors Urge: End a Basic Form of Sex Discrimination by Uniting the ERA and Abortion-Access Campaigns!" www.equality4women.org/Unite-ERA-and-Abortion-766.pdf (last accessed April 28, 2016).
CAWP. 2016. "Women in the U.S. Congress 2016." Center for American Women and Politics. New Brunswick, NJ: Rutgers University. http://cawp.rutgers.edu/women-us-congress-2016 (last accessed May 17, 2016).
"Cities for CEDAW." n.d. http://citiesforcedaw.org/ (last accessed January 6, 2016).
Comparative Constitutions Project. n.d. www.constituteproject.org/search?lang=en&q=domestic%20violence (last accessed January 6, 2016).
"Convention on the Elimination of All Forms of Discrimination against Women." n.d. New York: United Nations. www.un.org/womenwatch/daw/cedaw/history.htm (last accessed January 6, 2016).
de Beauvoir, Simone. 2011. *The Second Sex*. Translated by Constance Borde and Sheila Malovany-Chevallier. New York: Vintage.
de Gouges, Olympe. 1791. *The Declaration of the Rights of Woman and the Female Citizen*. www2.warwick.ac.uk/fac/arts/english/currentstudents/undergraduate/modules/full-list/special/en262/degouges (last accessed January 4, 2016).
de Tocqueville, Alexis. 1994. *Democracy in America*. New York: Knopf.
d'Entreves, Maurizio Passerin and Seyla Benhabib. 1997. *Habermas and the Unfinished Project of Modernity: Critical Essays on "The Philosophical Discourse of Modernity."* Cambridge, MA: MIT Press.
Djamba, Yanyi K. and Sitawa R. Kimuna (eds). 2015. *Gender-Based Violence: Perspectives from Africa, the Middle East, and India*. Cham, Switzerland: Springer.
Dobrowolsky, Alexandra and Vivien Hart (eds). 2003. *Women Making Constitutions: New Politics and Comparative Perspectives*. Houndmills, Basingstoke, Hampshire, UK: Palgrave Macmillan.
Donlan, Leni. 2008. *Working for Change: The Struggle for Women's Right to Vote*. Chicago: Raintree.
Francis, Roberta W. n.d. "The History Behind the Equal Rights Amendment." *The Equal Rights Amendment: Unfinished Business for the Constitution*. www.equalrightsamendment.org/history.htm (last accessed January 4, 2016).
Habermas, Jürgen. 1989. *The Structural Transformation of the Public Sphere: An Inquiry into a Category of Bourgeois Society*. Translated by Thomas Burger and Frederick Lawrence. Cambridge, MA: MIT Press.

Hegewisch, Ariane and Heidi Hartmann. 2015. *The Gender Wage Gap: 2014.* Institute for Women's Policy Research. www.iwpr.org/publications/pubs/the-gender-wage-gap-2014 (last accessed January 6, 2016).

hooks, bell. 1984. *Feminist Theory from Margin to Center.* Boston: South End Press.

"Instruments of International Law Concerning Women." n.d. Geneva, Switzerland: Inter-Parliamentary Union. www.ipu.org/wmn-e/law.htm (last accessed April 28, 2016).

Lang, Sara. 2015. "Chasing the Mythical Equal Rights Amendment." Women AdvaNCe. www.womenadvancenc.org/2015/09/04/chasing-the-mythical-equal-rights-amendment/ (last accessed January 5, 2016).

Madden, Barbara. 2015. "NC lawmakers Say 'No' Yet Again to Equality for Women." RATIFY ERA-NC. www.era-nc.org/?p=774 (last accessed January 6, 2016).

Mansbridge, Jane. 1986. *Why We Lost the ERA.* Chicago: University of Chicago Press.

Mill, John Stewart. 2000. *The Subjection of Women.* Orchard Park, NY: Broadview Press.

Obama, Barack. 2016. "Presidential Proclamation – Establishment of the Belmont-Paul Women's Equality National Monument." The White House, Office of the Press Secretary. www.whitehouse.gov/the-press-office/2016/04/12/presidential-proclamation-establishment-belmont-paul-womens-equality (last accessed April 28, 2016).

Office of the United Nations High Commissioner for Human Rights. 2012. "Born Free and Equal: Sexual Orientation and Gender Identity in International Human Rights Law." Geneva, Switzerland: United Nations. www.ohchr.org/Documents/Publications/BornFreeAndEqualLowRes.pdf (last accessed January 6, 2016).

"Protecting Survivors of Sexual Assault on Campus: Myths and Facts." 2014. National Women's Law Center. www.nwlc.org/resource/protecting-survivors-sexual-assault-campus-myths-and-facts (last accessed October 24, 2015).

"Report of the Woman's Rights Convention, held at Seneca Falls, N.Y., July 19th and 20th, 1848." 1997. *The Selected Papers of Elizabeth Cady Stanton and Susan B. Anthony – Volume 1: In the School of Anti-Slavery, 1840 to 1866,* Ann D. Gordon (ed.). New Brunswick, NJ: Rutgers University Press. http://ecssba.rutgers.edu/docs/seneca.html (last accessed January 4, 2016).

Siegel, Neil S. and Reva B. Siegel. 2013. "Equality Arguments for Abortion Rights." *UCLA Law Review Discourse* 60:160–170. www.uclalawreview.org/pdf/discourse/60-11.pdf (last accessed April 28, 2016).

Šimonović, Dubravka. "Introductory Note." Convention on the Elimination of All Forms of Discrimination against Women. New York: United Nations. http://legal.un.org/avl/ha/cedaw/cedaw.html (last accessed January 6, 2016).

"Tribal Communities." 2015. The United States Department of Justice, Office of Violence Against Women. www.justice.gov/ovw/tribal-communities (last accessed January 6, 2016).

"UN Women Welcomes New Human Rights Council Independent Expert on Sexual Orientation and Gender Identity." 2016. www.unwomen.org/en/news/stories/2016/6/human-rights-council-independent-expert-on-sexual-orientation-and-gender-identity#sthash.T3eE2r5P.dpuf UN Women website, 1 July (last accessed July 8, 2016).

"UN Working Group on the Issue of Discrimination Against Women in Law and in Practice Finalizes Country Mission to the United States." 2015. United Nations Office of the High Commission on Human Rights. www.ohchr.org/EN/NewsEvents/Pages/DisplayNews.aspx?NewsID=16872&LangID=E#sthash.n9kR3Vkq.dpuf (last accessed January 6, 2016).

United States Department of Justice, Federal Bureau of Investigation. 2015. *Hate Crime Statistics, 2014.* Washington, DC: Federal Bureau of Investigation. www.fbi.gov/about-us/cjis/ucr/hate-crime/2014/topic-pages/victims_final (last accessed January 6, 2016).

Vojdik, Valorie K. 2007. "Conceptualizing Intimate Violence and Gender Equality: A Comparative Approach." *Fordham International Law Journal* 31(2): 4.

Wollstonecraft, Mary. 1999. *A Vindication of the Rights of Woman: With Strictures on Political and Moral Subjects.* New York: Bartleby.com. www.bartleby.com/144/ (last accessed January 4, 2016).

6

HUMAN DIGNITY AND EQUALITY

Freedoms and Rights, Protection, Fairness, and Security

Judith R. Blau

In this, my objective is to provoke a discussion about reaffirming human rights, and to do so I take the ones with which we are familiar, namely, those that were first elaborated in the 1948 Universal Declaration of Human Rights. I then group them into categories. This discussion aims to underscore and reaffirm our collective understanding that human rights are universal and that they cohere because they are based on the transcendent principles of human dignity and equality. The motive behind this exercise is based on the observation that we—the world's peoples—face unprecedented crises; the most serious of these is climate change, and we can only face them together, united. A renewed affirmation of our shared and universal rights is appropriate, perhaps even necessary, to renew our shared commitments to human rights. Another reason to have this discussion is because the UDHR is specific, which is understandable given the context in 1948—the holocaust, the devastation of Hiroshima and Nagasaki, the immense loss of life in Europe and Japan. This may have been the case because it was better to have united the world around specifics in 1948 than to have articulated abstractions that might have been poorly understood. It includes, for example, the right to food and housing, the right to join a union, the right to freedom of opinion, and so forth. But perhaps what is now lacking are all-encompassing principles.

Nearly 70 years later, the world is very different. Intellectually, socially, and politically, people from all over the world can communicate, and do. That is to say that people from all corners of the world have gotten to know one another. Some of us casually meet in Geneva and New York for UN meetings, in Tokyo for trade talks, and in Athens to share ideas about climate change. It was recently announced that over one billion people use Facebook and emailing half way around the globe is a common experience. To give two other examples, Boston physicians are working in clinics in Liberia and Zimbabwean villages have wel-comed NGOs from Sweden to help deal with the drought. Yes, there are many positive things to say about the high degree of global interconnectedness. One of these is that we all can draw on a deep understanding of how to think and talk about human rights in more general terms than they could in 1948.

Yet Americans must not forget that the official definition of rights has not progressed since 1791. Nor should Americans forget that the US has posed a major obstacle in making the agreement at the COP21 an international treaty, weakening the agreement and giving other countries the excuse to dodge out of it. I highlight the year 2015 for that and other reasons.

The Year, 2015

It is especially important to talk about human rights now, following the catas-trophes of 2015, which imperiled human rights everywhere. Besides 2015 was a defining moment for truly recognizing the perils of climate warming. Briefly, now, let's recall 2015:

(1) The alarm was sounded—belatedly—that climate warming (that is, climate change) is posing extremely grave danger to all people, everywhere and to the planet.

(2) Huge numbers of refugees fled their home countries to seek safety; by the end of the year more than a million arrived in Europe, and several times that were registered in Egypt, Iraq, Jordan, and Lebanon.

(3) By the end of the year ISIS—or Daesh—controlled 50 percent of Syria, and much of Iraq.

(4) As the world peoples learned, during the year US police killed more than 1,000 black Americans.

(5) Oxfam International, the World Economic Forum, as well as French and American economists, have revealed the full extent of global economic inequalities—85 billionaires have the same wealth as the bottom half of the world's population. Such inequality is extreme in the US and it is aggravated because wages in the US have been stagnant for thirty-five years.

(6) At the same time, we need to recognize that the world has never been so tightly interconnected. This means, for example, that deadly infectious dis-eases quickly spread not only from one community to another, but from one country to another, and from one continent to another.

These are calamities. To be specific, these are *human rights calamities*. They bring great harm to many, many millions—even billions—of people. Each of these was preventable and each of these entails inequalities, as cause, or as consequence, or both. Inequalities in and of themselves are unjust but they also create distance between peoples, groups, and countries.

Elaboration

The heating of the planet, as noted in (1) has a history we shouldn't forget. Rich countries industrialized—at a relatively leisurely pace—steadily polluting the earth's air and oceans, contaminating the ground, and decimating the forests. Now poor countries are told they must not industrialize as the West did, but instead rapidly adopt expensive wind, sun, and tidal technologies; (2) and (3) are linked, of course. America's intervention in Afghanistan, Libya and Iraq ignited a reactionary backlash in the Middle East that now manifests itself in an unending stream of refugees; (4) The United States was harshly criticized at its 2015 Universal Periodic Review and again by a UN delegation in 2016 for the brutal treatment of black Americans;[1] (5) Extreme economic inequalities are global, but the US has the highest level of inequality compared with other developed countries, which is due to tax policies, the inordinate power of corporations who use their influence to create policies regarding wealthy individuals, and flat wages;[2] and (6) the unprecedented level of interconnectedness at all levels: cities, nations and continents, which brings many good things, such as almost universal internet access, but much that is bad as well, such as the rapid spread of contagious diseases.

Human Rights: A Background

Until the 1948 Universal Declaration of Human Rights, rights were understood to be best summarized in two eighteenth-century declarations: the 1789 French Declaration *des Droits de l'Homme et du Citoyen* and the 1791 Bill of Rights. Indeed, we could say that the French Declaration and the US Bill of Rights are similar because they both stress individual freedoms, with the latter emphasizing that the State (Congress) should not in interfere with individual freedoms. For example, Article 11 of the French Declaration states: "The free communication of ideas and opinions is one of the most precious of the rights of man. Every citizen may, accordingly, speak, write, and print with freedom, but shall be responsible for such abuses of this freedom as shall be defined by law."[3] And, similarly Article I of the Bill of Rights is: "Congress shall make no law... abridging the freedom of speech..." Article 19 of the UDHR goes further by emphasizing it is an individual right that is shared collectively: "*everyone* has the right to freedom of opinion and expression..." In fact, Articles 1–21 of the UDHR are, for the most part, clarifications of the French Declaration and the US Bill of Rights, yet with underlying philosophical differences, as evident in the noun, "*everyone.*"

Yet Articles 22 through 30 of the UDHR are dramatically different from the French Declaration and the US Bill of Rights, and these principles played a key role in constitutions that were written after 1948. In particular I am proposing that contemporary human rights can be grouped into four categories: twentieth century individual freedoms and rights, protection, fairness, and redistribution.

Freedoms and Rights: Number of Constitutions (out of 194) and Examples

First, there are freedoms and rights that originated in the Enlightenment and found expression in the 1789 *Declaration des Droits de l'Homme et du Citoyen* and the 1791 Bill of Rights. Now they are virtually universally affirmed, at least in principle. Below are examples from contemporary constitutions.

Fundamental Freedoms 191

Canada: Everyone has the following *fundamental freedoms*: freedom of thought, belief, opinion and expression, including freedom of the press and other media of communication.

Freedom of Opinion 163

Chile: Freedom to express *opinion and to inform*, without prior censorship, in any form and by any medium, without prejudice to responsibility [responder] for any crimes or abuses committed in the exercise of these freedoms, in conformity with the law, which must be of qualified quorum.

Freedom of Religion 182

Australia: The Commonwealth shall not make any law for establishing any religion, or for imposing any religious observance, or for prohibiting the free exercise of any religion, and no religious test shall be required as a qualification for any office or public trust under the Commonwealth.

Inalienable and Inviolable Rights 124

Andorra: The Constitution recognizes human dignity to be inalienable and therefore guarantees the inviolable and imprescriptible *rights* of the individual, which constitute the foundation of political order, social peace and justice.

Indonesia: Every person shall have the right to the freedom to believe *his/ her faith* (kepercayaan), and to *express his/her views* and thoughts, in accordance with his/her conscience.

Mali: Every person shall have the right to freedom of *thought, conscience, religion, cult, opinion, expression and creation within the law*.

Protections: Number of Constitutions (out of 194) and Examples

People who are temporarily or permanently vulnerable because of a handicap or frailty need protection, and there is virtually universal agreement about which people need protection. These include children, the disabled, handicapped, the elderly, and the chronically ill. These are states of being or conditions that cannot be helped.

Children 169

Cape Verde: All *children* shall have the right to the special protection of the family, society, and the State to guarantee conditions necessary for the whole development of their physical and intellectual capacities, and special care in case of orphans, abandoned *children*, or the emotionally deprived.

Disabled 70

Malta: *Disabled* persons and persons incapable of work are entitled to education and vocational training.

Aged 46

Cambodia: The *aged* without relatives and unable to support themselves, as well as invalids and the socially weak shall receive special protection from the State and society.

Mothers 44

Ghana: Special care shall be accorded to *mothers* during a reasonable period before and after child-birth; and during those periods, working *mothers* shall be accorded paid leave.

Handicapped 38

Honduras: The State shall support and promote the education of *handicapped* persons.

Pregnant Women 17

Slovakia: *Pregnant* women shall be entitled to special treatment, terms of employment, and working conditions.

Blind People 4

New Zealand: Regulations … may make provision for electors who are wholly or partially *blind* to vote by means of devices that enable them to vote without assistance despite the fact that they are wholly or partially *blind*.

Fairness: Number of Constitutions (out of 194) and Examples

Then, there are those who experience discrimination and/or are treated unfairly. Below a count of constitutions with 'fairness' provisions for particular groups and for each provision an example.

Racial Minorities 140

Singapore: It shall be the responsibility of the Government constantly to care for the interests of the *racial … minorities* in Singapore.

Religious Minorities 129

Togo: The Togolese Republic assures the equality before the law of all citizens without distinction of origin, of race, of sex, of social condition or of *religion*.

Refugees/Migrants/Stateless Persons 90

Ecuador: To propitiate the creation of Latin American and Caribbean citizenship; the free circulation of persons in the region; the implementation of policies that guarantee human rights of the people living along borders and *refugees*; and the common protection of Latin American and Caribbean citizens in countries of migratory transit and destination.

Albania: The fundamental rights and freedoms and the duties contemplated in this Constitution for Albanian citizens are also valid for foreigners and *stateless* persons in the territory of the Republic of Albania...

Language Minorities 82

Germany: German is the official language of the Republic without prejudice to the rights provided by Federal law for linguistic *minorities*.

Sexual Minorities 10

New Zealand: For the purposes of this Act, the prohibited grounds of discrimination are... *sexual orientation*, which means a heterosexual, homosexual, lesbian, or bisexual orientation.

Security: Number of Constitutions (out of 194) and Examples

Commonly and universally referred to as human rights (humanos derechos, droits de l'homme, etc.), the chief difficulty with this term is that there is cultural and societal variation in the salience of particular rights. To illustrate, many Americans justifiably feel they have no economic rights but with notable exceptions, they do have the right to speak and write as they please.[4] There is an exceptionally high overall level of economic well-being in Scandinavian countries yet in Norway, Sweden and Denmark there is very little diversity, and though diversity is not considered a human right per se, it is essential for human rights. UNESCO's Declaration on Cultural Diversity states: "Cultural rights are an integral part of human rights" and "The defense of cultural diversity is an ethical imperative, inseparable from respect for human dignity."[5]

Below I again report on the number of states (out of 194) that mention individual human rights in their constitutions, and quote from one constitution that mentions that particular one. To show the full range of human rights mentioned helps to clarify the basis of what people refer to when they say they have 'security.' In other words, some societies may promote—and their constitutions may guarantee—the right to food, the right to work, etc., thereby contributing to the security of their peoples.

Right to Work 136

Finland: The public authorities shall promote employment and work towards guaranteeing for everyone the *right to work*...

Right to Health Care 135

Belarus: Citizens of the Republic of Belarus shall be guaranteed the *right to health care*, including free treatment at state health-care establishments. The State shall make health care facilities accessible to all of its citizens.

Free Education 132

Nepal: Every citizen shall have the right to get *free education* up to the secondary level from the State, as provided in law.

Social Security 118

Indonesia: Every person shall have the right to *social security* in order to develop oneself fully as a dignified human being.

Rights of Children 106

Colombia: The rights of children take precedence over the rights of others.

Equal Pay for Equal Work 99

Greece: All workers, irrespective of sex or other distinctions, shall be entitled to *equal pay for work of equal value*.

Right to Strike 97

Kazakhstan: The right to individual and collective labor disputes with the use of methods for resolving them, stipulated by law including the *right to strike*, shall be recognized.

Right to Standard of Living 84

Angola: The state shall promote social development by: Ensuring that all citizens enjoy the benefits resulting from collective efforts in terms of development, specifically with regard to quantitative and qualitative *improvements to standards of living*.

Right to Rest and/or Leisure 82

Algeria: The *right to rest* shall be guaranteed. Statute shall determine the modalities of its exercise.

Right to Shelter 72

Kenya: Every person has the right to accessible and adequate *housing*, …

Right to Food 55

Haiti: The State recognizes the right of every citizen to decent housing, education, *food* and social security.

Consumer Protection 5

Spain: The public authorities shall guarantee the *protection of consumers* and users and shall, by means of effective measures, safeguard their safety, health and legitimate economic interests.

Right to the Benefits of Science 28

Guatemala: Every person has the right to participate freely in the cultural and artistic life of the community, as well as [to] benefit from the *scientific and technological progress of the Nation*.

Discussion

It is evident from these many examples that contemporary constitutions have advanced rights far, far beyond 1789 French Declaration *des Droits de l'Homme et du Citoyen* and the 1791 Bill of Rights. They include some or all of the human rights that were laid out in the 1948 Universal Declaration of Human Rights namely economic, social and cultural rights as well as political and civil rights. Like the UDHR, most constitutions stress individual rights—that is, for each and every person. Yet a few constitutions suggest that human rights for individuals can only be achieved collectively because the larger society has certain qualities that individuals cannot possess, or because a high degree of cooperation is required to achieve something that individuals cannot achieve on their own.

Peace, diversity, equality, and democracy are attributes of entire societies; while they can be enjoyed and affirmed by individuals, they can only be achieved by the collective. The most important example nowadays is slowing the rate of climate change. We must all cooperate to achieve this and we will all benefit if we do. Likewise, free riders will not only hurt themselves, but all of us. Exclusive focus on individual gain can only undermine cooperation, and the pursuit of the collective, common good.

There are two things to stress about the United States. First the US has the oldest statement of rights in the entire world, but it stops short at civil and political rights (while the French have moved on). Second, there were enough climate change deniers in the US Senate that the US did not approve a formal agreement to take aggressive action to slow climate change. Perhaps the problem is that selfish individualism dominates in the United States to such a degree that we have lost sight of the collective, common good.

Notes

1 US Universal Periodic Review, 2nd cycle. www.ohchr.org/EN/HRBodies/UPR/Pages/USSession22.aspxwww.ushrnetwork.org/sites/ushrnetwork.org/files/statement_to_the_media_by_the_united_nations_working_group_of_experts_on_people_of_african_descent_on_the_conclusion_of_its_official_visit_to_usa_19-2 (last accessed October 11, 2016).
2 See Robert B. Reich. 2015. *Saving Capitalism for the Many, Not the Few.* New York: Alfred A. Knopf.
3 See http://avalon.law.yale.edu/18th_century/rightsof.asp (last accessed October 11, 2016).
4 Julian Assange, Edward Snowden, and Chelsea Manning illustrate that free speech is not fully protected in the US.
5 UNESCO Universal Declaration on Cultural Diversity. 2 Nov 2001. http://portal.unesco.org/en/ev.php-URL_ID=13179&URL_DO=DO_TOPIC&URL_SECTION=201.html (last accessed October 11, 2016).

References

National Assembly of France. 1789. "Declaration of the Rights of Man." http://avalon.law. yale.edu/18th_century/rightsof.asp (last accessed October 11, 2016).

Reich, Robert B. 2015. *Saving Capitalism for the Many, Not the Few.* New York: Alfred A. Knopf.

United Nations Educational, Scientific and Cultural Organization. 2001. "UNESCO Universal Declaration on Cultural Diversity." http://portal.unesco.org/en/ev.php-URL_ID=13179&URL_DO=DO_TOPIC&URL_SECTION=201.html (last accessed October 11, 2016).

7

BEYOND WELFARE, WORKFARE, AND EMPLOYMENT

For a Basic Income as a Constitutional Amendment

Steven Panageotou

All Americans should have a right to be paid a guaranteed basic income. From Occupy protestors chanting slogans about the 1 percent, to Thomas Picketty's *Capital in the 21st Century*, discourse on economic inequality has become mainstream. According to the Institute for Policy Studies, "America's 20 wealthiest people [...] now own more wealth than the bottom half of the American population combined, a total of 152 million people in 57 million households" (Collins and Hoxie 2015). The widening gap between rich and poor is nothing new in the United States. According to Picketty (2014), economic inequality among Americans has risen sharply since the 1970s and 1980s. This ongoing trend towards growing economic inequality poses a significant obstacle to a healthy economy. As Stiglitz (2011) has said, "an economy in which *most* citizens are doing worse year after year—an economy like America's—is not likely to do well over the long haul."

Yet, the conventional solutions proposed by politicians range from stale to outright destructive. Democrats, with the most radical edge coming from Bernie Sanders, have endorsed raising the minimum wage, government investment to stimulate job growth, and higher taxes on the wealthy in a revamped welfare state. Republicans, however, have repeated the mantra of trickle-down economics by preaching the necessity of keeping wages low to keep workers competitive and taxes low to retain business competiveness. While the idea of a basic income is gaining traction among progressives and conservatives alike, politicians in the United States have yet to propose legislation for a basic income experiment, let alone a constitutional amendment that grants to all Americans a guaranteed minimal level of subsistence through a basic income program.[1] This stands in stark contrast to European countries, such as Finland, Switzerland, France, and the Netherlands, as well as Canada who are all either seriously considering or are already developing basic income experiments (Timothy 2016). The common ethos among Democrats and Republicans to rely on employment as the solution to economic inequality is maintained under assumptions that are called into question in the twenty-first century. The looming revolution in automation threatens to completely transform the entire labor market and will increasingly make large segments of the employed population obsolete (Srnicek and Williams 2015). What this means is that rising levels of economic inequality are rooted primarily in the structural transformation of the labor market in the twenty-first century. While a basic income program cannot promise to end economic inequality *per se* because it does nothing to limit the number of billionaires in the United States, basic income can compensate for the negative consequences resulting from unemployment, stagnating wages, and a thinning of the social safety net. In other words, basic income may be the key to not only averting an impending humanitarian crisis, but also to engendering a smooth transition to a post-work society.

The roots of economic inequality can be traced back to the early American Republic and the infancy of the United States. By forgoing a system of positive rights for citizens, the founding fathers actualized a system of negative rights that mandated individuals work to make a living, albeit without having to fear a tyrannical and overly-interventionist state. The result was growing economic inequality and a widening gap between the wealthy and poor that has haunted the United States for all of its history except for the unique post-World War II period that has since come to a close with the onset of neoliberalism (Reich 2015). The traditional repertoire of mechanisms to alleviate economic inequality used by the United States, comprising a combination of striving for full employment, an ideology that emphasizes a commitment to the work ethic and meritocratic principles, and a means-tested system of welfare for those at the bottom of society, has not and will likely not solve the trajectory of spiraling economic inequality in the future. Overall, there is a volatile mix of forces that will exacerbate economic inequality in the coming decades as many jobs being created today are characterized as precarious, automation threatens to dramatically reduce the pool of jobs in the near future, and the welfare state intended to provide assistance to the growing ranks of the poor is further scaled back. The post-2008 reality of unemployment, underemployment, and outright precarity among larger and larger segments of the population, especially among the youth, comes into conflict with neoliberal ideology that conditions people not only work in order to make a living, but also find in working a means of self-expression and identity formation. Faced with these challenges that are unfolding alongside a privatized healthcare system, rising rates of tuition, and the erosion of the welfare state, the traditional remedies to economic inequality are neutralized. A 'surplus population' of humans unable to find work and abandoned by the US Government is an increasing reality.

A movement for constitutional reform, and the introduction of a universal basic income as a constitutional amendment, could offer a fresh approach to an old problem. Basic income has been described as a system that provides "every citizen a livable amount of money without any means-testing" (Srnicek and Williams 2015: 118). As such, basic income is both *universal*, meaning that it is paid to each citizen or resident of a particular region and *guaranteed*, meaning that it is provided to all whether or not an individual is working (Widerquist, et al. 2013). By providing a minimal level of subsistence regardless of one's employment status, basic income has a close affinity with human rights values such as dignity, equality, and security.

The Rise and Fall of the Welfare State

The American Creed cultivated a citizenry opposed to a large and interventionist state, and instead promoted a civic tradition based in self-reliance and individualism in a context of perceived equality among citizens (Kalberg 2014). The "Protestant ethic," as Weber called it, nurtured an ethos that extolled the value of work among Americans (2002). This work ethic predisposed Americans to work longer hours than those in other industrialized nations, which was functional for an expanding capitalist economy that required a vast pool of laborers to serve as a workforce for the emerging American bourgeoisie. The commitment to the work ethic also served as an impediment to the construction of a welfare state in early America, as the responsibility for one's living was expected to derive from one's ability to work. For those Americans unable to "pull themselves up by their bootstraps," the infrastructure of extensive voluntary association membership in early America, buttressed by Protestant moralism, facilitated a private philanthropy that functioned as a welfare system for poor Americans (Lipset 1996). Even as a welfare state developed in the United States, the legacy of individualism and the Protestant ethic have continuously undermined the total acceptance of a government-administered solution to the social problem of poverty.

The Great Depression and the resultant high rates of poverty and unemployment in the 1930s "brought about a fundamental change in the role of philanthropy. The state increasingly took over responsibility for welfare functions, for hospitals, for higher education, and many other activities" (Brinkley 1996: 5). Viewed as a structural problem, Franklin Delano Roosevelt oversaw the construction of an active and interventionist welfare state to address the poverty and unemployment resulting from what was perceived to be a flawed capitalist system.

Following World War II, the state was purposed with establishing the milieu in which the economy could grow and therefore offer Americans the opportunity to insert themselves within the labor market to make a living. Through the adoption of Keynesian fiscal and monetary policies, the government became a means to stimulate consumer demand by augmenting the purchasing power of Americans through public spending. The Keynesian model combined with a vital welfare system, strong unions, and a booming consumer economy were major factors in sustaining what Harvey (2005: 10) called the postwar "class compromise between capital and labor" that engendered sustained economic growth during the 1950s and 1960s. Full employment was generally secured and the postwar economic boom conferred a rising standard of living to most Americans (Reich 2015).

Because the postwar economy "generated a plethora of middle-class jobs that paid reasonably well and were inherently secure," the welfare state emerged as a patchwork of programs to provide assistance primarily "to those who did not work—widows and children, the elderly, the disabled and seriously ill, and those who had lost their jobs" (Reich 2015: 133). Despite some programs that provided direct cash transfers, welfare relief was not intended to be a substitute for the income gained through employment. Jobs were available and high wages did not need supplementing. Instead, welfare programs generally targeted nonworkers and functioned as a "safety net of last resort" that offered limited benefits and conferred a negative social stigma (Esping-Andersen 1990: 22). The means-tested nature of such programs targeted segments of the population that had to prove their poverty or inability to work. The purpose of designing welfare programs to be means-tested and offer the bare minimum needed for survival was to scare laborers into staying employed and discipline welfare recipients to seek employment (Srnicek and Williams 2015).

The postwar formula for engendering high rates of economic growth and reductions in economic inequality broke down in the 1970s as "unemployment and inflation were both surging everywhere, ushering in a global phase of 'stagflation'" (Harvey 2005: 12). As growth rates slowed, profits plummeted, and the interests of elites threatened, "the owners and managers of capital...opened a long struggle for a fundamental restructuring of the political economy of postwar capitalism" (Streeck 2014: 27). Lurking in the shadows of academia and public policy, a doctrine emphasizing the ideals of personal freedom, self-reliance, and deeply opposed to state intervention, garnered international support as the solution to the global economy's ills. With the election of Ronald Reagan as president of the United States and Paul Volcker appointed as the chairman of the Federal Reserve, neoliberalism entered the mainstream of US politics. The postwar Keynesian political economic order abruptly collapsed in October 1979 as the Federal Reserve, under the discretion of Volcker, raised interest rates to quell inflation. Reagan continued the assault on the postwar class compromise by "further deregulation, tax cuts, budget cuts, and attacks on trade union and professional power...The long decline in real wage levels then began in earnest" (Harvey 2005: 25). The United States, and other advanced capitalist countries, "shed the responsibility they had taken on in mid-century for growth, full employment, social security and social cohesion, handing the welfare of their citizens more than ever over to the market" (Streeck 2014: 31).

The ideological shift that accompanied the transition into neoliberalism accorded to the state a diminished role in providing social services to citizens.

A consensus of conservative intellectuals, known as the 'overload theorists,' identified the growing demands of citizens on an overburdened state to be the central problem plaguing advanced capitalist countries during the economic crises of the 1970s. The danger was an "excess of democracy," in which "the advanced welfare state took on more and more tasks, for which additional revenue was needed" (Schäfer 2013: 172). In addition to accruing large government deficits to fund welfare programs, it was feared that if welfare benefits provided too many resources and too much comfort, the effect on the work ethic would be corrosive—recipients would lose the incentive to work and instead live off the public dole. The solution was to roll-back the services provided by the welfare state by slashing social expenditure, privatizing state assets, and liberalizing markets to meet the needs of individuals that the government had previously provided (Schäfer 2013). As a consequence, the welfare state that had once been integral to maintaining social peace during the postwar period underwent a fundamental dismantling that has continued into today.

From Welfare to Workfare

Ronald Reagan initiated welfare reform in the 1980s by enacting legislation to cut funding for Aid to Families with Dependent Children (AFDC), which provided cash entitlements for poor families with children (Whitman 1987). Yet, comprehensive welfare reform did not occur until the 1990s. Fulfilling his promise to "end welfare as we know it," Bill Clinton (2006) signaled the nail in the coffin for the welfare state when he signed into law in 1996 the Personal Responsibility and Work Opportunity Reconciliation Act (PRWORA). The goal of welfare reform has been twofold: first, to reduce what many perceive to be the dependency and complacency of welfare recipients to rely on government assistance by increasing the requirements that must be satisfied when receiving aid. The reality today is that "the unemployed have to fulfill an increasingly long list of conditions in order to gain even minimal benefits: attending training, constantly applying for jobs, listening to advice, and even working for free" (Srnicek and Williams 2015: 101). Second, as revenue from the collection of taxes has fallen since the 1980s as a result of persistent tax cuts, high public debts have been managed by recourse to slashing funding, mainly through rolling back the welfare state and cutting spending on welfare programs and entitlements (Streeck 2014).

By mandating that individuals work to receive benefits and placing a lifetime limit of five years, the PRWORA symbolized and institutionalized the transition from welfare to workfare. As its moniker suggests, the Act revived the traditional American values of personal responsibility, self-reliance, and the work ethic. While the postwar welfare state had generally provided relief to the nonemployed, according to Reich (2015: 138), "Now, those who are out of work receive very little. By 2014, only 26 percent of jobless Americans were receiving any kind of jobless benefit." In effect, the legacy of the 1996 PRWORA was to fundamentally restructure the welfare system such that employment has increasingly become a requirement to receive aid. According to a 2015 report by the UC Berkeley Labor Center, 73 percent "of enrollees in America's major public support programs are members of working families" (Jacobs, et al. 2015). Known as 'the working poor,' the pattern in the twenty-first century is for low-wage workers to supplement their incomes through workfare aid. Despite the meager workfare benefits, many American families still struggle to survive. According to Edin and Shaefer's (2015: xiii) examination of American poverty, "in 2011, more than 4 percent of all households with children in the world's wealthiest nation were living in poverty so deep that Americans don't believe it even exists in this country." Contrary to popular belief, the poverty only imaginable in developing countries is being experienced by a growing segment of Americans.

In addition to transforming welfare into workfare, the entirety of the welfare system, at both a federal and state level, has come under attack in recent years leading to a thinning of the social safety net. After failing to reach a bipartisan agreement for reducing the budget deficit, automatic spending cuts, known as 'the sequester,' took effect in March 2013. The target has been to reduce the federal deficit by $1.2 trillion over the next ten years. Split evenly between both defense and non-defense spending, funding has been cut to welfare programs such as Medicare, Section 8 housing vouchers, aid for Women, Infants, and Children (WIC), Head Start, and the Low Income Home Energy Assistance Program (LIHEAP) (Matthews 2013).

At a state level, a pattern is emerging whereby states manage budget deficits by slashing public spending, particularly through welfare cutbacks and mandating stricter workfare requirements. Determined not to raise taxes, one pillar of Arizona Governor Doug Ducey's plan to reduce the $1 billion budget deficit is to cut at least $4 million from the federally funded Temporary Assistance for Needy Families (TANF) program by reducing the lifetime limit for welfare recipients to twelve months, the shortest window of any state, among cuts to other public programs and public universities. Reinforcing workfare at a state level, the new budget plan will also mandate that Medicaid recipients have a job, and recipients will lose those benefits after five years (Associated Press 2015). Similarly, in Kansas and Missouri new legislation will reduce the lifetime limit on receiving TANF benefits to thirty-six and forty-five months, respectively, and tighten up regulations that require TANF recipients to work, apply for jobs, participate in job-training programs, or volunteer (Ranney 2015; Young 2015).

The drop in welfare recipients experienced in some states, such as the significant drop in enrollment that Maine experienced after imposing a three-month limit on food stamps for "able-bodied adults without minor dependents," does not mean that people are economically stable with well-paid jobs (Bidgood 2015). Rather, drops in welfare enrollment occur despite the poor remaining poor. The state's punitive apparatus, comprising its laws and courts that disproportionately target poor Americans, militarized police force, and system of mass incarceration, is deployed to manage and control this surplus population who are often pushed into the informal economy or illegal activities to survive (Srnicek and Williams 2015). For those working, the growing problem is that because employment opportunities tend to offer such low wages, many workers must supplement their incomes through workfare assistance. The problem, however, is that such a system reinforces a deepening of poverty, rather than providing a mechanism to overcome poverty.

More than the recipients of public assistance, the major benefactors of welfare reform are employers who can pay low wages and be assured that the government will provide supplemental assistance through workfare programs. "As a result, taxpayers are providing not only support to the poor but also, in effect, a huge subsidy for employers of low-wage workers, from giants like McDonald's and Walmart to mom-and-pop businesses" (Cohen 2015). Furthermore, requiring individuals to work to receive aid will soon confront a problem as the pool of jobs becomes dramatically reduced as automation unfolds.

The Future of Employment

What will the United States do when it sees the ranks of the unemployed, underemployed, and poor swell to unprecedented proportions, which is a recipe for a stagnant economy and social malaise? This is not simply a question of morality, although there is a clear moral dimension to the rising number of people living below the poverty level in a nation that has no shortage of prosperity. This situation spells disaster for a capitalist system that relies on a large base of consumers to purchase commodities produced through the market to maintain the stability of the system and fuel economic growth. Capitalism functions by paying wages and having those workers buy back the commodities produced through the market (Karatani 2014). Capitalism needs humans to consume, but no longer needs as many humans to work, so a striking contradiction results when an increasingly large segment of the labor force is either underpaid or unemployed and therefore does not have enough money to consume at the level required to sustain economic growth.

The structural transformation of the economy wrought by the ascent of neoliberal ideology in the 1980s is at the heart of the 'crisis of work' that the United States faces in the coming years. This looming crisis is defined by "a lack of formal or decent jobs for the growing numbers of the proletarian population" (Srnicek and Williams 2015: 91). The trends since the 2008 financial crisis have only exacerbated these underlying processes that, if left unchecked, will further result in increased economic inequality and a growing surplus population of humans that have few prospects for stable, well-paid employment and only minimal public assistance.

According to Reich (2015: 161):

> The so-called recovery from the Great Recession has been among the most anemic recoveries in American economic history, especially given how far the economy fell in 2008 and 2009. The ongoing problem is inadequate overall demand…After the crash of 2008, most Americans did not have the resources to buy enough goods and service to convince businesses to invest, expand, and hire. Hence, unemployment remained unusually high and most households' incomes stagnated or dropped.

Although a modest recovery is underway in the United States, bringing down the rate of unemployment, wages are stagnant and wealth continues to remain concentrated in the hands of a few (Reich 2015).

It is important to examine the types of jobs that are currently returning to the United States. While the 2008 Great Recession resulted in a significant loss of middle-class jobs, the jobs that have been created during the recovery have primarily been characterized as precarious because they stipulate "casual working hours, low and stagnant wages, decreasing job protections, and widespread insecurity" (Srnicek and Williams 2015: 93). According to the National Employment Law Project, "Low-paying industries such as retail and fast food accounted for 22 percent of the jobs lost in the Great Recession. But they generated 44 percent of the jobs added between the end of the recession and 2013" (Reich 2015: 134). In addition, these jobs tend to be nonunionized and offer little employee benefits.

Without strong unions and because corporations with massive capital reserves have been able to transform their economic power into political power, corporations have exerted pressure on politicians to keep the federal minimum wage unchanged, which over time has meant that inflation has steadily eroded the value of the minimum wage (Reich 2015). In effect, productivity increases have not been translated into higher wages. "Since 1979, the nation's productivity has risen by 65 percent, but workers' median compensation has increased by just 8 percent" (Reich 2015: 123). Workers have compensated for the low wages by accumulating higher and higher levels of private debt, specifically credit card debt and student loan debt (Schrager 2014). Without personal savings, "a full 34 percent of full-time workers live paycheque-to-paycheque" (Srnicek and Williams 2015: 94). The result is a growing portion of poor Americans who "work diligently, often more than forty hours a week, sometimes in two or more jobs. Yet they and their families remain poor" (Reich 2015: 134). These are often the same people forced to supplement their wages through socially stigmatizing workfare assistance.

The problems associated with precarious employment are augmented by the parallel trend in automation, which threatens to completely transform the entirety of the labor market and make human labor increasingly superfluous. Every aspect of the economy is subject to automation including:

Data collection (radio-frequency identification, big data); new kinds of production (the flexible production of robots, additive manufacturing, automated fast food); service (AI customer assistance, care for the elderly); decision making (computational models, software agents); financial allocation (algorithmic trading); and especially distribution (the logistics revolution, self-driving cars, drone container ships and automated warehouses). In every single function of the economy – from production to distribution to management to retail – we see large-scale tendencies towards automation (Srnicek and Williams 2015: 111).

According to research conducted by Oxford University, a whopping 47 percent of total US employment "is in the high risk category" and subject to complete automation in the next twenty years (Benedikt and Osborne 2013). Automation will not only affect working-class service and retail sector jobs, but middle-class and upper-class professional jobs are also subject to automation. Furthermore, the giant corporations dominating the leading growth sectors of the economy, including Facebook, Amazon, Twitter, and Instagram, "simply do not create jobs on the scale of classic firms like Ford and GM. In fact, new industries currently only employ 0.5 percent of the American workforce—hardly an inspiring record of job creation" (Srnicek and Williams 2015: 100). In effect, recourse to a growing economy based on full employment no longer looks feasible in the face of the structural transformation of the labor market. Even if employment does seem to increase, as a recent report indicated robust job growth in November 2015, many of these workers are not earning enough, even through workfare assistance, to get out of poverty (Stilwell 2015).

The necessity for individuals to earn a living through employment stands in stark contrast to the twenty-first century reality of precarious jobs and automated labor. Compounding the lack of (good) jobs is the erosion of the welfare state and the rise of workfare that has resulted in large segments of the population forced to work and collect a meager amount of public assistance to survive. Fewer job opportunities and a thinning of the social safety net have resulted in a cycle of poverty. According to Reich (2005: 138), "the poverty rate in 2013 was 14.5 percent, well above its levels of 11.3 percent in 2000 and 12.5 percent in 2007." The American Dream is fading as "43 percent of children born into poverty in the United States will remain in poverty for their entire lives" (Reich 2005: 139).

With the incomes of the vast majority of Americans shrinking and prospects for secure employment decreasing, a new surplus population is being produced, which presents a problem, and possibly a threat, for the existing capitalist system. If the present trends continue, this rising surplus population will continue to be managed through the state's punitive apparatus, which will have to grow to meet the challenge of a rising segment of those who are dispossessed and discontent. This outcome remains most likely so long as the looming crisis of overproduction and underconsumption is not confronted directly and politically.

One possible way to escape from this authoritarian future is to fundamentally reformulate the nature of economic rights in the United States. By transforming negative economic rights into positive economic rights, specifically through the implementation of a basic income, the current trajectory of economic inequality could be stymied. Basic income, by redistributing capital into the pockets of all Americans regardless of employment, could boost consumption and provide a "countervailing power" to a capitalist system that is organized more and more according to the interests of the elite (Reich 2015: 214). As such, basic income constitutes a qualitatively different kind of social policy to address economic inequality than employment, minimum wage hikes, and welfare.

Basic income could be established as a positive right that is both universal and guaranteed, which provides the policy with a radical force. By providing a minimum level of subsistence regardless of an individual's employment status, basic income seeks to "uncouple work and income" (Dahms 2005: 185). A basic income would be guaranteed whether or not an individual held a job, and individuals could choose to work rather than be forced to work. Basic income could establish a system where one's employment is no longer a measure of a human's value, which would be advantageous in time when employment is precarious and subject to automation. As such, basic income has the potential to fundamentally alter the nature of labor in modern societies, and furthermore, can only be successful in ending economic inequality if it does indeed transform the role of labor in the United States (Dahms 2015). With a basic income, automation is not something to be feared but welcomed, and even demanded, as citizens would experience an unprecedented level of leisure time and still be provided with the means to survive (Srnicek and Williams 2015). According to Dahms (2005: 235), "Basic income is bound to *strike at the very heart of the work society* – and the system of control it conceals." In addition, as people take on risks they never would in the existing system because of fear of failure and the inevitable setbacks that result, innovation could boom.

Conclusion: Towards a Basic Income

Basic income may be the most viable strategy for translating the wealth produced by capitalism into a more equitable distribution of resources for everyone. This is not simply a socialist system. Actually, basic income can work within the existing capitalist system, and even more, can serve to strengthen the American economy by redistributing wealth in such a way that the consumer basis of American society can be reinforced. In effect, people would have more money to consume, which is exactly how the United States was able to engender more social equality during the so-called 'Golden Age.'

The biggest obstacles to implementing a basic income are political, ideological, and cultural, not financial. According to most research, basic income "would be relatively easy to finance through some combination of reducing duplicate programmes, raising taxes on the rich, inheritance taxes, consumption taxes, carbon taxes, cutting spending on the military, cutting industry and agriculture subsidies, and cracking down on tax evasion" (Srnicek and Williams 2015: 123). The political obstacle arises because most mainstream politicians are committed to the traditional solutions of employment to address economic inequality. In the era of 'no-tax-increase' pledges, a public policy of basic income is often perceived as a waste of taxpayer funds on a system that will only engender dependency and reduce the incentive to work. Such sentiments, however, are misguided as the more equitable redistribution of funds could spur economic activity leading to a general reduction in poverty and savings for government.

The ideological and cultural obstacles stem from the deeply ingrained work ethic that is at the foundation of the American Creed. More than a means for survival, it has been normalized in the alienated society of the United States for individuals to derive their value and self-conception from their work. However, the growing dissatisfaction with employment terms, the unraveling opportunities for advancement, and the erosion of the welfare state all provide the impetus for individuals to overcome the dominant ideology and construct an alternative vision of a post-work society.

A basic income program is not entirely incompatible with twenty-first century American society. In fact, Alaska's Permanent Fund Dividend Program already resembles a basic income policy that is administered at the state level. In this program, "the state of Alaska invests a portion of its oil revenue in a fund, and distributes a portion of the returns to that fund to each resident, each year. The Permanent Fund Dividend makes a regular, unconditional, in-cash payment to every US citizen who lives in the state of Alaska for the full year. In that sense, it is a Basic Income" (Widerquist, et al. 2013: xxi). However, because the Dividend disburses payments that average between $1,000 and $2,000 per person each year, the income provides far less than is needed to meet the basic needs of each individual. In this sense, it constitutes a partial basic income. Nevertheless, Alaska's Permanent Fund Dividend Program is extremely popular and provides one example of how a basic income could be administered. Concrete proposals for a nationwide basic income in the United States vary. While there is no consensus for how much a basic income should provide every American each year, it is generally agreed that a basic income policy would be "large enough to meet a person's basic needs," such as food, water, and shelter (Widerquist, et al. 2013: xiv). The experiments underway in European countries are intended to meet this requirement. For example, the Netherlands will introduce a basic income experiment in twenty municipalities that will grant around $900 a month to recipients (Boffey 2015). Whether or not politicians in the United States will endorse a nationwide basic income program anytime soon, the hype about basic income is growing worldwide.

Although not a once-and-for-all solution to social problems, basic income could realize economic freedom in an entirely new way and establish the necessary infrastructure for further debate about the nature of social issues. Basic income can be conceived as a preparatory stage that will facilitate the improvement of the social conditions of all members of society without altering or destroying the past achievements of modern society. In this way, people could be provided with the means and have the time to further involve themselves politically, which is necessary for a healthy democracy. As such, basic income could be a catalyst for further qualitative change. Towards this end, I propose a constitutional amendment that would provide to all residents of the United States a guaranteed basic income.

Note

1 As will be discussed, Alaska's Permanent Fund Dividend constitutes the United States' only *partial* basic income program in existence. No *full* basic income program exists as of 2016 in the United States.

References

Associated Press. 2015. "Arizona Sharply Limits Welfare to Twelve Months." *The Arizona Republic*. www.azcentral.com/story/news/arizona/politics/2015/05/19/arizona-sharply-limits-welfare/27602007/ (last accessed February 23, 2016).

Bidgood, Jess. 2015. "States Tighten Conditions for Receiving Food Stamps as the Economy Improves." *The New York Times*. www.nytimes.com/2015/04/12/us/politics/states-tighten-conditions-for-receiving-food-stamps-as-the-economy-improves.html (last accessed February 25, 2016).

Boffey, Daniel. 2015. "Dutch City Plans to Pay Citizens a 'Basic Income', and Greens say it Could Work in the UK." *The Guardian*. www.theguardian.com/world/2015/dec/26/dutch-city-utrecht-basic-income-uk-greens (last accessed April 5, 2016).

Brinkley, Alan. 1996. *The End of Reform*. New York: Vintage Books.

Clinton, Bill. 2006. "How We Ended Welfare, Together." *The New York Times*. www.nytimes.com/2006/08/22/opinion/22clinton.html (last accessed February 29, 2016).

Cohen, Patricia. 2015. "Working, but Needing Public Assistance Anyway." *The New York Times*. www.nytimes.com/2015/04/13/business/economy/working-but-needing-public-assistance-anyway.html (last accessed February 25, 2016).

Collins, Chuck and Josh Hoxie. 2015. "Billionaire Bonanza: The Forbes 400 and the Rest of Us." *Institute for Policy Studies*. www.ips-dc.org/billionaire-bonanza/ (last accessed February 22, 2016).

Dahms, Harry F. 2005. "Globalization or Hyper-Alienation? Critiques of Traditional Marxism as Arguments for Basic Income." *Current Perspectives in Social Theory* 23: 205–276.

Dahms, Harry F. 2015. "Which Capital, Which Marx? Basic Income between Mainstream Economics, Critical Theory, and the Logic of Capital." *Basic Income Studies* 10(1): 115–140.

Edin, Kathryn J. and H. Luke Shaefer. 2015. *$2.00 a Day: Living on Almost Nothing in America*. Boston, MA: Houghton Mifflin Harcourt.

Esping-Andersen, Gøsta. 1990. *The Three Worlds of Welfare Capitalism*. Cambridge: Polity Press.

Frey, Carl Benedikt and Michael A. Osborne. 2013. "The Future of Employment: How Susceptible Are Jobs to Computerisation?" *Oxford University Working Paper*. www.oxfordmartin.ox.ac.uk/downloads/academic/The_Future_of_Employment.pdf (last accessed February 25, 2016).

Harvey, David. 2005. *A Brief History of Neoliberalism.* New York: Oxford University Press.

Jacobs, Ken, Ian Perry and Jenifer Macgillvary. 2015. "The High Public Cost of Low Wages." *UC Berkeley Labor Center.* http://laborcenter.berkeley.edu/the-high-public-cost-of-low-wages/ (last accessed February 24, 2016).

Kalberg, Stephen. 2014. *Searching for the Spirit of American Democracy: Max Weber's Analysis of a Unique Political Culture, Past, Present, and Future.* Boulder, CO: Paradigm Publishers.

Karatani, Kojin. 2014. *The Structure of World History: From Modes of Production to Modes of Exchange.* Durham, NC: Duke University Press.

Lipset, Seymour Martin. 1996. *American Exceptionalism: A Double-Edged Sword.* New York: W.W. Norton & Company, Inc.

Matthews, Dylan. 2013. "The Sequester: Absolutely everything you could possibly need to know, in one FAQ." *The Washington Post.* www.washingtonpost.com/news/wonk/wp/2013/02/20/the-sequester-absolutely-everything-you-could-possibly-need-to-know-in-one-faq/ (last accessed February 21, 2016).

Nash, Kate. 2012. "Towards a Political Sociology of Human Rights," in *The Wiley-Blackwell Companion to Political Sociology,* Edwin Amenta, Kate Nash, and Alan Scott (eds): 444–453. Malden, MA: Wiley-Blackwell.

Picketty, Thomas. 2014. *Capital in the Twenty-First Century.* Cambridge, MA: The Belknap Press of Harvard University Press.

Ranney, Dave. 2015. "Brownback says Welfare Reform Aims to Break 'Cycles of Dependency'." *Kansas Health Institute.* www.khi.org/news/article/brownback-says-welfare-reform-aims-to-break-cycles-of-dependency (last accessed February 22, 2016).

Reich, Robert B. 2015. *Saving Capitalism: For the Many, Not the Few.* New York: Alfred A. Knopf.

Schäfer, Armin. 2013. "Liberalization, Inequality and Democracy's Discontent," in *Politics in the Age of Austerity,* Armin Schäfer and Wolfgang Streeck (eds): 169–195. Malden, MA: Polity Press.

Schrager, Allison. 2014. "Consumer Debt Hits an All-Time High." *Bloomberg Business.* www.bloomberg.com/bw/articles/2014-09-30/consumer-debt-hits-an-all-time-high (last accessed January 29, 2016).

Srnicek, Nick and Alex Williams. 2015. *Inventing the Future: Postcapitalism and a World Without Work.* Brooklyn, NY: Verso.

Stiglitz, Joseph E. 2011. "Of the 1%, by the 1%, for the 1%." *Vanity Fair.* www.vanityfair.com/news/2011/05/top-one-percent-201105 (last accessed April 12, 2016).

Stilwell, Victoria. 2015. "Job Growth in U.S. Exceeds Forecast, Foreshadowing Rate Increase." *Bloomberg Business.* www.bloomberg.com/news/articles/2015-12-04/payrolls-in-u-s-increased-more-than-forecast-in-november (last accessed February 20, 2016).

Streeck, Wolfgang. 2014. *Buying Time: The Delayed Crisis of Democratic Capitalism.* Brooklyn, NY: Verso.

Sunstein, Cass R. 2005. "Why Does the American Constitution Lack Social and Economic Guarantees?" in *American Exceptionalism and Human Rights,* Michael Ignatieff (ed.): 90–110. Princeton, NJ: Princeton University Press.

Timothy, Joe. 2016. "CANADA: Ontario is Ready to Test a Basic Income." *Basic Income Earth Network.* www.basicincome.org/news/2016/04/canada-ontario-is-ready-to-test-a-basic-income/ (last accessed April 5, 2016).

Weber, Max. 2002. *The Protestant Ethic and the "Spirit" of Capitalism.* New York: Penguin Books.

Whitman, David. 1987. "The Key to Welfare Reform." *The Atlantic.* www.theatlantic. com/past/docs/unbound/flashbks/welfare/whitmaf.htm (last accessed February 25, 2016).

Widerquist, Karl, Yannick Vanderborght, José A. Noguera, and Jurgen De Wispelaere. 2013. "Introduction: The Idea of an Unconditional Income for Everyone," in *Basic Income: An Anthology of Contemporary Research*, Karl Widerquist, Yannick Vanderborght, José A. Noguera and Jurgen De Wispelaere (eds): xii–xiv. Hoboken, NJ: Wiley-Blackwell.

Young, Virginia. 2015. "Missouri Legislature Enacts Limit on Welfare Benefits over Nixon's Veto." *St. Louis Dispatch.* www.stltoday.com/news/local/govt-and-politics/missouri-legislature-enacts-limit-on-welfare-benefits-over-nixon-s/article_22e44a54-b286-50e5-8236-fdaf93c1b2e3.html (last accessed February 22, 2016).

8

PRESERVING ECONOMIC SECURITY

Housing, Food, and Medical Care

Steven L. Foy

A common American way of maintaining inequality is to categorize basic human rights as luxuries (Rosenberg n.d.). In this view, their attainment is the sole (or at least primary) responsibility of the individual rather than the birthright of humanity. For example, the Fair Labor Standards Act sets the federal minimum wage at $7.25 per hour, but wage data from the American Community Survey suggests that more than 37 percent of US families make less than a living wage—one that would provide for basic human needs (Nadeau and Glasmeier 2015). Progress toward a living wage has proven difficult to achieve; as of December 2010, only 125 municipalities in the United States passed any sort of living wage law, and such laws do not necessarily cover all workers (National Employment Law Project 2011). Despite estimates that a living wage ordinance would cost most firms less than 2 percent of their total production costs, an underlying counterpoint emerges—usually less directly argued but sometimes stated as blatantly as in the headline by blogger Matt Walsh: "Some people don't deserve a living wage" (Bernstein 2003; Walsh 2013). If even a basic wage may be constructed as a luxury and excluded from sufficient protection, then other, more indirect elements of economic stability may face even greater scrutiny.

Issue 1: Access to Affordable Housing

Owning a home has long been a mainstay of the "American Dream" and a central component of long-term economic security (Christie 2014; Rossi 1980). Generally, one's home is one's greatest financial asset, not only providing the opportunity to create equity that can be liquidated through sale but also providing living space that can be rented out for ongoing income (Megbolugbe and

Linneman 1993). However, confidence in home ownership has eroded in the wake of the recent US housing crisis, and home ownership rates have reached twenty-year lows (Joint Center for Housing Studies of Harvard University 2015). In July 2015, home ownership fell to 63.4 percent—the lowest rate since 1967. Meanwhile, the homeowner vacancy rate (or the percentage of available homes for purchase) fell to 1.8 percent—the lowest rate in the last decade—signaling a decline in home-buying demand (Callis and Kresin 2015; Olick 2015). Moreover, although home ownership has historically been promoted in developed countries via tax incentives or other governmental programs, political support for funding such initiatives has waned more recently (Megbolugbe and Linneman 1993).

Certain groups face especially arduous barriers in buying and maintaining ownership over homes. Although rising rent costs are motivating an increasing number of millennials to purchase houses, student debt and difficulty saving sufficient funds for a down payment have previously joined with delayed family formation to disincentivize such purchases (Gopal and Gittelsohn 2015). Racial and ethnic minorities often also face discrimination in housing markets (Reskin 2012), and predominantly black and Latino neighborhoods face higher rates of foreclosure (Hall, Crowder, and Spring 2015; Sharp and Hall 2014).

Difficulty accessing affordable housing may necessitate renting, but that too has become more difficult in the wake of the recent economic downturn. For example, in 2014, there was a gap of approximately 47,698 between the number of renter households earning $25,000 or less per year and the number of affordable housing units available (i.e., housing units available to rent for less than 30 percent of a household's annual income) in Austin, Texas (BBC Research and Consulting 2014). Micro-rental units help ease the situation by providing smaller, less expensive housing options, but their construction is often stymied by minimum size requirements and other regulations as well as by opposition from existing homeowners in proposed locations (Infranca 2014). In the second quarter of 2015, the rental vacancy rate across the US (or the percentage of available rental units) dropped to 6.8 percent—the lowest rental vacancy rate in the last decade. Meanwhile, rental prices grew by 5 percent (Olick 2015). Thus, across the country, those attempting to access affordable housing via rental are facing rising costs coupled with diminishing availability.

Representing Access to Affordable Housing as a Luxury

The extent to which affordable housing for the working class is reconstituted as a luxury can be seen via the commonality of arguments deprioritizing housing subsidization in favor of meeting the expectations of the already-housed. Returning to the example of the problems Austin, Texas has had with meeting affordable housing needs, when a low-income housing project was proposed for a wealthy, northwestern neighborhood, Jay Wiley, who was running for Austin City Council, started a petition to demonstrate his opposition. The petition expressed concern about public safety, traffic, and strains on local schools, but proposed no clear alternative for providing needed housing (Stephens 2015).

Although developers frequently tout affordable housing development goals in their mission or business statements, they may be hampered by negative responses from community residents (Scally and Tighe 2014). A recent survey of affordable housing developers in New York found that, out of 75 nonprofit and for-profit developers, 70 percent reported community opposition to afford-able development (Scally and Tighe 2014). Among these developers, 12 percent almost always and 31 percent frequently experienced community opposition, ranging from unorganized individual responses to coordinated efforts by neigh-borhood associations, utilizing legal challenges, letters to the editor, yard signs, petitions, social media, flyers, and a variety of other mechanisms (Scally and Tighe 2014).

The language utilized by such responses to affordable housing development often reflects a view of its recipients as undeserving of the right to equitable hous-ing options. In their survey of New York housing developers, Corianne Scally and Rosie Tighe (2014) found that one-fifth of their respondents mentioned that community opposition to building centered around negative perceptions of expected housing recipients, who were characterized as "those people," "welfare recipients," and "homeless." Community opposition has even threatened the crea-tion of housing options for low-income senior citizens, as was the case when affluent residents in Darien, CT reacted in angry protests (Prevost 2013).

Even when those in need of affordable housing achieve it, they may still face structural conditions intended to remind them of others' perceptions of their relatively undeserving status. Vinnie Roscigno (2009) found that landlords also discriminate in their maintenance of units, and residential associations discrimi-nate in their enforcement of rules. In New York City, a luxury apartment com-plex (whose offerings start at a cost of $1.07 million for a one-bedroom) offered 55 apartments for rent to those with low incomes for $833 per month. However, the developers ensured that none of the apartments for rent to low-income resi-dents were accessible by the main entrance; low-income residents had to use a side entrance colloquially referred to as the "poor door" (Rooney and Fox 2015).

The Right to Housing in International Constitutions

To determine the extent to which countries other than the United States have enshrined housing rights in their constitutions, I utilized Constitute's database to conduct keyword searches of "abode," "apartment," "domicile," "dwelling," "home," "house," "housing," "property," and "residence" which yielded 194 con-stitutions. Sixty of these constitutions (31 %) contained language relevant to the right to housing.

Of the sixty constitutions containing language relevant to the right to hous-ing, forty-two (70%) *directly establish* a right to housing that is *universally available* to citizens of the country (as when Angola's Constitution indicates that "Every citizen shall have the right to housing"). Three constitutions (5%) *directly establish* a right to housing that is *conditional* (as when Brazil's Constitution grants a right to housing specifically to former World War II combatants). Eight constitutions (13%) *imply* a right to housing that is *universal* (as when Panama's Constitution indicates that the "State shall establish a National Housing Policy in order to provide housing for all people..."). Seven constitutions (12%) *imply* a right to housing that is *conditional* (as when the People's Republic of Korea's Constitution indicates that the "State shall provide all *working* (emphasis added) people with every condition for obtaining...housing," requiring people work to receive this provision).

Issue 2: Access to Food Security

A number of Americans live in "food desert[s]"—"areas of poor access to the provision of healthy affordable food where the population is characterized by deprivation and compound social exclusion" and "those areas of cities where cheap, nutritious food is virtually unobtainable" (Wrigley, et al. 2002). Although real wages have stagnated, food prices continue to rise (Desilver 2014). According to the United States Department of Agriculture's Economic Research Service (n.d.), supermarket prices are expected to rise by two to three percent in 2016. Eating healthily, though becoming more financially feasible for many Americans, remains challenging for a large minority. Mayuree Rao and colleagues (2013) estimated the added cost of healthier eating at approximately $547.50 per person per year, admitting that this would pose a "big barrier" for about 30 to 40 percent of the US population (Shaw 2014). Further, the cost of organic foods (which offer a way to avoid pesticides linked to respiratory problems, skin conditions, birth defects, cancer, and other maladies) is higher than the cost of conventional food, as its production often includes the costs of crop rotation to sustain soil fertility, higher per unit labor input, transportation costs to keep organic foods separate from conventional foods to avoid contamination, and other added expenses (Food and Agriculture Organization of the United Nations n.d.; Center for Ecogenetics and Environmental Health n.d.).

Inability to keep pace with the rising food costs can lead to household food insecurity—a lack of "consistent, dependable access to enough food for active, healthy living" (Coleman-Jensen, et al. 2015). In 2014, 14 percent of US households experienced food insecurity, while 5.6 percent had very low food security, necessitating the reduction of food consumption and non-normative patterns of eating (Coleman-Jensen, et al. 2015). Lack of nourishment associated with food insecurity can also result in other negative economic repercussions via healthcare in the long term, as food insecurity is associated with an increased risk of hospitalization, cardiovascular disease, diabetes, and a host of other problems (RTI International 2014).

Even when food is accessible, it may not be sufficiently healthy due to economic forces. Although about one person out of every seven lacks sufficient protein and energy from the food he or she consumes, and even more people suffer from deficiencies in micronutrients, less nutritious food may be more profitable for food producers (Godfray, et al. 2010). Highly processed food and drink with high added fats and sugars tend to yield comparatively higher profit margins, so they have become growth areas (Desjardins 2010; Finkelstein and Zuckerman 2008). Insider Monkey, a company that aims to inform investors, included ice cream, sugar processing, candy, and chocolate in their top five high-margin food products to build a business around, and the fast food industry spends more than $5 million per day advertising to children (Erbar 2014; Federal Trade Commission 2008).

Representing Food Security as a Luxury

Historically, access to food has often been constructed as a luxury and used to differentiate between social classes. As part of a public banquet held by ancient Roman emperor Domitian, baskets of food were distributed to all, but the common people received smaller meal baskets with lesser goods. At other public dinners, commoners were only given a serving of wine (Corbier 2013). The aristocracy also had access to more and higher-quality food than the masses among the Celts and the Egyptians (Alcock 2006). Unskilled laborers spent all but 3 percent of their wages on bread in 1789 France, while the wealthy enjoyed champagne, pastries, and other delicacies.

Much remains unchanged. According to the United Nations' World Food Programme (n.d.), the world already produces enough food to feed its entire population, and North America has enjoyed a food surplus in net intra-regional trade in the past several decades, so overpopulation is not inherently a barrier to nutrition (The Economist Online 2012). Yet, securing food access for those in need is still often framed as an unreasonable extravagance in the US. At the heart of the issue may be the implication of food scholar Paul Thompson (2015) that directing resources at hunger necessitates decreasing the ability of the already food secure to enjoy more objectively excessive pursuits—some related to food (such as patronizing high-end restaurants) and others not. In other words, luxury by the food secure is seen as threatened by attempts to create food security for others, so others' food security is, in turn, framed as luxury. This may partially explain recent pushback against food insecurity; since 2013, at least 22 cities have passed ordinances outlawing sharing food with the homeless across places as different from each other as California and Texas. In one attention-garnering episode labeled "biscuitgate," Raleigh, NC, church members were threatened with arrest if they continued distributing sausage biscuits and coffee to people lined up in a local park (Willoughby 2014).

There are clear economic advantages to restrict universal access to food. When food becomes a commodity, scarcity allows those with plenty to reap the rewards. In ancient Rome, the implementation of a monetary system created business interest in decreasing demand and increasing prices (Corbier 2013: 130). In the modern US, although farm subsidies allow for crop diversification and growing rotations to avoid overtaxing particular tracts of land, they also decrease the food supply and allow for greater profit; between 2007 and 2011, the US Government provided $3,000,000 to 2,300 farms on which no crops were grown (The Economist 2015).

The Right to Food Security in International Constitutions

To determine the extent to which countries other than the United States have enshrined food rights in their constitutions, I returned to Constitute's database to conduct keyword searches as follows: "bread," "food," "meal," "meat," "nourishment," "nutrition," "nutritious," "sustenance," "vegetable," and "water" yielded 109 constitutions. Thirty-seven of these constitutions (34%) contain language relevant to food security.

Of the thirty-seven constitutions containing language relevant to the right to food security, eighteen (49%) *directly establish* a right to food that is *universally available* to citizens of the country (as when Bolivia's Constitution states that "Every person has the right to water and food..."). Seven constitutions (19%) *directly establish* a right to food that is *conditional* (as when Guatemala's Constitution guarantees the right to food to children and to the elderly). Seven constitutions (19%) *imply* a right to food that is *universal* (as when Hungary's Constitution states that everyone has the right to physical and mental health and says that Hungary will "promote effective application of the right...by ensuring access to healthy food and drinking water..."). Five constitutions (14%) *imply* a right to food that is *conditional* (as when Cuba's Constitution notes that the "Power of the people... guarantees" that no children will lack food without including a right to food for adults).

Issue 3: Access to Affordable Medical Care

Medical costs pose a significant challenge to US economic security. At the macro-level, the US spends more than twice as much per capita on healthcare as the average developed country (Peter G. Peterson Foundation 2016). Due to a lack of centralized pricing, costs are substantially higher in the US than in peer countries for everything from routine office visits to normal delivery of babies and angiograms (Klein 2013).

At the micro-level, the cost of healthcare is a major contributor to economic hardship. In a 2014 national poll from the *New York Times*/CBS News, 46 percent of respondents described the cost of basic medical care as a hardship, 33 percent indicated that their out-of-pocket costs had "gone up a lot" in the last few years, and 13 percent said that they were "much less likely" to go to the doctor if sick or injured than was the case in the past few years. Twenty-five percent of respondents said yes to the question of whether they had halved pills or skipped doses of medicine to reduce their financial burden (Rosenthal 2014). As medical bills rise, some are proposing consumer health care loans that would operate similarly to home mortgages to increase the affordability of medication (Montazerhodjat, Weinstock, and Lo 2016). Already, families are more likely to turn to payday loans with substantial fees which further destabilize their economic conditions (Bickham and Lim 2015). The situation is exacerbated by insurance barriers. Costs for many individual medical expenses are higher for the uninsured at the point of sale, but 48 percent of uninsured adults indicate that their primary impediment in attempting to obtain health insurance is its cost (Kaiser Family Foundation 2015).

The burden of healthcare costs can lead to disastrous economic consequences. Medical care costs were a factor in approximately 46.2 percent in 2001 and 62.1 percent in 2007 of US bankruptcies; 77.9 percent of those who experienced medical bankruptcies were insured at the onset of illness (Himmelstein, et al. 2009). Moreover, the odds of bankruptcy occurring as a result of medical debt were 2.38 times higher in 2007 than in 2001 (Himmelstein, et al. 2009).

Representing Medical Care as a Luxury

Access to healthcare in the US is frequently framed as a luxury rather than as a right and often in blunt fashion; in a 2009 editorial for the *Wall Street Journal*, Anthony Daniels commented that when he denies the right to health care and someone replies by asking whether he thinks it is acceptable for people to die in the street, he will "then ask my interlocutor whether he can think of any reason why people should not be left to die in the street, other than that they have a right to health care" (Daniels 2009). In a 1993 town hall meeting, responding to President Clinton's health plan, Canadian American philosopher Dr. Leonard Peikoff (1993) suggested that rights other than the explicit rights to life, liberty, property, and the pursuit of happiness were no more deserved than "a right to a trip to Disneyland, or a meal at McDonald's..."

Public opinion has fluctuated, indicating a split between those who frame healthcare as a right and those who do not. In 2007, nearly two-thirds of Americans supported a governmental guarantee of health insurance for all Americans (Toner and Elder 2007). Now, most Americans (52%) believe that the federal government is not responsible for ensuring access to healthcare, with 70 percent of Democrats and those leaning Democrat viewing the federal government as responsible and 75 percent of Republicans and those leaning Republican viewing the federal government as not responsible for ensuring access to healthcare (Wilke 2013).

The justifications for denying a right to healthcare are multifarious but tend to revolve primarily around the practicality of implementation and the potential burden imposed on others. Some have suggested that the establishment of a right to healthcare implies government fulfillment of that right and have expressed skepticism about the US Government's capability to do so (Daniels 2009). Peikoff (1993) suggests that a right to healthcare represents an unfair burden on others. In line with this thinking, Senator Rand Paul stated "With regard to the idea of whether or not you have a right to healthcare, you have to realize what that implies...I'm a physician, that means you have a right to come to my house and conscript me, it means you believe in slavery" (Jacobson 2015).

The Right to Medical Care in International Constitutions

To determine the extent to which countries other than the United States have enshrined the right to medical care in their constitutions, I returned to Constitute's database to conduct searches using the words "dental," "dentist," "doctor," "health," "hospital," "medical," "medicine," and "nurse" which yielded 186 constitutions. One hundred and thirty-one of these constitutions (70%) contain language relevant to medical care.

Of the 131 constitutions containing language relevant to the right to medical care, ninety-seven (74%) *directly establish* a right to medical care that is *universally available* to citizens of the country (as when Albania's Constitution states that "Citizens enjoy in an equal manner the right to health care from the state"). Two constitutions (2%) *directly establish* a right to medical care that is *conditional* (as when Djibouti's Constitution specifically establishes the right to examination by a doctor of one's choice but only for persons "made the object of a measure deprivative of [their] liberty"). Twenty-eight constitutions (21%) *imply* a right to medical care that is *universal* (as when Latvia's Constitution states that the "State shall protect human health and guarantee a basic level of medical assistance for everyone"). Four constitutions (3%) *imply* a right to medical care that is *conditional* (as when Gambia's Constitution states that "Disabled persons shall be entitled to protection against...discrimination, in particular as regards access to health services"). Here, the right to medical care is implied by the protection against discrimination in accessing health services, and that protection is conditioned upon status as a disabled person.

How it will Work

Constitutions from across the world bear witness to how egalitarian values can inform the meaningful enshrinement of rights relevant to economic security. As presented in this chapter, numerous constitutions explicitly or implicitly acknowledge universal or conditional rights in the areas of housing (60), food security (37), and medical care (131). Beyond important symbolic functions, such acknowledgement often has tangible effects on future policy creation and enforcement. Constitutional revision is often a necessary first step toward substantive legislative change (Focus Ireland n.d.). Moreover, specific constitutional language protecting a right provides an easier judicial path to recompense for its violation (Knuth and Vidar 2011).

While research on the direct effect of incorporating constitutional rights on the outcomes those rights are meant to address is limited, constitutional protection may be correlated with important population benefits in some cases. For example, in countries whose constitutions incorporate a right to health, the state pays for a higher percentage of healthcare costs, meaning that out-of-pocket proportions are lower for patients (Kavanagh 2015). Additionally, constitutions that incorporate an overt, enforceable right to health are significantly associated with decreased mean infant and under-five mortality rates, and the relationship is even stronger when countries are more democratically governed (Matsuura 2013). Thus, constitutional protections addressing affordable access to housing, food, and medical care offer the prospect of not only subsequent legal protections with opportunities for judicial enforcement but also measureable improvements in quality of condition for a country's inhabitants. By specifically enshrining the right to affordably access these critical components of economic security, the United States will more accurately reflect the oft-repeated cliché that the US is the "greatest country on Earth" (Ernst 2013).

References

Alcock, Joan P. 2006. *Food in the Ancient World.* Westport, CT: Greenwood Press.

BBC Research and Consulting. 2014. "2014 Comprehensive Housing Market Analysis: City of Austin." http://austintexas.gov/sites/default/files/files/NHCD/2014_Comprehensive_Housing_Market_Analysis_-_Document_reduced_for_web.pdf (last accessed August 19, 2015).

Bernstein, Jared. 2003. "Higher Wages Lead to More Efficient Service Provision—The Impact of Living Wage Ordinances on the Public Contracting Process." http://lecet.org/Legislative/prevailing_wage/Higher%20wages%20lead%20to%20more%20efficient%20service%20provision.pdf (last accessed November 12, 2016).

Bickham, Trey and Younghee Lim. 2015. "In Sickness and in Debt: Do Mounting Medical Bills Predict Payday Loan Debt?" *Social Work in Health Care* 54(6): 518–531.

Callis, Robert R. and Melissa Kresin. 2015. "Residential Vacancies and Homeownership in the Second Quarter." *US Census Bureau News.* www.census.gov/housing/hvs/files/qtr215/currenthvspress.pdf (last accessed August 18, 2015).

Center for Ecogenetics and Environmental Health. n.d. "Fast Facts about Health Risks of Pesticides in Food." http://deohs.washington.edu/ceeh/sites/deohs.washington.edu.ceeh/files/documents/FF_Pesticides.pdf (last accessed April 29, 2016).

Christie, Les. 2014. "Owning a Home No Longer the American Dream." *CNNMoney.* http://money.cnn.com/2014/06/04/real_estate/american-dream-homes/ (last accessed August 18, 2015).

Coleman-Jensen, Alisha, Matthew P. Rabbitt, Christian Gregory, and Anita Singh. 2015. "Household Food Security in the United States in 2014." *United States Department of Agriculture Economic Research Service.* www.ers.usda.gov/media/1896836/err194_summary.pdf (last accessed November 19, 2015).

Corbier, Mireille. 2013. "The Broad Bean and the Moray: Social Hierarchies and Food in Rome," in *Food: A Culinary History*, Jean-Louis Flandrin (ed.): 128–140. New York, NY: Columbia University Press.

Daniels, Anthony. 2009. "Is There a 'Right' to Health Care?" *The Wall Street Journal*. www.wsj.com/articles/SB10001424052970203517304574306170677645070 (last accessed November 23, 2013).

Desilver, Drew. 2014. "For Most Workers, Real Wages Have Barely Budged for Decades." *Pew Research Center*. www.pewresearch.org/fact-tank/2014/10/09/for-most-workers-real-wages-have-barely-budged-for-decades/ (last accessed November 19, 2015).

Desjardins, Ellen. 2010. "The Urban Food Desert: Spatial Inequality or Opportunity for Change?" in *Imagining Sustainable Food Systems: Theory and Practice*, Alison Blay-Palmer (ed.): 87–114. Burlington, VT: Ashgate.

Erbar, Pablo. 2014. "10 High Margin Food Products to Build a Business Around." *Insider Monkey*. www.insidermonkey.com/blog/10-high-margin-food-products-to-build-a-business-around-332858/ (last accessed November 19, 2015).

Ernst, Douglas. 2013. "Obama: It's a 'Cliché' to Say America is the 'Greatest Country on Earth.'" *The Washington Times*. www.washingtontimes.com/news/2013/may/15/obama-its-cliche-say-america-greatest-country-eart/ (last accessed May 1, 2015).

Federal Trade Commission. 2008. "Marketing Food to Children and Adolescents: A Review of Industry Expenditures, Activities, and Self-Regulation: A Federal Trade Commission Report to Congress." www.ftc.gov/reports/marketing-food-children-adolescents-review-industry-expenditures-activities-self-regulation (last accessed April 29, 2016).

Finkelstein, Eric A. and Laurie Zuckerman. 2008. *The Fattening of America: How the Economy Makes Us Fat, if it Matters, and What to Do About It*. Hoboken, NJ: John Wiley & Sons, Inc.

Focus Ireland. n.d. "Putting a 'Right to a Home' in Our Constitution." www.focusireland.ie/files/prhc.pdf (last accessed May 2, 2016).

Food and Agriculture Organization of the United Nations. n.d. "Why is Organic Food More Expensive than Conventional Food?" www.fao.org/organicag/oa-faq/oa-faq5/en/ (last accessed April 26, 2016).

Godfray, H. Charles J., John R. Beddington, Ian R. Crute, Lawrence Haddad, David Lawrence, James F. Muir, Jules Pretty, Sherman Robinson, Sandy M. Thomas, and Camilla Toulmin. 2010. "Food Security: The Challenge of Feeding 9 Billion People." *Science* 327: 812–818.

Gopal, Prashant and John Gittelsohn. 2015. "Rising Rents Are Finally Forcing Millennials to Buy Houses." *Bloomberg*. www.bloomberg.com/news/articles/2015-03-25/millennials-start-shift-to-homeownership-as-rents-soar (last accessed May 1, 2015).

Hall, Matthew, Kyle Crowder, and Amy Spring. 2015. "Variations in Housing Foreclosures by Race and Place, 2005–2012." *The ANNALS of the American Academy of Political and Social Science* 660(1): 217–237.

Himmelstein, David U., Deborah Thorne, Elizabeth Warren, and Steffie Wollhandler. 2009. "Medical Bankruptcy in the United States, 2007: Results of a National Study." *The American Journal of Medicine* 122(8): 741–746.

Infranca, John. 2014. "Housing Changing Households: Regulatory Challenges for Micro-Units and Accessory Dwelling Units." *Stanford Law & Policy Review* 25: 53–90.

Jacobson, Louis. 2015. "Did Rand Paul Equate a Right to Health Care with Slavery?" *Politifact*. www.politifact.com/punditfact/statements/2015/may/27/sarah-silverman/did-rand-paul-equate-right-health-care-slavery/ (last accessed November 23, 2015).

Joint Center for Housing Studies of Harvard University. 2015. "The State of the Nation's Housing 2015." www.jchs.harvard.edu/sites/jchs.harvard.edu/files/jchs-sonhr-2015-full.pdf (last accessed August 19, 2015).

Kaiser Family Foundation. 2015. "Key Facts about the Uninsured Population." http://kff.org/uninsured/fact-sheet/key-facts-about-the-uninsured-population/ (last accessed November 20, 2015).

Kavanagh, Matthew M. 2015. "The Right to Health: Institutional Effects of Constitutional Provisions on Health Outcomes." *Studies in Comparative International Development* 50(4): 1–37.

Klein, Ezra. 2013. "21 Graphs that Show America's Health-Care Prices Are Ludicrous." *The Washington Post.* www.washingtonpost.com/news/wonk/wp/2013/03/26/21-graphs-that-show-americas-health-care-prices-are-ludicrous/ (last accessed November 20, 2015).

Knuth, Lidija and Margret Vidar. 2011. "Constitutional and Legal Protection of the Right to Food Around the World." *Food and Agriculture Organization of the United Nations.* www.fao.org/docrep/016/ap554e/ap554e.pdf (last accessed May 1, 2016).

Matsuura, Hiroaki. 2013. "The Effect of a Constitutional Right to Health on Population Health in 157 Countries, 1970–2007: The Role of Democratic Governance – Working Paper No. 106." *Harvard Initiative for Global Health Program on the Global Demography of Aging.* https://cdn1.sph.harvard.edu/wp-content/uploads/sites/1288/2013/10/PGDA_WP_106.pdf (last accessed May 1, 2016).

Megbolugbe, Isaac F. and Peter D. Linneman. 1993. "Home Ownership." *Urban Studies* 30(4/5): 659–682.

Montazerhodjat, Vahid, David M. Weinstock, and Andrew W. Lo. 2016. "Buying Cures Versus Renting Health: Financing Health Care with Consumer Loans." *Science Translational Medicine* 8(327): 1–8.

Nadeau, Carey and Amy K. Glasmeier. 2015. "Update: New Data, New Findings, Always Clarifying the Message Based on User Feedback." *Living Wage Calculator.* http://livingwage.mit.edu/articles/5-update-new-data-new-findings-always-clarifying-the-message-based-on-user-feedback (last accessed June 20, 2015).

National Employment Law Project. 2011. "Local Living Wage Laws and Coverage." www.nelp.org/content/uploads/2015/03/LocalLWLawsCoverageFINAL.pdf?nocdn=1 (last accessed June 21, 2015).

Olick, Diana. 2015. "Homeownership Rate Drops to 63.4%, Lowest Since 1967." *CNBC.* www.cnbc.com/2015/07/28/home-ownership-rates-drop-to-lowest-since-1967.html (last accessed August 18, 2015).

Peikoff, Leonard. 1993. "Health Care is Not a Right." *Americans for Free Choice in Medicine.* www.afcm.org/hcinar.html (last accessed November 23, 2015).

Peter G. Peterson Foundation. 2016. "United States Per Capita Healthcare Spending is More Than Twice the Average of Other Developed Countries." www.pgpf.org/chart-archive/0006_health-care-oecd (last accessed May 3, 2016).

Prevost, Lisa. 2013. *Snob Zones: Fear, Prejudice, and Real Estate.* Boston, MA: Beacon Press.

Rao, Mayuree, Ashkan Afshin, Gitanjali Singh, and Dariush Mozaffarian. 2013. "Do Healthier Foods and Diet Patterns Cost More than Less Healthy Options? A Systematic Review and Meta-Analysis." *BMJ Open* 3: 1–16. http://bmjopen.bmj.com/content/3/12/e004277.short (last accessed November 12, 2015).

Reskin, Barbara. 2012. "The Race Discrimination System." *Annual Review of Sociology* 38: 17–35.

Rooney, Ben and Emily Jane Fox. 2015. "Luxury New York Apartment Accepts 'Poor Door' Applications." *CNNMoney*. http://money.cnn.com/2015/02/19/luxury/luxury-rental-poor-door/ (last accessed August 15, 2015).

Roscigno, Vincent J. 2009. "The Complexities and Processes of Racial Housing Discrimination." *Social Problems* 56(1): 49–69.

Rosenberg, Emily. n.d. "American Freedom and the World: External Threats, Internal Dissent." *Historical Society of Pennsylvania*. http://digitalhistory.hsp.org/pafrm/essay/american-freedom-and-world-external-threats-internal-dissent (last accessed April 29, 2016).

Rosenthal, Elisabeth. 2014. "How the High Cost of Medical Care is Affecting Americans." *The New York Times*. www.nytimes.com/interactive/2014/12/18/health/cost-of-health-care-poll.html (last accessed November 20, 2015).

Rossi, Peter H. 1980. *Why Families Move*, 2nd ed. Beverly Hills: Sage.

RTI International. 2014. "Current and Prospective Scope of Hunger and Food Security in America: A Review of Current Research." www.rti.org/pubs/full_hunger_report_final_07-24-14.pdf (last accessed November 19, 2015).

Scally, Corianne Payton and J. Rosie Tighe. 2014a. "NIMBY: Where, When, and to Which Developers It Happens." *Rooflines*. www.rooflines.org/3675/nimby_where_when_and_to_which_developers_it_happens/ (last accessed August 19, 2015).

Scally, Corianne Payton, and J. Rosie Tighe. 2014b. "Who, Why, and How Communities Oppose Affordable Housing." *Rooflines*. www.rooflines.org/3701/who_why_and_how_communities_oppose_affordable_housing/ (last accessed August 19, 2015).

Sharp, Gregory and Matthew Hall. 2014. "Emerging Forms of Racial Inequality in Homeownership Exit, 1968–2009." *Social Problems* 61(3): 427–447.

Shaw, Jonathan. 2014. "The Price of Healthy Eating." *Harvard Magazine*. http://harvardmagazine.com/2014/03/the-price-of-healthy-eating (last accessed November 19, 2015).

Stephens, Alexis. 2015. "Austin Housing Debate Pits Traffic Concerns against Equitable Development." *Next City*. https://nextcity.org/daily/entry/austin-affordable-housing-equitable-development (last accessed November 12, 2015).

The Economist Online. 2012. "How to Feed a Planet." *The Economist*. www.economist.com/blogs/graphicdetail/2012/05/daily-chart-17 (last accessed November 20, 2015).

The Economist. 2015. "Milking Taxpayers: As Crop Prices Fall, Farmers Grow Subsidies Instead." *The Economist*. www.economist.com/news/united-states/21643191-crop-prices-fall-farmers-grow-subsidies-instead-milking-taxpayers (last accessed November 20, 2015).

Thompson, Paul B. 2015. *From Field to Fork: Food Ethics for Everyone*. New York, NY: Oxford University Press.

Toner, Robin, and Janet Elder. 2007. "Poll Shows Majority Back Health Care for All." *The New York Times*. www.nytimes.com/2007/03/01/washington/01cnd-poll.html. (last accessed November 20, 2015).

US Department of Agriculture Economic Research Service. n.d. "Food Price Outlook, 2016." www.ers.usda.gov/data-products/food-price-outlook/summary-findings.aspx#foodCPI (last accessed November 19, 2015.)

Walsh, Matt. 2013. "Some People Don't Deserve a Living Wage." http://themattwalshblog.com/2013/11/07/some-people-dont-deserve-a-living-wage/ (last accessed August 11, 2015).

Wilke, Joy. 2013. "Majority in US Say Healthcare Not Gov't Responsibility." *Gallup*. www.gallup.com/poll/165917/majority-say-healthcare-not-gov-responsibility.aspx (last accessed June 8, 2016).

Willoughby, Karen L. 2014. "More Cities Say, 'Don't Feed the Homeless.'" *Christian Examiner*. www.christianexaminer.com/article/more.cities.saying.dont.feed.the.homeless/47526.htm (last accessed November 20, 2015).

World Food Programme. n.d. "What Causes Hunger?" www.wfp.org/hunger/causes (last accessed November 20, 2015).

Wrigley, Neil, Daniel Warm, Barrie Margetts, and Amanda Whelan. 2002. "Assessing the Impact of Improved Retail Access on Diet in a 'Food Desert': A Preliminary Report." *Urban Studies* 39(11): 2061–2082.

9

WHAT LATIN AMERICA AND THE CARIBBEAN TEACH THE UNITED STATES ABOUT CONSTITUTIONALIZING ENVIRONMENTAL HUMAN RIGHTS

K. Russell Shekha and Leah Edwards

At the end of the 2015 United Nations Climate Conference, or COP21, the 196 attending parties negotiated the Paris Agreement ("Adoption of the Paris Agreement" 2015). The main goal was placing a cap of 2° Celsius on increasing average global temperatures. President Barack Obama said, "…the Paris agreement establishes the enduring framework the world needs to solve the climate crisis. It creates the mechanism, the architecture, for us to continually tackle this problem in an effective way." He also suggested that, "We'll have a strong system of transparency, including periodic reviews and independent assessments, to help hold every country accountable for meeting its commitments." The Paris Agreement needed fifty-five countries to sign so it could enter into force; by April 29, 2016, 177 countries had signed it, and sixteen had ratified.

The President's optimistic statement about institutional architecture is a direct inspiration for this study. The COP21 and resulting commitments by the US and other countries led us to the foundational inquiry of this study—What can the US learn from Latin American and Caribbean countries about constitutional environmental rights (CERs)?[1] We examine these rights through the critical lens of the sociology of human rights, and by integrating overlapping debates in environmental sociology. The sociology of human rights provides new ways to understand and explain the intersections of constitutional politics, socio-economic policies and cultural programs, and social and environmental justice movements that shape the environmental trajectories of countries in the Americas. Similarly, environmental sociology critiques the impacts of capitalist development on environmental degradation, weighs world systems arguments of global, ecological stratification and world society's emphasis on global normative environmentalism. The sub-discipline also examines struggles for environmental justice and citizenship across contexts (see Pellow and Brehm 2015 for an overview of environmental sociology). Thus, the sociology of human rights benefits from environmental sociology because it provides:

> precious insights into both the rights conditions for and the rights claims of nation-states, peoples, groups, and communities in the Global South. This proves significant for our understanding not only of third generation collective rights ... but also of rights bundles... (Frezzo 2014: 133).

The reason we argue the US can learn much about environmental rights from countries in the Americas is because these countries began including CERs into their regimes and political systems during the last thirty to forty years. What we show in this chapter, echoed throughout this volume in different forms, is that CERs do what President Obama suggests. CERs institutionalize the architecture, mechanisms, and accountability necessary to ensure the human right to a healthy and clean environment. However, we would be remiss to suggest there are only positives to be found when analyzing environmental rights struggles in the Americas. Thus, we also show that rights claims for CERs are not without political, economic, social and cultural costs most visible in ongoing pluralistic social movement mobilizations for the environment.

Most of the Western hemisphere is far outpacing US efforts to address environmental problems by framing them in the language of human or environmental rights and then institutionalizing environmental, human rights as constitutional provisions and articles. Table 9.1 shows this using the Constitute Project's (Elkins, Ginsburg, and Melton 2013) database of constitutions from thirty-five countries in the Americas,[2] that Latin American and Caribbean countries include environmental rights in great numbers, defined innovatively, imaginative in scope, expansive in coverage, and added over many years. Of these thirty-five countries, 77 percent (27) of countries in the Americas include "protection of environment," 46 percent (16) "protection of consumers," 54 percent (19) the "right to safe work environment," 49 percent (17) "limits in the employment of children," 60 percent (21) the "right to health care," 57 percent (20) the "right to reasonable standard of living," 54 percent (19) the "right to shelter," and 23 percent (9) sustainable development (Elkins, Ginsburg, and Melton 2013). This list demonstrates the variation in substance (discussed further below) and in representation of CERs. However, these illustrative data suggest something very powerful. The US and Canada sit in curious company with the small (populations less than two million) island countries of the Bahamas, Dominica, Grenada, St. Kitts and Nevis, St. Vincent and Grenadines, and Trinidad and Tobago as the only countries in the Americas with none of the CERs listed above.

The lack of any of the above rights is worrisome given the recent commitment by the US to reduce its own carbon footprint by embracing the 2015 Paris Accords. Yet, a growing body of literature suggests ratification of international

TABLE 9.1 Presence of Environmental Rights Bundles in Latin American and Caribbean Constitutions

Country	Environment	Consumer	Safe Work	Child Labor	Health Care	Living Std.	Shelter	Sustain. Develop
Antigua & Barbuda	Yes	No	No	No	No	Yes	No	No
Argentina	Yes	Yes	Yes	No	No	Yes	Yes	No
Bahamas	No	No	No	No	No	No	No	No
Barbados	Yes	No	No	No	No	No	No	No
Belize	Yes	No	Yes	No	Yes	Yes	No	No
Bolivia	Yes	Yes	Yes	Yes	Yes	Yes	Yes	Yes
Brazil	Yes	Yes	Yes	Yes	Yes	Yes	Yes	No
Canada	No	No	No	No	No	No	No	No
Chile	Yes	No	No	Yes	Yes	No	No	No
Colombia	Yes	Yes	No	Yes	Yes	Yes	Yes	Yes
Costa Rica	Yes	Yes	Yes	Yes	No	Yes	Yes	No
Cuba	Yes	No	Yes	No	Yes	No	Yes	No
Dominica	No	No	No	No	No	No	No	No
Dominican Republic	Yes	Yes	Yes	Yes	Yes	Yes	Yes	Yes
Ecuador	Yes	Yes	Yes	Yes	Yes	Yes	Yes	Yes
El Salvador	Yes	Yes	Yes	Yes	Yes	Yes	Yes	Yes
Grenada	No	No	No	No	No	No	No	No
Guatemala	Yes	Yes	Yes	Yes	Yes	Yes	Yes	No
Guyana	Yes	No	No	No	Yes	Yes	Yes	No
Haiti	Yes	No	No	Yes	Yes	No	Yes	No
Honduras	Yes	Yes	Yes	Yes	Yes	Yes	Yes	No
Jamaica	Yes	No	No	No	No	No	No	No
Mexico	Yes	Yes	Yes	Yes	Yes	Yes	Yes	Yes
Nicaragua	Yes	Yes	Yes	Yes	Yes	Yes	Yes	No
Panama	Yes	No	Yes	Yes	Yes	Yes	Yes	No
Paraguay	Yes	Yes	Yes	Yes	Yes	Yes	Yes	No
Peru	Yes	Yes	No	No	Yes	No	No	Yes
Saint Lucia	Yes	No	Yes	No	No	Yes	No	No
St. Kitts & Nevis	No	No	No	No	No	No	No	No
St.Vincent & Grenadines	No	No	No	No	No	No	No	No
Suriname	Yes	Yes	Yes	No	Yes	No	No	No
Trinidad & Tobago	No	No	No	No	No	No	No	No
United States	No	No	No	No	No	No	No	No
Uruguay	Yes	No	Yes	Yes	Yes	No	Yes	No
Venezuela	Yes	Yes	Yes	Yes	Yes	Yes	Yes	Yes
Total (Americas)	27	16	19	17	21	20	19	9

(Continued.)

Table 9.1 (*cont.*)

Country	Environment	Consumer	Safe Work	Child Labor	Health Care	Living Std.	Shelter	Sustain. Develop
Total as % of Americas	77%	46%	54%	49%	60%	57%	54%	23%
Total (World)★	153	47	83	79	135	83	72	42
Total as % of World	17%	35%	23%	22%	16%	24%	26%	20%

Note: ★The Constitute Project includes 194 constitutions; updated June 2016.

human rights treaties alone does not lead to improved national human rights practices (see Cole 2015).While the US is a leader in internationalizing environmental rights by ratifying the Paris Accords, without significant constitutional improvements, this commitment is subject to the whims and idiosyncrasies of electoral politics. Critics of Obama's handling of the Paris Accords already point to ways to undo and undermine them. Steven Groves (2016) states the Paris Accords should be brought to Congress as an international treaty citing Article II of the US Constitution. Despite admitting Congress would not have ratified the Paris Accords, he suggests it should develop legislation denying the EPA or other programs to take any steps towards the commitments made in the ratification of the Paris Accords.This is just one example of how easy it is in the US to seriously threaten implementation of commitments not protected by the constitution.

The twenty-seven countries in the Americas and the Caribbean including protection of the environment in their constitutions show implementation of the Paris Accords to be less politically uncertain because of CERs. This does not mean stronger constitutions fully protect countries from political manipulation. The International Rights of Nature Tribunal in Paris during COP21 condemned Ecuador for ongoing oil exploitation in the Yasuní National Park, using the 2008 constitution to shame Ecuador for violating the "rights of nature". Thus, we show that Latin American and Caribbean countries provide strategies for creating institutional architecture, procedural mechanisms, substantive definitions, transparency and accountability to the environment to deter political manipulations.

Yet, the question of the efficacy of CERs remains. One debate in environmental sociology recently pointed to the issue of efficacy in the question of global environmentalism's impact and preceded a growing trend in environmental sociology to explore the impacts of the world society on environmental policy and degradation (Buttel 2000; Frank, Hironaka, and Schofer 2000). While one study (Frank, Hironaka, and Schofer 2000) found that world society theory best explains a growing sense that the nation has a basic responsibility to environmental protection, a response by Buttel (2000) suggested that properly accounting for domestic factors leading to environmental protection by the nation needs greater attention. Buttel (2003) continues to suggest that domestic activism is the most important predictor for positive domestic environmental policy and that there is no substitute for international agreements adaptable enough to work with all varieties of national institutional frameworks. However, there is a current surge in studies suggesting the importance of the international environmental movements for positively affecting domestic environmental policy and mobilization (Longhofer and Schofer 2010; Longhofer, et al. 2016; Murdie and Urpelainen 2015; Pacheco-Vega 2015; Schofer and Hironaka 2005).

Constitutional Environmental Rights in the Americas

In this section, we investigate the part of the rights cycle of most interest to sociologists (Frezzo 2014), how countries implement environmental rights claims into the political system as CERs. What types of environmental protections do the Americas include in their constitutions? What can the US learn from the variety of environmentally oriented constitutional rights that proliferate in the Americas? Considering the sociological definition of CERs we proposed above, we acknowledge the variety of ways that countries ascribe environmental rights into constitutions. Especially considering that CERs spilled out of third-generation, collective rights to include individuals and the Mother Earth it is important to assess both the number of occurrences and the language of environmental protections throughout the Americas.

Table 9.1 shows seven different subgroups of rights that the Constitute Project (Elkins, Ginsburg, and Melton 2013) defines that we suggest are environmental rights bundles including "protection of environment" defined above. We include an eighth category 'sustainable development' based on our own search of the database. Below we provide discussions and examples of six other "social rights" subtopics from the Constitute Project that we demonstrate are environmental rights bundles situated in different places on the spectrums discussed above.

A strong example of a CERs bundle is the right to a safe work environment. The Constitute Project defines "Right to safe work environment" as a constitutional guarantee that "Grants individuals the right to work in environment free of preventable hazards. This may include an obligation on the state to provide safe working conditions." Based on the sociological definition of CERs above we might stop there and declare this a rights bundle. However, it is important to look to examples from the nineteen countries in the Americas that include a safe work environment.

Several examples show the range that countries in the Americas articulate a safe work environment. Antigua and Barbuda, Belize, and Saint Lucia include this right only in the Preamble defining it with the same language "that labour should not be exploited or forced by economic necessity to operate in inhumane conditions." Guyana includes this right as a specific article but not as a fundamental right. Other countries, such as Argentina, El Salvador, and Guatemala define safe work environments as part of their fundamental rights packages, sometimes bundling them with civil, political, economic and social rights. However, these examples do not include any language suggestive of environmental protections or guarantees. Most countries including this, such as Bolivia, Brazil, Cuba, and Nicaragua, define it as fundamental, as bundled with other civil and social rights, and use language such as "hygiene," "health," "environmental," and "safety" suggesting a focus on ecological conditions of workplaces. Mexico specifies protections for groups such as artisans and domestic workers and indicates procedural mechanisms in the form of penalties. The 2015 Dominican Republic Constitution expands environmental citizenship stating, "The public powers shall promote the dialogue and agreement between workers, employment, and the State…shall… promote the creation of petitions integrated by employers and workers for the attainment of these goals" (Art. 62).

"Limits in the employment of children" is another example of a CERs bundle, that "Protects children against exploitation in the workplace." This may be in the form of a ban on child workers, or as a requirement for additional protections for child workers (Elkins, Ginsburg, and Melton 2013). This rights bundle includes civil, economic, and social rights protections and is also part of the third generation rights protecting children as a group at risk of exploitation and rights abuses. Table 9.1 shows that seventeen countries in the Americas (49%) include this, which is 22 percent of the seventy-nine countries around the world including this right.

On the surface, the presence of environmental protections is not as clear, but examples from specific countries in the Americas demonstrate that this is also an environmental right. Brazil, Colombia, Ecuador, El Salvador, Guatemala, Honduras, Mexico, and Panama explicitly prohibit unhealthy or dangerous work for children. Other countries, such as Haiti, may not define child labor rights using health or safety, but state "Special laws govern the work of minors…" Thus, this does not mean that child labor legislation does not include environmental rights. Chile also suggests legislation may prohibit child labor but protects employers stating "Any discrimination that is not based on personal skills or capability is forbidden, notwithstanding that the law may require Chilean citizenship or age limits in certain cases" (Art. 19). These examples demonstrate that countries in the Americas often bundle child labor rights with CERs.

While some merely advocated for including consumer protections as human rights (Deutch 1994), we suggest protection of consumers is a CER. The Constitute Project defines "protection of consumer" as a constitutional right that "Addresses consumer rights or consumer protection. Protects consumers from harmful products and/or predatory or unethical business practices." Table 9.1 shows that sixteen countries (46%) in the Americas include this, which is 35 percent of the world's countries including consumer protections. This right to a protection from harmful products is interesting because it is clearly environmental in definition, and aimed at arguably the largest collective in all capitalist economies, the consumer. However, it also defines consumer protections for individuals. That is, the definition includes both the civil rights and economic rights of the individual and the collective right to a healthy environment. This is important when considering the longstanding debate within environmental sociology between the political economy perspectives. The ecological modernization thesis suggests that despite environmental degradation, modernization and globalization also result in countries and corporations embracing policies to protect the environment. The treadmill of production perspective, discussed above, is the competing theory suggesting that intensified capitalist development lead to increased environmental degradation (Pellow and Brehm 2015).

The Ecuadorian Constitution provides the strongest constitutional environmental protections of consumers. This constitution includes an entire section, "5. Users and Consumers," Articles 56–60 devoted to protection of consumers. Consumer protection also includes part of Article 66 of "6. Rights to Freedom" which specifies the right to quality public goods. The Bolivian Constitution focuses on two main points: the supply of food and "products in general" and to reliable information about such products. In other articles however, Bolivia addresses many related concerns, such as the Law of Mother Earth and GMO bans. Therefore, while the article on consumer protection may be sparse, the thoroughness of the constitution in other respects allows civil society to protect consumers themselves. Costa Rica's Constitution stipulates regulation of monopolies and prohibits monopolies that threaten the freedom of commerce, agriculture and industry.

Three other rights categories demonstrate the wide applicability of CERs bundles. The Constitute Project defines the "Right to healthcare" as a social right that "Obligates the state to provide health care to its citizens, or provides individuals with the general right to health care. In some cases, health care must be provided by the government free of charge" (Elkins, Ginsburg, and Melton 2013). Table 9.1 shows that twenty-one countries in the Americas (60%), which is 16 percent of the 135 countries of the world, include this right. The "Right to a reasonable standard of living" is a social right, which "Grants individuals the right to a standard of living in concordance with a basic understanding of human dignity. May also refer to adequate well-being, suitable existence, or life worthy of a human being." Table 9.1 shows that twenty countries in the Americas (57%), which is 24 percent of the eighty-three countries of the world including this right. The "Right to shelter" "Grants individuals the right to adequate shelter or housing. Often framed in terms of facilitating family life." Nineteen (54%) constitutions in the Americas include CERs to shelter, 26 percent of the world's countries that include shelter.

While not part of the Constitute Project's list of rights topics, we searched for 'sustainable development' in the database. Interestingly, and a reflection of the changing landscape of global politics and normative commitments to environmental stewardship and rights, eight (23%) constitutions in the Americas include sustainable development, which is 20% of the world's. Bolivia and Ecuador, with arguably the strongest protections of the environment as Hayward (2005) defines and we discuss below, do not include sustainable development as part of the sections on rights. Nor do El Salvador, Peru, Guyana states that it will "secure sustainable development and use of natural resources while promoting justifiable economic and social development" (Art. 149J, 2, C), as part of its fundamental rights package, which the nation includes as a rights bundle with state protection from pollution and guarantees to conservation. This is suggestive of procedural mechanisms for enforcement (Art. 149J).

What can the United States learn from all of this? We believe the lessons for the US are twofold. First, we show that the Americas provide many models for CERs. We recognize the political landscape of the US is markedly different from many of these countries. However, Gargarella's (2011) analysis of grafting social rights onto hostile constitutions developed in the liberalism-conservatism historical context suggests that perhaps Latin American countries are useful models for national self-reflexivity in the US. Indeed, the Chicago Boys certainly made their mark using Chile as an experiment for the present-day neoliberal capitalist system, which was arguably possible because of its constitutional democracy. Below we point to new CERs implemented during General Pinochet's dictatorship. Regardless, the US is reluctant as a nation to update its federal constitution and Bill of Rights. A prime example of this is that while 60 percent of countries in the Americas have the right to health care in their constitutions, the US was mired in a politically exhausting and costly battle around the Affordable Care Act. Most importantly, we show conclusively through the human rights enterprise and the sociology of human rights that CERs are *for the people*. That is, throughout the many variations of environmental rights bundles in the Americas there is a consistent theme of protection for specific groups of peoples that are often historically marginalized, oppressed, or seemingly without power. CERs can empower these people by opening political opportunities for environmental justice often simultaneously with other types of social justice and human rights work.

Protection of the Environment

The Constitute Project's (Elkins, Ginsburg, and Melton 2013) category "protection of environment" is most consistent with the scope of the environmental rights definition Hayward (2005) provides. This scope means that countries in the Americas articulate their commitment to protect the environment along the spectrums we used to provide a sociological definition of CERs. Within this section, we focus on Ecuador and Bolivia in detail because of their innovations in constitutional environmental rights. By exploring these examples, we develop a critique of the protection of environment in constitutional democracies set within the context of modernizing, global capitalist economies. We analyze strong commitments to protecting the environment in Ecuador and Bolivia which allow us to answer the question of what the US can learn from these countries. This provides the final starting point that this chapter offers—a theoretically and empirically grounded conversation about the US's commitment to environmental rights.

Ecuador

The 2008 Ecuadorean Constitution's "protection of environment" (Elkins, Ginsburg, and Melton 2013) is also one of the strongest in Latin America. Rights to food, water, and a healthy environment make up the first few Articles in the section on fundamental rights based on the *sumak kawsay*, or good way of life. Before that the constitution states "Natures shall be the subject of those rights that the Constitution recognizes for it" (Art. 10). The constitution includes CERs in sections on education, housing, health, communal rights, rights to freedom, and most significantly in the "Rights of Nature" (7). CERs include comprehensive substantive and procedural rights, focuses on individuals, collectives with special emphasis on indigenous and rural areas, and the innovative, ecocentric rights of nature (*Pachamama*). Substantive rights include clean water, healthy food, ecological health and sustainability, freedom from pollution, clean technologies, and alternative energies. A strong statement forbids chemical, biological, and nuclear weapons, organic pollutants and internationally prohibited agrochemicals, as well as GMOs and experimental biological technologies that might be harmful to human health, food sovereignty, or ecosystems. The document includes a series of substantive environmental rights for collectives such as indigenous communities and groups. Procedural, democratic rights include environmental education, a responsibility and mechanisms for citizens and communities to report environmental problems, and special provisions for large communities and indigenous groups. Ecuador's CERs in the 2008 constitution cannot be captured adequately here and begin in Title 1, 1, Article 3 and end in Title VIII (International Relations), 1, Article 416 (Ecuador Constitution 2008).[3]

Ecuador is the first nation to ascribe CERs directly to nature. Nature, or *Pachamama*, has the right to exist and be restored when damaged. Procedural rights empower peoples to demand that the state upholds and respects nature's rights. Ecuador eschewed the more common anthropocentric format in favor of an ecocentric constitutional framework, meaning that its commitment to CERs makes it one of the strongest in the world (Akchurin 2015).

Reasons for this innovation in CERs included an historical emphasis on environmental protection, strong environmental and indigenous movements that often overlapped, and a new opening for the political left when President Rafael Correa took office in 2006 on a platform of constitutional reform (Akchurin 2015). Akchurin (2015) points to early conservationism in the forms of constitutional protections of places known for natural beauty as part of a package protecting national artistic treasures in 1945, and making the Galápagos the first national park in 1959. This led eventually, after an oil boom and increases in exports of other natural resources throughout the 1970s, to the nation's second environmentally oriented constitutional reform. In 1984, Ecuador included rights to a pollution-free environment. As internal infrastructures for environmental protections increased in the 1970s through the 1990s, so did mobilizations of scientifically oriented environmentalists, justice-oriented *ecologista* movements, and indigenous movements demanding *plurinacionalidad*, or a plurinational state. These historical developments combined set the stage for the articulation of the rights of nature in Ecuador's 2008 Constitution (Akchurin 2015). Thus, as the human rights enterprise (Armaline, et al. 2015) suggests, Ecuador's innovation in constitutionalizing rights of nature is a mix of long historical processes and the skillful use of political opportunities that opened during Correa's administration by an alliance of environmental justice and rights activists consisting of lawyers, policy makers, and social movement actors (Akchurin 2015).

However, CER's do not always ensure environmental protections or respect for nature's rights. As Akchurin (2015) points out, the Ecuadorian government continues export industries based on environmental exploitation such as oil drilling in the Yasuní National Park. At the same time, an Ecuadorean judge ended a seventeen-year battle over environmental contamination by Texaco-Chevron ordering the company to pay $9 billion dollars in damages (Whittemore 2011). This is interesting considering the Secoya people (among others) battled the company over environmental contamination starting well before the 2008 constitutional reforms (Vickers 2003). CERs do not guarantee freedom from political or civil rights abuses for indigenous groups seeking protections of their lands. Despite political opportunities early in Correa's administration, some suggest the President is backpedaling. Correa overturned fundamental rights to water to open lands to mining processes that are environmentally destructive, and shut down social movement organizations that protest new mining operations (Whittemore 2011).

Bolivia

Bolivia's "Protection of the environment" (Elkins, Ginsburg, and Melton 2013) is among the two most expansive compared to every other nation in the Latin American and Caribbean regions. Bolivia's Constitution demonstrates CER bundles defined explicitly as fundamental, for individuals, indigenous and multicultural communities, the general population, economic organizations and institutions, governmental agencies from autonomous regions to the central state, and the Mother Earth. Protection of the environment is wide in scope, encompassing renewable and nonrenewable natural resources, food sovereignty and security, biodiversity, wild fauna and domestic animals, prohibitions on weapons that affect the environment, nuclear and toxic waste, sustainable development, and tourism. It also includes specificity within these categories. Bolivia's constitutional protection of the environment is also one of the strongest in comparison to other countries because of the procedural mechanisms specified that increase democratic participation and empower environmental citizenship. These environmental protection mechanisms include ways to promote and educate, normative and legal definitions, mandates for responsibility and obligations, specification of powers, jurisdiction, and liability, as well as prioritization of the Amazonian areas. The details above illustrate the strength of environmental protection in the Bolivian Constitution but cannot capture the entirety of these rights specified across twenty-four Articles beginning in Part I, Title I, I, Article 3 and ending in Part IV, Title II, IX, Article 402 (Plurinational State of Bolivia Constitution 2009).[4]

There are many reasons for Bolivia's comprehensive constitutional protections of the environment. Failed hydrocarbon and gas policies and a Constitutional Assembly promised by President Mesa combined with prolonged water and gas wars between social movements and the state led to political and economic instability. Protestors demanding both procedural and substantive environmental rights helped set the stage for eventual constitutional reforms under President Morales, the nation's first indigenous president, who opened up political opportunities for those on the left. For example, in 2006, President Morales appointed Abel Mamani, a known activist in the struggle for water rights, as the first Minister of Water. With Morales nationalizing natural gas, the move to put the control of water back into the hands of the Cochabamba peoples signaled his administration's resistance to international neoliberalism (Perreault 2008). Indigenous movements for autonomy and self-governance of natural resources, ecological conservation, and land rights throughout the decades before the 2009 Constitution (Ruiz-Mallén, et al. 2015) contributed to the comprehensive CERs. They thoroughly detailed environmental rights for collectives in the document. Protestors fought for better resource regulation and for an anti-neoliberal agenda. The 2009 Constitution passed with 61 percent of the population voting in favor (Hammond 2011).

Following adoption of the new Constitution, Bolivia hosted the First Peoples' World Conference on Climate Change and the Rights of Mother Earth in 2010 as a response to the perceived failures of COP15 in Copenhagen. The Conference, held in Cochabamba to commemorate the 2000 Cochabamba Water War, drew over 35,000 people. Interestingly, the Cochabamba Accords included commitments to keeping average global temperatures from rising more than 1° Celsius (Turner 2010), which is even lower than the 2015 Paris Agreement's 1.5° goal ("Adoption of the Paris Agreement" 2015).

While the Bolivian Constitution is newer than the Ecuadorean, scholars still point to inherent tensions between an economy based on natural resources and a new constitution based on CERs and human rights (Schilling-Vacaflor 2011).

Adding to this, Gudynas (2013) suggests the Morales administration abandoned *bien vivir*, part of the rights of nature philosophy of indigenous peoples in the nation, as a development agenda emerged again. That said, he is careful to state that there have been positive changes in Bolivia since the 2009 Constitution and 2010 Conference on Mother Earth, but that the Morales administration is neither a socialist alternative nor a return to neoliberalism.

Why Constitutional Environmental Rights in the US?

We believe the work in this volume shows the US capacity for considering constitutional updates. Given the recent, historic Paris Agreement on climate change there are more opportunities for demanding the US's Constitution or Bill of Rights match the times. Looking at the commitment of Latin American and Caribbean nations to CERs, we can see a large variety of models for the US to draw upon. Most of these countries ascribed environmentally oriented rights in great numbers and with creative implementation. Other countries include CERs more directly such as in Bolivia and Ecuador (*Pachamama* and *Bien Vivir*). Treating the environment as a public good, or a commodity to use, remains a problem in cases of environmental protection in the US. Latin American countries show workable alternatives to this model by situating environmental rights as fundamental human rights, comprehensively substantive and procedural, and occasionally extend them from the individual to nature herself. Many of these countries include CERs as responses to demands from social and indigenous movements.

A definition of CERs grounded in the sociology of human rights as a rights bundle (Frezzo 2014) and in the human rights enterprise (Armaline, et al. 2015) allows for the necessary dynamic, contested processes that are unique to each country while pointing to areas where histories of countries converge. These convergences unveil new possible opportunities for mobilization and policy. Gargarella (2011) shows how the classic liberal-conservative debates characterizing constitutional developments and grafting social rights in Latin American countries are potentially applicable to the US. While this study emphasizes national processes leading to new CERs, studies emphasizing world society normative institutionalization may not be wrong either. That is, if Latin American and Caribbean countries can articulate, and follow up on, commitments to the environment through innovative and creative CERs, all while capturing international audiences' imagination and support, then why should the US be any different? We do not suggest that this provides the only template for how the US might deepen its commitment to environmental human rights. We believe this contribution to *Humans Rights Of, By, and For the People* provides another starting point for how we as a country might follow up on the Paris Accords to institutionalize the architecture, mechanisms, and accountability necessary to ensure the human right to a clean environment. As we have shown, countries in Latin American and the Caribbean demonstrate definitively that CERs provide that necessary national institutionalization of environmental rights through constitutional status.

Notes

1 We use the acronym for Constitutional Environmental Rights (CERs) based on its usage in a growing body of scholarship in this field such as Tim Hayward's *Constitutional Environmental Rights* (2005).
2 The Constitute Project (Elkins, Ginsburg, and Melton 2013) is a database of most of the world's constitutions, translated into English with drop-down "Topics" that include an impressive list of "Rights and Duties." The database allows for filtering by region. The Americas region includes: Antigua and Barbuda, Argentina, Bahamas, Barbados, Belize, Bolivia (Plurinational State of), Brazil, Canada, Chile, Colombia, Costa Rica, Cuba, Dominica, Dominican Republic, Ecuador, El Salvador, Grenada, Guatemala, Guyana, Haiti, Honduras, Jamaica, Mexico, Nicaragua, Panama, Paraguay, Peru, St. Kitts and Nevis, St. Lucia, St. Vincent and the Grenadines, Suriname, Trinidad and Tobago, United States of America, Uruguay, and Venezuela (Bolivarian Republic of).
3 For the full text of Ecuador's Constitutional chapters and Articles within the "protection of environment" category in the Constitute Project go to www.constituteproject.org/search?lang=en&country=Ecuador&key=env (last accessed October 11, 2016).
4 For the full text of Bolivia's Constitutional s and Articles within the "protection of the environment" category in the Constitute Project go to www.constituteproject.org/search?lang=en&country=Bolivia&key=env (last accessed October 11, 2016).

References

"Adoption of the Paris Agreement." 2015. FCCC/CP/2015/L.9/Rev.1. United Nations Framework Convention on Climate Change.

Akchurin, Maria. 2015. "Constructing the Rights of Nature: Constitutional Reform, Mobilization, and Environmental Protection in Ecuador." *Law & Social Inquiry* 40(4): 937–968.

Armaline, William T., Davita S. Glasberg, and Bandana Purkayastha. 2015. *The Human Rights Enterprise: Political Sociology, State Power, and Social Movements.* Cambridge: Polity Press.

Buttel, Frederick H. 2000. "Ecological Modernization as Social Theory." *Geoforum* 31: 57–65.

Buttel, Frederick H. 2003. "Environmental Sociology and the Explanation of Environmental Reform." *Organization & Environment* 16(3): 306–344.

Cole, Wade M. 2015. "Mind the Gap: State Capacity and the Implementation of Human Rights Treaties." *International Organization* 69(02): 405–441.

Deutch, Sinai. 1994. "Are Consumer Rights Human Rights." *Osgoode Hall Law Journal* 32(3): 537–578.

Elkins, Zachary, Tom Ginsburg, James Melton. 2013. "Constitute: Constitutional Text for Scholars and Drafters." Data Collection. www.constituteproject.org/ (last accessed October 11, 2016).

Elkins, Zachary, Tom Ginsburg, James Melton, Robert Shaffer, Juan F. Sequeda, and Daniel P. Miranker. 2014. "Constitute: The World's Constitutions to Read, Search, and Compare." *Web Semantics: Science, Services and Agents on the World Wide Web* 27: 10–18.

Frank, David John, Ann Hironaka, and Evan Schofer. 2000. "The Nation-State and the Natural Environment over the Twentieth Century." *American Sociological Review* 65(1): 96–116.

Frezzo, Mark. 2014. *The Sociology of Human Rights*. Cambridge: Polity Press.

Gargarella, Roberto. 2011. "Grafting Social Rights onto Hostile Constitutions." *Texas Law Review* 89: 1537–1555.

Groves, Steven. 2016. "The Paris Agreement Is a Treaty and Should Be Submitted to the Senate." *The Heritage Foundation*. www.heritage.org/research/reports/2016/03/the-paris-agreement-is-a-treaty-and-should-be-submitted-to-the-senate (last accessed October 11, 2016).

Gudynas, Eduardo. 2013. "Development Alternatives in Bolivia: The Impulse, the Resistance, and the Restoration." *NACLA Report on the Americas* 46(1): 22–26.

Hammond, John L. 2011. "Indigenous Community Justice in the Bolivian Constitution of 2009." *Human Rights Quarterly* 33(3): 649–681.

Hayward, Tim. 2005. *Constitutional Environmental Rights*. Oxford: Oxford University Press.

Longhofer, Wesley and Evan Schofer. 2010. "National and Global Origins of Environmental Association." *American Sociological Review* 75(4): 505–533.

Longhofer, Wesley, Evan Schofer, Natasha Miric, and David John Frank. 2016. "NGOs, INGOs, and Environmental Policy Reform, 1970–2010." *Social Forces* 94(4): 1743–1768.

Murdie, Amanda and Johannes Urpelainen. 2015. "Why Pick on Us? Environmental INGOs and State Shaming as a Strategic Substitute." *Political Studies* 63(2): 353–372.

Pacheco-Vega, Raul. 2015. "Transnational Environmental Activism in North America: Wielding Soft Power through Knowledge Sharing?" *Review of Policy Research* 32(1): 146–162.

Pellow, David N. and Hollie Nyseth Brehm. 2015. "From the New Ecological Paradigm to Total Liberation: The Emergence of a Social Movement Frame." *The Sociological Quarterly* 56(1): 185–212.

Perreault, Tom. 2008. "Popular Protest and Unpopular Policies: State Restructuring, Resource Conflict, and Social Justice in Bolivia," in *Urban and Industrial Environments: Environmental Justice in Latin America: Problems, Promise, and Practice*, David V. Carruthers (ed.): 239–262. Cambridge, MA: The MIT Press.

Ruiz-Mallén, Isabel, Christoph Schunko, Esteve Corbera, Matthias Rös, and Victoria Reyes-García. 2015. "Meanings, Drivers, and Motivations for Community-Based Conservation in Latin America." *Ecology & Society* 20(3): 393–406.

Schilling-Vacaflor, Almut. 2011. "Bolivia's New Constitution: Towards Participatory Democracy and Political Pluralism." *European Review of Latin American and Caribbean Studies* 90: 3–22.

Schofer, Evan and Ann Hironaka. 2005. "The Effects of World Society on Environmental Protection Outcomes." *Social Forces* 84(1): 25–47.

Turner, Terisa E. 2010. "From Cochabamba, A New Internationale and Manifesto for Mother Earth." *Capitalism Nature Socialism* 21(3): 56–74.

Vickers, William T. 2003. "The Modern Political Transformation of the Secoya," in *Millennial Ecuador: Critical Essays on Cultural Transformations and Social Dynamics*, Norman E. Whitten Jr. (ed.): 46–74. Iowa City, IA: University of Iowa Press.

Whittemore, Mary Elizabeth. 2011. "The Problem of Enforcing Nature's Rights Under Ecuador's Constitution: Why the 2008 Environmental Amendments have No Bite." *Pacific Rim Law & Policy Journal Association* 20(3): 659–691.

10

REVISE NOW!

Judith R. Blau

It is imperative to revise the US Constitution, and there are two exceedingly pressing reasons to do so. First, dramatically increasing inequalities mean that the well-being of 99 percent of Americans is at risk (if not 99.1 percent, and even 99.01 percent). Second, these 99 percent (or 99.1 percent, and even 99.01 percent) face growing risks because of rapid acceleration of climate warming and disruption. That is, unless the rights of Americans are ensured constitutionally, poor Americans—which is to say, the vast majority of Americans—will be at high risk as the temperature rises. According to a recent report of the Intergovernmental Panel on Climate Change (n.d.), poor Americans will face grave health problems, go hungry, and lose their homes to floods. In other words, there is a calamity on our doorstep if we don't both dramatically curb greenhouse gasses and dramatically reduce runaway inequalities. These two are inexorably linked, as I will explain.

Background: Inequality and Climate Change in the US

Inequality in the US:[1]

- The top 0.1 percent of all families owns 22 percent of the wealth.
- The richest 1 percent has more wealth than the bottom 90 percent.
- Put another way, the top 0.1 percent and the bottom 90 percent own virtually the same share of the nation's wealth.
- 400 Americans have more wealth than half of all Americans combined.
- 99 percent of all new income is going to the top 1 percent.
- The wealth of the Wal-Mart Walton family in 2013 equaled the wealth of the bottom 42 percent of Americans combined.

- The top 0.1% of American families now own roughly the same share of wealth as the bottom 90%.
- The poverty rate in 2014 for children under age 18 was 21.1 percent.

Oxfam International (2014) may have been the first to sound the alarm on recent dramatic increases in worldwide inequality, but its 2014 conclusions have been confirmed by an increasing number of economists who replicated Oxfam International's estimate, both for the world (Piketty 2014) and for the US (Saez 2015; Stiglitz 2015; Reich 2015).

Climate change in the US:[2]

- Since 1901, the average surface temperature across the contiguous 48 states has risen at an average rate of 0.13°F per decade.
- In 2013, US greenhouse gas emissions totaled 6,673 million metric tons (14.7 trillion pounds) of carbon dioxide equivalents. This 2013 total represents a 6 percent increase since 1990.
- Seven of the top 10 warmest years on record for the contiguous 48 states have occurred since 1998; 2012 was the warmest year on record.
- Since 1993, however, average sea levels have risen at a rate of 0.11 to 0.14 inches per year—roughly twice as fast as the long-term trend.
- From 2000 through 2014, roughly 20 to 70 percent of the US land area experienced conditions that were at least abnormally dry at any given time.
- Nationwide, unusually hot summer days (highs) have become more common over the last few decades.
- As the climate continues to warm, average annual temperatures in Alaska are projected to increase an additional 2 to 4°F by the middle of this century.

Inequality: Projections

One reason for the alarm is that the incomes of the top 0.01 percent are increasing faster than the top 0.1 percent or top 1 percent (Thompson 2014). None can project what inequality will look like in five years, ten years, or even next year. It depends on, say, whether the taxes of the people in the highest income brackets are increased, or whether or not there is a recession. Progressive economists (and socialists such as Bernie Sanders) have highlighted the egregious disparities between rich and poor Americans; this, indeed, may increase pressure on politicians to enact new tax laws.

Climate Change: Projections

Climate change or warming will only get worse. The best estimate of the sea level rise at America's shores by the year 2100 is between 14.1 and 32.5 feet. (The lack of precision is due to uncertainty as to whether the West Antarctic Ice Sheet is stable or not.) In one scenario, this affects the homes of more than 20 million people, which is more than half the current population. Put another way, the total area affected includes an estimated 1,485 municipalities, 21 of which are cities that exceed 100,000 residents (Strauss, Kulp, and Levermann 2015). Sea-level rise is just one of many components of climate change. Scientists predict extreme droughts in some places as well as torrential rains elsewhere (Union of Concerned Scientists n.d.).

Inequality and Human Rights

The concentration of wealth and high rates of poverty or impoverishment might seem abstract because they are described and measured by a single numerical value, namely by the Gini coefficient (or sometimes by the Theil index). Recently, economists (e.g., Balakrishnan, Heintz, and Elson 2015) have pointed out that inequality in America is a human rights violation, often suggesting (contrary to traditional thinking) that it has nothing to do with differences in merit or effort. Instead, the suggestion is that the gap between the poor and the rich is arbitrary, a function of racial or regional differences (urban vs. rural, or North vs. South), or a matter of luck, namely being born into a rich or poor family. For example, the poor are poor because they only can afford to eat less healthy foods, take fewer holidays, have higher rates of chronic illness, and are less likely to have medical insurance.

Who Causes Climate Change?

Globally, the richer countries of the West—the US and European countries— both historically and contemporaneously—are most responsible for producing emissions that warm the climate (World Bank n.d.). Likewise, rich Americans are responsible for producing more emissions than poor Americans because they fly more (Cohn 2014), are less likely to take public transportation (Maciag 2014), and use more appliances that require electricity (Edin and Shaefer 2015). There are nearly 1.5 million American households with practically no cash income.

Inequalities and Climate Change

There will be nothing random or egalitarian or even democratic about this, which is to say that not every one of the 20 or so million Americans will be equally affected. In fact—as I will conjecture—something like 99.99 percent might lose their homes in the floods while 0.01 percent will be spared that fate.

Let us say (and it is plausible; see ArcGIS 2015) that the Atlantic Ocean overflows the banks of the East River and laps up onto the FDR Drive. It is also plausible— even likely—that if you are rich enough to own a penthouse on Manhattan's East Side that you will simply move—the chances are pretty good that you also own a penthouse in London or maybe even a chateau in Tuscany. So you move. But as the Atlantic rises further, it pushes against the Harlem River which overflows its banks. Water crashes down on 155th Street, flooding the Bronx, and then onto Harlem. It gets worse. There are food shortages, and the 99.01 percent in the Bronx and Harlem go hungry (see Gregory, Ingram, and Brklacich 2005). There are no guarantees whatsoever that the top 1 percent or the top 0.1 percent or the top 0.01 percent will not hoard America's food supply. In fact they will. Why wouldn't they?

Conclusions: Other Countries' Constitutions and the US Constitution

To sum up some of the points from Chapter 6:

- There is nothing in the US Constitution that ensures that people will not go hungry: 14 percent of Americans are already food insecure.
- There is nothing in the US Constitution that protects children, the disabled, the elderly, and women.
- There is nothing in the US Constitution that ensures or protects positive rights—right to education, right to a home, right to medical care, right to a decent wage, and so forth.

In other words, the US is an outlier, failing to protect basic rights that protect everyone, and particularly those who are vulnerable or at risk. Moreover, US tax laws benefit the rich and corporations, which indirectly benefits the rich. Yet some countries go further than spelling out positive rights. Box 10.1 contains a list of thirteen countries (out of 194) with constitutions that spell out that inequality is unacceptable and/or must be reduced. Although the dates when countries added these provisions to their constitutions are not known, it is plausible that these were added in response to recent and growing concerns about global economic inequality.

Box 10.2 contains a list of eight countries (out of 194) with constitutions that spell out that efforts should be undertaken to deal with the climate or climate change. There is no question that such provisions and language are new, responding to the recent and growing concern about the warming of the planet. To be sure, general abstract language in constitutions needs to be accompanied by policies and widespread practices that reduce CO_2 and methane emissions, including investments in solar energy and wind turbines, investment in public transportation, fuel-efficient cars, policies that encourage local gardens, policies that encourage bicycle riding, and technologies for composting toilets and reduction of beef consumption.

In sum, constitutions matter. They embody best practices, universal standards, protections for the most vulnerable, and highlight standards and expectations for the future. They teach tolerance. Most of all, any state constitution embraces everyone and unites them in a shared vision that everyone is different and equal.

BOX 10.1 CONSTITUTIONS THAT REFER TO INEQUALITY

Bangladesh

The State shall adopt effective measures to remove social and economic *inequality* between man and man and to ensure the equitable distribution of wealth among citizens, and of opportunities in order to attain a uniform level of economic development throughout the Republic.

Bolivia

To promote policies of equitable distribution of wealth and of the economic resources of the country, for the purpose of preventing *inequality*, social and economic exclusion, and to eradicate poverty in its multiple dimensions.

Chad

However, the customs contrary to the public order or those that promote *inequality* between citizens are prohibited.

Croatia

The extent of such restrictions shall be adequate to the nature of the danger, and may not result in the *inequality* of persons in respect of race, color, gender, language, religion, national or social origin.

Ecuador

The State shall adopt affirmative action measures that promote real equality for the benefit of the rights-bearers who are in a situation of *inequality*.

To prevent the concentration or hoarding of production inputs and resources, promote their distribution, and eliminate privileges or *inequality* in access to these inputs.

Ethiopia

The historical legacy of *inequality* and discrimination suffered by women in Ethiopia is taken into account; women, in order to remedy this legacy, are entitled to affirmative measures. The purpose of such measures shall be to provide special attention to women so as to enable them compete and participate on the basis of equality with men in political, social and economic life as well as in public and private institutions.

Madagascar

...the elimination of all forms of injustice, of corruption, of *inequality* and of discrimination;

Nepal

It shall be the economic objective of the State to make the national economy self-reliant, independent, and developing it towards socialism oriented economy with equitable distribution of resources and means, by ending all forms of economic exploitation and *inequality*, with maximum utilization of available resources and means through the participation of cooperatives, and public and private sector for sustainable development, and to build an exploitation-free society by fair distribution of the achievements made so far.

Niger

The State makes of the creation of wealth, of growth and of the fight against *inequality* a major axis of its interventions.

Serbia

Any inciting of racial, ethnic, religious or other *inequality* or hatred shall be prohibited and punishable.

Slovenia

Human rights and fundamental freedoms may be suspended or restricted only for the duration of the war or state of emergency, but only to the extent required by such circumstances and inasmuch as the measures adopted do not create *inequality* based solely on race, national origin, sex, language, religion, political or other conviction, material standing, birth, education, social status or any other personal circumstance.

Somalia

In assigning a drafting project mentioned in Clause (5), the Oversight Committee shall prioritize the project as follows...Accord high priority to a project that aims at changing the behaviors that constitute a social problem concerning: *Inequality* in quality of life of different segments of the Somali population, including income *inequality, inequality* in health care delivery, and *inequality* in education;

Thailand

With a view to setting up of a democratic regime of government with the King as the Head of State which is suitable for Thai context, establishing the trustworthy and fair election system, establishing the efficient mechanism for prevention and suppression of corruption, eliminating economic and social *inequality* for sustainable development, enabling State mechanism to provide public services thoroughly, efficiently and effectively, and strengthening law enforcement rigorously and fairly.

Source: Constitute: www.constituteproject.org/?lang=en
Note: The word "equality" is used in 167 constitutions, but these are not included here.

BOX 10.2 CONSTITUTIONS THAT REFER TO CLIMATE OR CLIMATE CHANGE

Bolivia

To protect agricultural and agro-industrial production from natural disasters, inclement *climate*, and geological catastrophes. The law shall provide for the creation of agricultural insurance.

Dominican Republic

The formulation and execution, through law, of a plan of territorial ordering that ensures the efficient and sustainable use of the natural resources of the Nation, in accordance with the necessity of adaptation to *climate* change, is a priority of the State,

Ecuador

The State shall adopt adequate and cross-cutting measures for the mitigation of *climate* change, by limiting greenhouse gas emissions, deforestation, and air pollution; it shall take measures for the conservation of the forests and vegetation; and it shall protect the population at risk.

Nepal

Increasing investment in the agricultural sector by making necessary provisions for sustainable productivity, supply, storage and security, while making it easily available with effective distribution of food grains by encouraging food productivity that suits the soil and *climate* conditions of the country in accordance with the norms of food sovereignty.

Sri Lanka

National policy on land use will be based on technical aspects (not on political or communal aspects), and the Commission will lay down general norms in regard to the use of land, having regard to soil, *climate*, rainfall, soil erosion, forest cover, environmental factors, economic viability, &c.

Tunisia

The state guarantees the right to a healthy and balanced environment and the right to participate in the protection of the *climate*.

Venezuela

It is a fundamental duty of the State, with the active participation of society, to ensure that the populace develops in a pollution-free environment in which air, water, soil, coasts, *climate*, the ozone layer and living species receive special protection, in accordance with law.

Vietnam

The State has a policy to protect the environment; manage, and effectively and stably use natural resources; protect the nature and biodiversity; take initiative in prevention and resistance against natural calamities and response to *climate* change.

Source: Constitute: www.constituteproject.org/?lang=en
Note: The word "environment" is mentioned in 146 constitutions and "mother earth" in three constitutions, but these are not included here.

Notes

1 Kertscher, Tom. 2015 (Fact-checked data).
2 If anything, these are conservative estimates; see Environmental Protection Agency n.d.

References

ArcGIS. 2015. Sea Level Planning Tool—New York City. www.arcgis.com/home/item. html?id=bc90ddc4984a45538c1de5b4ddf91381 (last accessed October 9, 2016).
Balakrishnan, Radhika, James Heintz, and Diane Elson. 2015. "What Does Inequality Have to Do with Human Rights?" Political Economy Research Institute. www.peri.umass. edu/fileadmin/pdf/working_papers/working_papers_351-400/WP392.pdf (last accessed October 9, 2016).
Cohn, Emily. 2014. "Chris Rock: If Poor People Knew How Rich Rich People Are, There Would Be Riots." *Huffington Post Business*. www.huffingtonpost.com/2014/12/ 01/chris-rock-inequality-rich-people_n_6248392.html.(last accessed October 9, 2016).
Comparative Constitutions Project. n.d. www.constituteproject.org/ (last accessed October 9, 2016).
Edin, Kathryn J. and H. Luke Shaefer. 2015. *$2.00 a Day: Living on Almost Nothing in America*. New York: Houghton Mifflin.
Environmental Protection Agency. n.d. "Climate Change Indicators in the United States." www3.epa.gov/climatechange/science/indicators/weather-climate/temperature.html (last accessed October 9, 2016).

Gregory, P. J, J. S. I. Ingram, and M. Brklacich. 2005. "Climate Change and Food Security." *Philosophical Transactions of the Royal Society: Biological Sciences* 360(1463): 2139–2148.

Intergovernmental Panel on Climate Change. n.d. *Working Group II. Impacts, Adaptations and Vulnerabilities.* http://The Worl'dwww.ipcc.ch/ipccreports/tar/wg2/index.php?idp=674 (last accessed October 9, 2016).

Kertscher, Tom. 2015. "Bernie Sanders, in Madison, claims top 0.1% of Americans have almost as much wealth as bottom 90%." *PolitiFact.* www.politifact.com/wisconsin/statements/2015/jul/29/bernie-s/bernie-sanders-madison-claims-top-01-americans-hav/ (last accessed October 9, 2016).

Kulikowski, Laurie. 2015. "The 11 Most Obscenely Expensive Homes in the World and Their Filthy Rich Owners." *The Street.* www.thestreet.com/story/12942112/3/the-11-most-expensive-homes-in-the-world-and-their-rich-owners.html (last accessed October 9, 2016).

Maciag, Mike. 2014. "Public Transportation's Demographic Divide." *Governing.* www.governing.com/topics/transportation-infrastructure/gov-public-transportation-riders-demographic-divide-for-cities.html (last accessed October 9, 2016).

National Alliance to End Homelessness. n.d. "Snapshot of Homelessness." www.endhomelessness.org/pages/snapshot_of_homelessness (last accessed October 9, 2016).

Oxfam International. 2014. "Even It Up: Time to End Extreme Inequality." www.oxfam.org/sites/www.oxfam.org/files/file_attachments/cr-even-it-up-extreme-inequality-291014-en.pdf (last accessed October 9, 2016).

Piketty, Thomas. 2014. *Capital in the Twenty-First Century.* Translated by Arthur Goldhammer. Cambridge: Belknap Press.

Reich, Robert B. 2015. *Saving Capitalism for the Many, Not for the Few.* New York: Alfred A. Knopf.

Saez, Emmanuel. 2015. "Striking it Richer: The Evolution of Top Incomes in the United States." http://eml.berkeley.edu/~saez/ (last accessed October 9, 2016).

Stiglitz, Joseph E. 2015. *The Great Divide: Unequal Societies and What We Can Do About Them.* New York: W. W. Norton.

Strauss, Benjamin H., Scott Kulp, and Anders Levermann. 2015. "Carbon Choices Determine US Cities Committed to Futures Below Sea Level." *Proceedings of the National Academy of the United States of America.* www.pnas.org/content/112/44/13508.full (last accessed October 9, 2016).

Thompson, Derek. 2014 "The Rise and Rise and Rise of the .01 Percent in America." *The Atlantic.* www.theatlantic.com/business/archive/2014/02/the-rise-and-rise-and-rise-of-the-001-percent-in-america/283793/ (last accessed October 9, 2016).

Union of Concerned Scientists. n.d. "Global Warming Impacts." www.ucsusa.org/our-work/global-warming/science-and-impacts/global-warming-impacts#.VyOWS-Q8Iik (last accessed October 9, 2016).

World Bank. n.d. "CO_2 Emissions: Metric Tons Per Capita." http://data.worldbank.org/indicator/EN.ATM.CO2E.PC (last accessed October 9, 2016).

Zeveloff, Julie and Gus Lubin. 2012. "The 25 Biggest Landowners in America." *Business Insider.* www.businessinsider.com/the-25-biggest-landowners-in-america-2012-10 (last accessed October 9, 2016).

PART III
Towards Action

11
WHY A SOCIOLOGY OF HUMAN RIGHTS?

Mark Frezzo

How can we analyze and advocate human rights at the same time? How can we balance our obligation to uphold scholarly standards with our desire to advance the cause of human rights in the real world? With a view to situating this volume in the context of ongoing debates on social scientific rigor and ethical commitments, this chapter examines the growing interest in human rights in the university system in the United States, the institutionalization of the sociology of human rights as a field of research, teaching, and service, and the implications of the nascent field for interpreting major documents in the human rights canon.

In the process, this argues for the need to revise the Constitution of the United States in reference to the cutting-edge human rights norms that find expression not only in the classics of the human rights canon (which establish a framework for augmenting first-generation civil and political rights and second-generation economic and social rights), but also in more recent documents: the 1972 Declaration of the United Nations Conference on the Human Environment (Stockholm Declaration), the 1979 United Nations Convention on the Elimination of All Forms of Discrimination Against Women (CEDAW), the 1992 Rio Declaration on Environment and Development, and the 2007 Declaration on the Rights of Indigenous Peoples (DRIP).

Taken together, these documents deepen second-generation economic and social rights for peoples in the Global South, women across the world, and indigenous peoples everywhere. At the same time, they give greater definition to third-generation cultural and environmental rights—collective rights belonging to communities, groups, and peoples in the United States, as well as in the Global South. Completely absent from the constitution and from other Enlightenment-era documents, rights to cultural and environmental preservation became prominent courtesy of struggles against colonialism, Western financial and cultural domination, and the pervasive environmental destruction associated with consumerism. Owing to a number of interrelated factors—including a constitution that emphasizes first-generation civil and political rights for individuals and a political culture that celebrates possessive individualism—it can be challenging for inhabitants of the United States to think and talk about collective rights. For this reason, sociologists often call attention to community-based organizations, social movement organizations (SMOs), and non-governmental organizations (NGOs) that support third-generation cultural and environmental rights. This leads them to incorporate ideas that reflect the experiences and struggles of non-Western societies.

As this chapter suggests, sociologists have a particular way of analyzing human rights documents. More precisely, sociologists examine not only the *social contexts* in which such documents are debated, drafted, and enacted, but also the *social impacts* of such documents (in the form of new institutions and altered power relations) (Frezzo 2015). The practice of reading human rights texts *sociologically*—in addition to *legally*—reveals what is "at stake" in debates on and struggles over human rights in the age of globalization. In a nutshell, sociologists look beyond legal verbiage to ascertain how human rights documents influence the framing practices of SMOs and NGOs and the laws, social programs, and institutions created by states.

Sociology and Constitutional Reform

What would happen if we were to examine the constitution through the lens of the sociology of human rights? When placed in the trajectory of Enlightenment and post-Enlightenment thought, the US Constitution appears as both a *forerunner* and a *laggard* in its stance on human rights. The constitution is a forerunner insofar as it transfers sovereignty from the monarchy to the people and establishes civil and political rights (initially for only a small percentage of the population). The constitution is a laggard—even though various amendments have addressed some of the egregious exclusions—because it has not been revised to meet the demands of the contemporary world. Accordingly, this assumes the acknowledgement of a paradox: even though the US Constitution was originally conceptualized as a living, breathing, evolving document, citizens of the United States tend not to embrace the idea that it should be revised to meet the demands of the current period. We could point to the widespread veneration of the "Founding Fathers" and the concomitant fetishization of the constitution—both of which figure prominently in the political culture of the United States—as factors that inhibit discussion of comprehensive constitutional reform. We could also point to the widespread suspicion of internationalist impulses—an unfortunate legacy of the Cold War. Notwithstanding the decisive role of the United States in establishing the United Nations system, there has been little discussion of the merits and deficiencies of the Universal Declaration of Human Rights (UDHR).

However, as many of the authors included in this volume demonstrate, the situation is beginning to change. Increasingly, community-based activists, SMOs, and their NGO allies are framing their demands in reference to human rights documents—beginning with the UDHR. In so doing, they often draw—whether implicitly or explicitly—on postcolonial, feminist, and environmentalist critiques of the omissions and abuses of Enlightenment thought, as well as the deliberate misapplications and unintended consequences of scientific research and technological advancement. This opens the possibility of moving beyond the Enlightenment belief in the inevitability of 'progress' toward a more grounded understanding of how greater economic and social equality, acceptance of different gender and sexual identities, cultural pluralism, and environmental sustainability can be achieved.

Though far from automatic or guaranteed, advances can be accumulated as the outgrowths of unpredictable social struggles. Phrased differently, SMOs and their NGO allies can build on previous legislative and judicial achievements. That these struggles are frequently framed in terms of human rights is clear from the recent history of the United States, with the victory of the LGBT movement in achieving marriage equality figuring prominently in current discussions. In arguing that state prohibitions of same-sex marriage violated the Due Process and Equal Protection clauses of the 14th Amendment, the Supreme Court's decision, on June 26, 2015, effectively settled the issue of marriage. As the culmination of nearly two decades of struggle since the passage of the 1996 Defense of Marriage Act, the decision testified not only to the power of the Supreme Court to protect the interests of minority groups, but also to the importance of codifying human rights at the level of the constitution (as an impetus to policymaking).

Let us examine, albeit briefly, the limitations of the Supreme Court's decision. Needless to say, this required reference to the 14th Amendment, adopted in 1868 as a means of elaborating citizenship rights. However, the Supreme Court's decision did not require a new constitutional amendment to establish same-sex marriage as a right. Nor did it address the longstanding problem of discrimination against the LGBT community in employment and housing. Finally, the Supreme Court's decision did not protect the LGBT community from "religious freedom acts" passed by a number of states. In the end, court decisions—though essential to advancing and protecting the rights of the LGBT community—cannot take the place of new legislation and new institutions.

To recapitulate, the overall argument is as follows: policymaking—whether undertaken by Congress, state legislatures, or by city councils—proves indispensable for social change. For this reason, there is a long history of militating for legislation among human rights-oriented SMOs. At the same time, new legislation—no matter how favorable to historically underrepresented, exploited, or marginalized segments of the population—is not necessarily permanent. For this reason, opponents of workers' rights, women's rights, civil and political rights for persons of color, and LGBT rights continually seek to repeal such legislation and/or to challenge it in the court system.

As the Supreme Court's 2013 gutting of the 1965 Voting Rights Act testifies, legislative gains can be precarious. Legislation is subject not only to modification by the Supreme Court, but it can also be modified or even repealed with changing electoral tides. In contrast, constitutional amendments can solidify the achievements of SMOs and their NGO allies by stimulating or even compelling legislation on the part of elected officials. In the period in which the constitution was drafted, debates centered exclusively on civil and political rights. Such were the limitations of the European Enlightenment. In the contemporary period, economic/social rights and cultural/environmental rights have been placed on the agenda by an array of SMOs and NGOs not only in the United States and elsewhere in the Global North, but also in the Global South. Technological changes associated with globalization have brought these popular forces into closer contact with one another, stimulating productive dialogues across political and cultural divides.

In this light, the normative argument that runs throughout the book is as follows: we need to revise the constitution to make it more consistent, not only with the revised constitutions of other countries (e.g., the 1996 Constitution of South Africa, which expressly prohibits discrimination on the basis of race, ethnicity, social status, gender, sexual orientation, disability, age, and other personal characteristics), but also with recent human rights treaties and declarations (South African Government n.d.). How would this process work? In revising the constitution, we would solidify past legislative gains—including those that came with the New Deal (1933–1938), the 1964 Civil Rights Act, the 1965 Voting Rights Act, the 1965 Social Security Amendments, the 1990 Americans with Disabilities Act, and the 2010 Patient Protection and Affordable Care Act. At the same time, revising the constitution would promote the creation of new packages of legislation to bring to fruition such economic/social rights as the right to a living wage or the right to a free education from kindergarten through college and such cultural/environmental rights as the right to inhabit ancestral lands, the right to receive an education in an indigenous or minority language, the right to use clean waterways for subsistence, transport, and recreation, and the right/responsibility to protect the earth as an end-in-itself.

In other words, the practical argument that runs through this volume is as follows: amidst a more congenial political culture and a more fertile climate for human rights thinking, a popular coalition would convince policymakers to place an array of new constitutional amendments (like those presented in this book) on the docket. Then, in accordance with Article V of the US Constitution, the House of Representatives and the Senate would vote in favor of the amendments by at least a two-thirds majority. Finally, in keeping with Article V of the US Constitution, at least three-fourths of the states would vote in favor of the amendments. While this would not magically change social conditions overnight, it would provide grassroots movements with the tools with which to pressure progressive lawmakers into funding new programs and creating new institutions.

Doubtless, contentious politics in the name of adding economic/social and cultural/environmental rights to the constitution would not replace electoral politics. But it would change electoral politics for the better. More to the point, it would precipitate a process of improving conditions for poor and working-class persons, women, minority communities, immigrants, the LGBT community, persons living with disabilities, and many others.

As this book argues, academics have a significant role to play in creating an auspicious climate for constitutional reform. Accordingly, it makes sense to reflect on the potential contributions of academics in general, and of sociologists in particular. Since the advent of the United Nations system in 1945, academics in numerous disciplines have played prominent roles in the human rights community. In the same period, many sociologists have devoted their research to public policy outcomes in welfare and developmental states across the world. When unchecked by social policy, economic inequality and poverty can rip the fabric of a society. For this reason, sociologists have begun to treat economic inequality and poverty not only as social problems, but also as *human rights violations*. This shift in mindset is auspicious for sociologists who wish to connect with grassroots movements on one side and policymakers on the other. Like their counterparts in the other social sciences, sociologists have the capacity to serve as a bridge between the worlds of activism and policymaking. This does not involve telling either activists or policymakers how to do their jobs; instead, it involves demonstrating how sociological research can illuminate the power of human rights norms.

Human Rights and the Academy in the United States

When we hear the phrase "human rights community," we ordinarily think of lawyers defending the rights of aggrieved persons, Amnesty International campaigning on behalf of prisoners of conscience, Human Rights Watch reporting on human rights abuses in conflict zones, Oxfam International pushing for the alleviation of poverty in the Global South, and the UN General Assembly passing resolutions to advance new interpretations of the human rights canon. In addition, we might imagine the International Criminal Court investigating political officials for crimes against humanity and military officers for war crimes in the aftermath of interstate wars, civil conflicts, or ethnic cleansing. Digging deeper, we might think of SMOs, like the Zapatistas in Mexico, the World Social Forum in Brazil, Occupy Wall Street in the United States, and anti-austerity groups in Greece, opposing neoliberal economic policies in the name of human rights. Or we might think of Black Lives Matter activists calling attention to police brutality against African Americans. Regardless, the roles of academics—in the humanities, the social sciences, social work, education, law, medicine, the natural sciences, and engineering—might not immediately come to mind. Nevertheless, academics—in their research, teaching, and service—are important members of the human rights community. More precisely, they are active participants in the "epistemic community" insofar as they have a "shared belief or faith in the verity and applicability of specific forms of knowledge or specific truths" (Haas 1992: 3, 4ff.). The form of knowledge in question is that of human rights.

Though they operate within distinct disciplinary cultures and thus employ different theories and methods in their work, these academics share a commitment to the human rights canon—UN treaties and declarations that serve as reference points for SMOs, NGOs, and policymakers across the globe. Some of these scholars are satisfied with the existing human rights canon; others wish to add to it. This is not surprising, since most documents in the human rights canon remain aspirational, yet couched in the language of a different era. In any case, scholars undertake exegesis of such canonical texts as the 1948 UDHR, the 1966 International Covenant on Civil and Political Rights (ICCPR), and the 1966 International Covenant on Economic, Social, and Cultural Rights (ICESCR)— the three pillars of what was meant to serve as the "International Bill of Rights." But textual exegesis is only the first step. The next step is to analyze how the actualization of a given set of rights—taking the three major measures in the Human Development Index (namely, the right to a living wage, the right to the highest level of healthcare available, and the right to the highest level of education available) as examples—would improve the wellbeing of the population and alter power relations within the country. Academic research proves indispensable for such assessments.

How do academics contribute to this epistemic community built around human rights? Academics produce research that influences NGO staff, journalists, foreign relations and public policy think tanks, government policymakers, jurists, and UN officials. Such research covers everything from poverty and economic inequality to interstate relations, social exclusion, cultural and religious differences, and environmental degradation. Moreover, academics teach courses on an array of human rights *abuses* (including ethnic cleansing and forced migration, false imprisonment and torture, unequal access to education and jobs, race and gender discrimination, and illegal dumping of toxins) and human rights *remedies* (including international treaties and institutions, constitutional reform, public policy initiatives, alternative development programs, urban renewal, and ecological preservation). In keeping with a trend in the university system, many of these courses emphasize civic engagement and global citizenship, and hence require students to undertake service-learning projects that apply human rights acumen to the real-world puzzles and dilemmas. Finally, in the spirit of service, academics convene at conferences to build human rights-oriented research agendas into their home disciplines, to forge links across disciplines and universities, to defend the rights of persecuted intellectuals, and to undertake community outreach.

What prompted academics based in the United States to implement programs in human rights? Notwithstanding the establishment of the United Nations Educational, Scientific, and Cultural Organization (UNESCO) in 1945 and the ratification of the UDHR, the ICCPR, and the ICESCR in the ensuing two decades, it took some time for scholars based in the United States to organize research clusters around human rights. With the rise of Area Studies (with foci on the Cold War antagonists of the United States, the Soviet Union and China), considerable intellectual energy and acumen has been devoted to the perceived need to promote the objectives 'development' and 'modernization' in the Third World. Over time, the emergence of dissenting voices within the development consensus opened a space for considering the role of geopolitical, cultural, and environmental factors in influencing the pathways of newly independent countries. Within the university system, Peace Studies, Labor Studies, Women's Studies, African American Studies, Latino/a Studies, LGBT Studies, and Environmental Studies paved the way for interdisciplinary programs in human rights. In effect, these fields can be interpreted as institutional expressions of the peace and anti-nuclear movement, the working-class movement, the women's movement, the civil rights movement, the LGBT movement, and the green movement respectively. To this day, these interdisciplinary fields differ from their disciplinary counterparts in permitting—and often encouraging—a commitment to *social engagement* (however conceived). Depending on the focus of the program, this might mean inviting organization leaders to speak on campus, placing students in internships with labor unions or NGOs, or requiring students to undertake service-learning projects with community-based organizations. As university leaders across the United States have recognized, service-learning programs help students not only to empathize with underrepresented groups, but also to embrace differences in a multicultural society.

The history of such interdisciplinary domains merits further consideration. With the rapid expansion of the university system after 1945, and especially with the upheavals of the late 1960s and early 1970s, many students and professors not only became activists, but also longed to make their intellectual work more relevant to a rapidly changing world. For its part, social movement research—an interdisciplinary field that cuts across sociology, political science, and anthropology—reflects the realization that mass mobilizations merit being studied not as 'irrational crowds' engaged in 'riotous behavior,' but rather as organized, systematic, and sustained attempts to change society (in reference to a normative schema). The normative schema may fall to the left, the center, or the right of the political spectrum. The schema may be secular or religious in orientation. It goes without saying that some SMOs are committed to the non-violent pursuit of human rights, while others—including the nationalist and xenophobic SMOs in the United States and the European Union that have emerged in response to the challenges of globalization—are fundamentally opposed to human rights. Such SMOs are equally worthy of study. Nevertheless, the important breakthrough for the field consists in the recognition that SMOs—understood as manifestations of human agency—influence electoral politics and contribute, whether indirectly or directly, to policy outcomes, as well as to cultural shifts. It is not surprising that many social movement researchers would convey to their students an enthusiasm for engaging in contentious politics—an avenue of agency that can be just as influential as electoral politics.

This dovetails with the mission of service-learning initiatives, regardless of disciplinary focus: to inspire students to apply the insights of classroom knowledge to address social problems. For example, in the author's (Frezzo) upper-division undergraduate course on the Sociology of Human Rights, students learn to analyze such social problems as poverty, economic inequality, structural racism, cultural exclusion, and environmental degradation as multifaceted *human rights problems*. This helps them to investigate multifaceted *human rights remedies*: packages of civil/political, economic/social, and cultural/environmental rights, called "rights bundles," that acknowledge the interconnectedness of different "spheres" of human life. While classroom learning is crucial, students report arriving at a higher level of understanding when they actualize their insights through community outreach—whether joining an Amnesty International campaign or proposing a constitutional amendment to formalize free university education as a right for all inhabitants of the United States. Owing to problems with the political culture—including anti-intellectualism, lack of civility, the power of corporate mass media to shape public opinion, the primacy of "dark money" in electoral campaigns, and partisan gridlock among elected officials—students often find it challenging to bracket two-party politics. In the service-learning component of the course, students learn to think beyond "Democrats versus Republicans" and "liberals versus conservatives" in order to excavate underlying human rights issues. In the process, students acquire experience in analyzing issues from a social scientific perspective, debating policy matters in a civil manner, and serving as human rights educators in the local community. Owing to initiatives at numerous universities, service-learning courses are becoming more popular—especially in interdisciplinary programs.

In sum, what these interdisciplinary programs share is a belief in the importance of marshaling scholarly expertise—whether in the humanities, the social sciences, the natural sciences, or an applied field—not only for the advancement of particular constituencies, but also for the improvement of the human condition. As we shall see, this mission proves consistent with Article 15 of the ICESCR, which stipulates that all human beings have the right to enjoy the benefits of scientific research and technological advances (while implying the universal right to be protected from the excesses of science and technology). Naturally, social movement researchers and other interdisciplinary scholars (e.g., scholars in African American Studies, Latino/a Studies, Peace Studies, and Women's Studies) routinely differ on the question of how to advance human welfare. Some are more inclined than others to align with SMOs and NGOs that work in their areas of expertise. Some are more inclined than others to offer policy prescriptions.

Reasonable persons may disagree on the nature and degree of engagement (Blau and Iyall Smith 2006; Blau and Moncada 2009). If addressed in a civil manner, such disagreements can be conducive to growth: scholars leaning toward the analysis pole often need to be reminded of the normative impulses latent in all research, while those leaning toward the advocacy pole often need to be reminded of the power of critical detachment. Within the aforementioned fields, analysis and advocacy converge in their shared emphasis on increasing popular partici-pation in debates on social policy. What is important is that the movement and praxis-oriented fields stress the role of popular participation in debates on values and social policy. Such debates lead inevitably to the methodical consideration of the nature, scope, and applicability of human rights norms, declarations, treaties, and institutions to the social context of the United States. Let us turn, then, to the role of sociology in promoting rigorous, yet engaged, research and teaching on human rights.

Sociology and Human Rights

Although sociologists have long been interested in human rights, it is only in the last decade that the American Sociological Association (ASA)—the profes-sional organization representing sociologists who work in the United States—has adopted public positions on human rights, and that the ASA has created a Section on Human Rights. These developments warrant consideration, since they relate directly to one of the main objectives of this volume—namely, to demonstrate the utility of sociological theories and methods for the analysis of debates on and struggles over the constitution and its complex relationship both with the Enlightenment tradition and with the human rights canon established after 1945. In recognition of the long-standing interest of sociologists in human rights, the ASA issued the 2005 "Statement on Human Rights on the Occasion of the ASA's Centenary." Taking the anniversary as "an opportunity to reiter-ate its strongest support for the basic civil and political freedoms of peoples," the ASA "anchored" its statement in the UDHR.[1] Representing an important breakthrough for sociologists focusing on human rights, the 2005 Statement emphasized the protection of sociologists' rights to pursue their research with-out encumbrance or persecution by governments. Notwithstanding its circum-scribed purview, the 2005 Statement closed by "[urging] all governments…to uphold the spirit and the substance" of all "international agreements that affirm the importance of full equality of all peoples and cultures; social and personal security; health care and education; freedom to join trade unions and otherwise assemble; a just wage and an adequate standard of living; and the freedom to participate in and benefit from scientific advancement" (ibid.). In addition to pointing to the need for a universal yardstick by which to measure the achieve-ments and failures of all governments, the closing of the 2005 Statement offered a trenchant challenge to the United States government in particular. To date, legislative achievements in these areas have not been bolstered by constitutional amendments.

In an effort to build on the precedent of the 2005 Statement, the scholarly NGO Sociologists Without Borders (SSF) drafted a document that would eventually become the 2009 "Statement Affirming and Expanding the Commitment of the American Sociological Association to Human Rights." In the 2009 Statement, the ASA "recognizes the full equality and dignity of all peoples and supports the rights of gay, lesbian, bisexual and transgendered persons, people with disabilities, and vulnerable children and adults."[2]

In addition, the ASA "recognizes the rights of all peoples to social and personal security; to gender equality; to freedom from discrimination; to join trade unions and otherwise assemble; to an adequate standard of living, including a decent job and a just wage, health care, housing, food and water, education; and to a sustainable environment" (ibid.). Drawing on the spirit of public sociology in the ASA, the 2009 Statement explicitly affirms the need for policy proposals to actualize the economic/social and cultural/environmental rights found not only in contemporary human rights declarations, but also in a number of revised constitutions. Confined to the professional obligations of sociologists—understood as defenders of society against market fundamentalism and fiscal austerity, institutionalized forms of discrimination, cultural exclusion, and environmental degradation—the 2009 Statement does not call for the revision of the constitution. But it encourages sociology professors and students to examine the United States through the lens of cutting-edge human rights norms.

While the 2005 and 2009 statements reflect the growing tendency among ASA members to connect the sociological enterprise to debates on and struggles for human rights, an intervening development expresses the emergence of the sociology of human rights as a distinct field of research, teaching, and service. Benefiting immensely from the ideas, energy, and enthusiasm of members and fellow travelers of SSF, the ASA human rights section was founded in 2008 "to promote and support critical, interdisciplinary, and international engagement with human rights scholarship, teaching and practice," while "foster[ing] human rights approaches to the sociological enterprise."[3] In addition to organizing regular paper sessions, special panels, and mini-conferences at the annual meetings of the ASA, the section on human rights serves as a forum for the discussion of ideas for research, teaching, and service. Fittingly, a number of authors in this volume have contributed to the establishment and expansion of the section on human rights. Moreover, various proposals to revise the US Constitution have figured prominently in the section discussions.

Conclusion

This chapter has argued that sociology offers a particular set of tools to activists and policymakers wishing to revise the US Constitution to meet the demands of the contemporary period. Chief among these tools are: a lens through which to analyze the social underpinnings and implications of human rights treaties and declarations, along with a gauge to measure the efficacy of different forms of engagement. In illuminating the norms, declarations, treaties, and institutions that comprise the human rights corpus, sociologists can foster a productive dialogue between activists and policymakers. Such a dialogue could assist the United States not only in confronting domestic problems, but also in altering its conduct as a global actor.

Notes

1 See www.asanet.org/news-events/asa-news/american-sociological-associations-statement-human-rights-occasion-asas-centenary (last accessed October 10, 2016).
2 See www.asanet.org/about/Council_Statements/Council%20Statement%20on%20Human%20Rights%20(August%202009).pdf (last accessed October 10, 2016).
3 See www.asanet.org/asa-communities/sections/human-rights (last accessed October 11, 2016).

References

American Sociological Association. 2005. "American Sociological Association's Statement on Human Rights on the Occasion of ASA's Centenary." www.asanet.org/news-events/asa-news/american-sociological-associations-statement-human-rights-occasion-asas-centenary (last accessed October 10, 2016).
American Sociological Association. 2009. "Statement Affirming and Expanding the Commitment of the American Sociological Association to Human Rights." www.asanet.org/sites/default/files/savvy/about/Council_Statements/Council%20Statement%20on%20Human%20Rights%20(August%202009).pdf (last accessed October 10, 2016).
American Sociological Association. n.d. "Section on Human Rights." www.asanet.org/asa-communities/sections/human-rights (last accessed October 10, 2016).
Blau, Judith and Alberto Moncada. 2009. *Human Rights: A Primer*. Boulder, CO: Paradigm Publishers.
Blau, Judith and Keri Iyall Smith (eds). 2006. *The Public Sociologies Reader*. Lanham, MD: Rowman and Littlefield.
Frezzo, Mark. 2015. *The Sociology of Human Rights*. Cambridge, UK: Polity.
Haas, Peter M. 1992. "Introduction: Epistemic Communities and International Policy Coordination." *International Organization* 46(1): 1–35.
South African Government. n.d. "The Constitution of the Republic of South Africa." www.gov.za/documents/constitution/constitution-Republic-South-Africa-1996-1 (last accessed October 10, 2016).

12

THE CONSTITUTION PROJECT

Implementing a Group Projects Structure

Davita Silfen Glasberg

Most students (and much of the population and popular media for that matter) in the United States tend to think of human rights issues as something that is of a concern elsewhere in the world, but not the US. They commonly argue that the US is the "gold standard" of human rights; after all, it was Eleanor Roosevelt, representing the US, who was at the vanguard of developing the Universal Declaration of Human Rights (UDHR). The US Constitution enumerates and protects our rights. Therefore, it is exceptional as the standard bearer of human rights for the rest of the world. Right?

Whether or not the US is the "gold standard" of human rights, and whether or not the constitution addresses human rights are empirical questions, we tell our students. So we at the University of Connecticut developed a sociology course, 'Human Rights in the United States,' to examine the question. After a few semesters, it became abundantly clear that the answer was no, the US is NOT the gold standard of human rights; that there are numerous violations of those articulated in the UDHR; and that the US has failed to ratify just about all of the international covenants and agreements concerning human rights, citing reservations and concerns (not the least of which is the right to sovereignty and economic and political interests). Many argue that signing such instruments is unnecessary, in part because of the conviction that the constitution provides for human rights.

Where do we go from here? After helping students understand the limits to the US "exceptionalism," and the fact that we hardly hold the top prize for human rights practices and enforcement, the lingering question at the end of the semester is always, "So, now what? Why is it important for me to know this depressing stuff if I don't know what to do with it?" I began to incorporate the concept of the human rights enterprise (Armaline, Glasberg, and Purkayastha 2011; 2015) throughout the curriculum, to help students see that there are always social justice movements, direct actions, and a variety of organized activities that people on the ground engage in to address human rights violations and deprivations, to push back against human rights from the top down (i.e., *de jure* human rights, but not necessarily *de facto* human rights), and to agitate for human rights even as the state may resist. I provide concrete historical examples, such as the abolition movement, the suffrage movement, the civil rights movement, the women's movement, and the gay rights movement. This helps students in that they now see that there is plenty of action taking place all the time; but they continue to believe that the US is still the only place on earth that has a constitution that protects their rights, even if imperfectly.

Once again, I tell them, that is an empirical question: is the US the only country with such a constitution? If it is not, what others may exist, and what do they look like? The Constitution Project offers a wonderful way to examine this question.

Structuring the Constitution Project for the Classroom

There are a variety of different approaches one could take in structuring an assignment or exercise around the Constitution Project. For example, one approach might be to organize a course around a specific theme for all the students of the class to explore together over the course of the full semester, such as the right to food, the right to shelter, the right to an education, the right to adequate compensation for work, the right to economic viability, etc. I organized my class using a different approach: Rather than having the entire class focus on a single issue I have mine organized into groups, each taking on a different issue. This was because the description of the course indicated that the course was intended to examine Human Rights in the United States in a more general way, rather than to focus on individual topics for the full semester. This was, clearly, an organizational and curricular constraint: we cannot stray too far from the catalog description of the course, even though we do have academic freedom to approach it as we see fit. What began as an institutional constraint quickly became a pedagogical benefit: students got into small groups to select topics on which to focus, and that provided them with a more intimate group dynamic. Furthermore, this structure allowed the full class to explore eleven different topics while dividing the labor to do so.

At the beginning of the semester I sent around a sign-up sheet for group projects with eleven potential topics that corresponded to the syllabus. As many as five students per group could sign up and they were free to alter the topic if they wished. For example, what began as a topic on Occupy Wall Street quickly changed to exploring the use of excessive force by the police force against people of color on the street (although the class often raised Occupy Wall Street in a variety of contexts throughout the semester); what began as child labor morphed into an examination of the treatment of Latin American children migrating to the US border.

The topics they ultimately chose were:

- National Security and the NSA (The right to privacy and freedom from torture)
- Rights of Immigrants (Citizenship and rights)
- Racial Profiling (The right to freedom from racism and racial discrimination)
- Equal Pay and Comparable Worth (The right to freedom from sexism and gendered discrimination)
- Same Sex Marriage (Sexual citizenship and human rights)
- Cultural Rights and Native Americans (Citizenship and the rights of indigenous populations)
- Living Wage vs. Minimum Wage (The right to a living wage)
- Hunger and Homelessness (The right to sustenance)
- Welfare Reform (The right to sustenance)
- Universal Health Care (The right to access to health and health care)
- Children at the Border (The rights of children)
- Protesting Police Use of Excessive Force (The right to freedom from torture and violence).

Most recently, students have chosen to examine other topics, including:

- Syrian Refugees and the Rights of Immigrants (Citizenship and rights)
- Reparations for Slavery (The right to freedom from racism and racial discrimination; the right to restitution)
- Transgender Rights (Sexual citizenship and human rights)
- Corporations as Citizens (Who has rights? What is a citizen? Are corporate rights human rights?).

After the students signed up I developed an email distribution list for each group to help them stay in contact with each other.

The Assignment

Each group was assigned a presentation date that corresponded with the appropriate unit on the syllabus. Their assignment was to prepare a presentation with the following elements:

- a clear statement of the human rights issue, linking it to the UDHR or other international human rights covenants and agreements
- the dimensions of the problem

- activism relating to the problem (including controversies, relative successes and failures)
- a list of bibliographic and additional sources
- three to four provocative discussion questions for the class.

They were told they could present this as a presentation or as a debate, and they were encouraged to be as creative as they wished in the format of the presentation, including, for example, PowerPoint, multimedia, poems, photographs, charts, and diagrams. If they chose to do this as a debate, half the group must present one side of the debate and the other half the opposite point of view (notably, none of the groups chose to engage in the debate format; all chose a presentation format, and all were highly creative!). Afterwards, they were required to send me a file of the presentation to be uploaded on our Blackboard Learning Management System for the class to review.

Then they wrote up a group paper in which they engage in a comparative analysis of the constitutions of three different countries, at least two of which must be on a different continent (to discourage them from looking exclusively at Western Europe) and compare how these countries' constitutions do or do not deal with the issue they're focusing on and compare that to the US. The paper was to be about eight to twelve pages in length, exploring the following:

- Identify which human rights in the Universal Declaration of Human Rights your group's topic concerned.
- What does the US Constitution say about such rights?
- What are the limitations or problems posed by the way the US Constitution addresses this issue?
- What do other countries' constitutions say about such rights? Make sure you compare and contrast at least three different countries, and that at least two of them are from different continents.
- How might you revise the US Constitution to address these rights?
- What would the implications be of such a revision?

I gave them the links to the relevant resources for this exercise, including the link to other countries' constitutions. The groups were given two weeks to complete their paper after their group presentation. I asked them to send it to me via email so I could post it on our Blackboard system for the class to share.

Challenges and Discoveries

Students were initially a bit overwhelmed getting started. Most had difficulty establishing a division of labor for the presentation, and some were quicker to resolve this issue than others. Two in particular sought some direction from me to help them develop a mechanism for dividing up the tasks. Almost all of them eventually broke down the research and the presentation by the elements required for the presentation.

Students found it challenging to identify which countries' constitutions to select for their comparative analysis. The restriction of the assignment requiring at least two of the three constitutions to come from different continents seemed to help them to a degree: most divided the labor along continental lines, with one student searching the link for constitutions among countries on one continent, and two other students each searching the constitutions of countries on one of two other continents. Some students developed an excel spreadsheet to compare and contrast elements of constitutions on the continent they were researching to help them select the one they thought would be the most intriguing to explore; but none of the groups shared these with me (they considered these to be like outlines, and those are not shared with the instructor, they reasoned). That's unfortunate. I am convinced that the next time I do this exercise I will require that they develop such a comparative spreadsheet and that it be turned in with their paper. I'm certain there is quite a lot of wonderful, rich data in that "outline"!

The following is the array of countries each group ultimately selected:

- National Security and the NSA (The right to privacy and freedom from torture):
  - France
  - South Africa
  - South Korea
- Rights of Immigrants (Citizenship and rights):
  - Germany
  - Nigeria
  - Japan
- Racial Profiling (The right to freedom from racism and racial discrimination):
  - Brazil
  - Russia
  - Egypt
- Equal Pay and Comparable Worth (The right to freedom from sexism and gendered discrimination):
  - Germany
  - South Africa
  - Burundi
- Same Sex Marriage (Sexual citizenship and human rights):
  - Argentina
  - Iran
  - Nigeria
- Cultural Rights and Native Americans (Citizenship and the rights of indigenous populations):
  - China
  - Australia
  - South Africa

- Living Wage vs. Minimum Wage (The right to a livable wage):
  - Mexico
  - Netherlands
  - China
- Hunger and Homelessness (The right to sustenance and shelter):
  - Germany
  - Japan
  - South Africa
- Welfare Reform (The right to sustenance):
  - Denmark
  - Canada
  - Mexico
- Universal Health Care (The right to access to health and health care):
  - Canada
  - Denmark
  - China
- Children at the Border (The rights of children):
  - Norway
  - South Africa
  - Syria
- Protesting Police Use of Excessive Force (The right to freedom from torture and violence):
  - Mexico
  - Russia
  - Hong Kong
  - Australia
- Syrian Refugees and the Rights of Immigrants (Citizenship and rights):
  - Iraq
  - Indonesia
  - Greece
- Reparations for Slavery (The right to freedom from racism and racial discrimination; the right to restitution):
  - Republic of Moldova
  - Ecuador
  - Mexico
- Transgender Rights (Sexual citizenship and human rights):
  - France
  - China
  - Saudi Arabia
- Corporations as Citizens (Who has rights? What is a citizen? Are corporate rights human rights?):
  - China
  - Germany
  - South Africa.

In addition to the challenge of selecting nations to compare, the groups often faced the difficulty that all students must confront in group projects: the problem of differential work habits and social loafing. Some groups worked quite well together; others suffered from internal tensions resulting from one member having more of a "Type-A" approach to work while another member preferred a more casual "laid-back" style of waiting until the last minute to provide material to the group. In one group the rest of the group absorbed the task of the more casual student, because they were keenly aware that they would all share the same grade for the group effort; but resentments simmered that the casual student would get to enjoy a grade to which s/he had not contributed. While this can be a toxic group dynamic, the group did rise to the occasion; ultimately, the casual student felt guilty for not providing a fair contribution to the presentation and volunteered to pick up more of the work for the paper. However, by that point, the rest of the group members were hesitant to let their grades rely on an unreliable student and they rejected the offer. The final group work was terrific, but not nearly as much fun for its members as it was for the other groups.

In one instance, a group member contributed well to the group presentation, but failed to participate adequately for the group paper. She repeatedly promised the group that her material was almost ready and would be added to the document right away, only to tell them she was not quite ready after all. Finally, she stopped responding to their emails altogether, and ultimately dropped the class without letting them know. They came to me in a panic about how to pick up the slack to complete the assignment. I decided the fair thing to do was to ask them to make constitutional comparisons between the US and only two other countries. This was a less-than-ideal solution, but I thought the only fair way to avoid penalizing two hard-working students for the failure of one.

Almost all the students reported that the exercise of looking at other countries' constitutions was challenging but illuminating: they discovered that almost all countries had a constitution, something that came as a surprise to most of them. They also developed a newfound respect for other countries around the world, certainly beyond the wealthier industrialized and post-industrialized countries of Western Europe: while the US Constitution enumerated quite a list of negative rights ("freedom from" a whole host of state intrusions, for example), almost all other countries' constitutions framed positive rights ("rights to" a wide range of political, civil, social, and economic rights). Students were surprised to discover that many countries in fact articulated rights to food, shelter, education, and health, and to a decent, living wage. These are things for which people in the US are expected to pay, and presumed to be personally responsible for obtaining; no one is expected to be anyone else's responsibility. In contrast, many countries' constitutions frame these rights as inalienable, regardless of one's ability to pay for them. Indeed, many groups noted that the countries they compared often explicitly framed their constitutions relative to the UDHR (see Appendix 2). Students marveled at how much better-developed and articulated these positive rights were in far-flung places, well beyond what they presumed at the beginning of the semester was the "gold standard" of human rights in the US Constitution. One of the notable insights students had after listening to several reports was that nations whose constitutions were written after the development of the UDHR were more likely to have embedded its provisions into their constitutions, or to have deliberately and consciously framed them in the context of the UDHR. They realized that the US Constitution was drafted well before the UDHR, so it was not framed in terms of human rights (especially cultural and civil rights) but rather in terms of individuals' liberties. They identified the historical cultural context in the US as one of competitive individualism rather than one of community. But they agreed that this did not mean the US Constitution had to be considered as "written in stone" and immune to change. In fact, at least a few noted that it is a "living document," as such, subject to change and growth with greater contemporary sophistication and knowledge of human rights.

They also discovered the distinction between *de jure* rights written into constitutions and *de facto* practice that defied those rights (both in the US and elsewhere). For example, the group that looked at Protesting Police Use of Excessive Force (The right to freedom from torture and violence) found that all the countries they compared had *de jure* expressions of constitutional rights to assembly, freedom of expression, and freedom from torture and violence; but they also found that some constitutions acknowledged caveats to these freedoms (including prohibitions against protests and expressions critical of the government), and all routinely violated those constitutional rights in practice on the streets. Students found that disconnect troubling, to say the least.

They also discovered that the theoretical framework that dominates much of human rights scholarship, in which the state imposes human rights from above and through written documents like constitutions, is far more complicated. For example, many countries' constitutions represent the intersection the institutions of state and religion (or, in some cases, the fusion of these institutions) such that political, civil, and social rights can be affected. For example, the group that examined the rights of sexual citizenship found that in all three constitutions they reviewed religious prohibitions against homosexuality infused the language of the constitution, and in most cases identified penal codes and often severe punishments for suspicion of homosexuality. The question of sexual citizenship and human rights, then, becomes compromised by cultural or religious tenets. Students wrestled with the tension between sexual citizenship and human rights, and the right to national sovereignty. This alerted students to an understanding that multiple institutions and cultural norms and practices frame how constitutions may or may not resonate with the Universal Declaration of Human Rights, and that the notion of human rights itself is far from unambiguous.

The idea that the concept of human rights is not without complicated gray areas also raised a troubling set of questions about cultural relativism with which students struggled: do human rights trump local cultures, or does the imposition of human rights violate local rights to sovereignty? For example, was it justifiable for some US states to maintain a system of slavery since it was an accepted part of their culture (and an important element of their economy), even if that violated the concept of the right to freedom from enslavement? Does cultural relativity make any and all practices defensible even these contradict the Universal Declaration of Human Rights? While students generally found slavery to be repugnant and an obvious violation of the right to human dignity and freedom from enslavement, they were uncomfortable with the idea that anyone could force another country to adopt a set of principles that violated local cultures. They were frustrated by the idea that there was not a clear, simple answer to this debate that has plagued human rights scholars in the literature as well.

Overall, students in all the groups concluded that neither the *de jure* US Constitution nor the *de facto* practices in the US were anywhere near the "gold standard" of human rights they had initially presumed. While some countries they studied shared lapses in their constitutions with those in the US, most appeared to do a better job of at least *de jure* acknowledging the values of the UDHR and attempted to frame their constitutions accordingly. In the US, the constitution historically predates the UDHR, and contemporary political leaders have remained unconvinced that the US Constitution as it currently stands is in any way inconsistent with the UDHR. That position notwithstanding, students decided that the only existing "gold standard" of human rights was the UDHR itself! As such, at least one student deemed the UDHR a sociological ideal type against which all constitutions may be measured.

Conclusion: What We Have Seen Can't Be Unseen: So What Next?

The biggest challenge students faced was what to do with their new insights relative to the US Constitution. They struggled with the gap between what could or should be and the practical political realities of transforming it. While they could see that the US Constitution was largely inadequate on the question of human rights, they had difficulty imagining how they might get around the centuries-old political process that frames constitutional changes and the daunting institutional forces and interests that would surely rally to prevent and subvert change.

We engaged in a long discussion of the power of social movements to prompt changes, many that were unimaginable a generation or two ago: voting rights for African Americans and women; rights to marry for same-sex and transgender couples; prisoners' rights; and the rights of people to feed the hungry in open public spaces, to name just a few. While these battles are far from perfect or settled, there have been significant inroads due to the persistent efforts of social movements.

Some students pointed with frustration to what they considered the "failures" of the Occupy Wall Street movement: after all that "noise" and disruption, they argued, what actually changed? Similarly, what has the Black Lives Matter movement changed? We discussed how social movements are not quick fixes, but are long processes involving persistence, patience, organization, and resources that work to bring a light to issues, raise consciousness, and ultimately affect change, even if in small increments at a time. After the Occupy movement, for example, we are alert and talking about severe inequality and the 1 percent. That's step one in social change. The Black Lives Matter movement has succeeded in resurrecting a vocal civil rights/anti-racism movement that has already succeeded in an increased use of body cameras on police around the country to document police behavior on the street, and an increase in public demands for accountability. Several campus administrators have been fired for ignoring racism on campus, police commissioners have been disciplined, some police officers have been arrested and at least one has been jailed for racist violence against citizens. Although the semester ended before the US Supreme Court's landmark decision regarding the right to marriage for same-sex and transgender persons or the similar determination in Ireland, it represents another example for future semesters of the effect social movements' persistence can have on the evolution of human rights, in the US and around the world.

We discussed how social movements are often characterized by two-steps forward and one-and-a-half steps back. While setbacks may be frustrating, and feel like losses, so long as we're still that half-step forward we are indeed making progress, and percolating human rights from below. I do believe that's the best we can expect after a single semester: plant a seed and instigate curiosity about other constitutions and questions about why the US Constitution can't be just as good or better. That's not a bad start!

References

Armaline, William T., Davita Silfen Glasberg, and Bandana Purkayastha (eds). 2011. *Human Rights in Our Own Back Yard: Injustice and Resistance in the United States*. Philadelphia: University of Pennsylvania Press.

Armaline, William T., Davita Silfen Glasberg, and Bandana Purkayastha. 2015. *The Human Rights Enterprise: The State, Resistance, and Human Rights*. Cambridge, UK and Malden, MA: Polity Press.

13

FOR A DECOLONIZED US CONSTITUTION

Keri E. Iyall Smith

Many chapters in this book encourage us to look to the modern concept of human rights to find inspiration for amendments to the US Constitution, which will expand the rights of all who live within its boundaries. Another source of inspiration can be found in the norms, structures, and practices of indigenous peoples. Decolonizing the US Constitution will lead to a constitution that prioritizes community, downplays the individual, expands participation, and thinks holistically about the needs of our societies for the good of all. The process of decolonization involves all aspects of society working towards freedom and transformation, seeking to reveal a new society, which "engenders indigenous knowledge" (Lee 2013: 118). Decolonization is also a disruption of the colonial structures, institutions, and policies to reconnect to indigenous homelands, cultures, and communities (Corntassel 2012). Through this disruption, patriarchy, the racial hierarchy, and capitalism will be undone and replaced by a holistic model acknowledging, realizing, and embodying the indigenous knowledge of all.

In this chapter I will propose a path to decolonize the US Constitution, looking to indigenous traditions to learn about the importance of kinship, leadership traits, equality, restorative justice, and the traditional roles of nature. I will then critically analyze the US Bill of Rights—looking specifically at ways that its language suggests an adversarial relationship between the government and citizens and ways that it may demonstrate cooperation. By looking to indigenous nations to envision a decolonized US Constitution, this chapter concludes with a glance at how life might be different for all within the US by integrating the traditions and practices of indigenous peoples.

Decolonizing Our Minds

Upon their contact with indigenous peoples, Europeans naïvely believed they had found groups of people who lived without morals, were lawless, uncivilized, and uneducated. This might have made the genocide to follow less of a moral quandary, but the reality could hardly be further from the truth. Indigenous peoples lived regulated lives. They managed the forest and its resources. Hidden meadows created by indigenous peoples still exist, encircled by tall, broad cedar trees. These meadows might have been sites of cultivation, markets, or large structures. Indigenous peoples knew the value of dignity, justice, and peace. Community and children were highly valued. Leadership was selected with great care through community-based decision making. Leaders had strict codes regulating their decision making and answered to the group. All community members played a role in the group's survival.

While for some assimilated indigenous nations this past is quite distant, in other communities the ties to the past remain strong and people are committed to live according to the teachings of their elders. Through decolonization, indigenous knowledge on kinship, leadership, equality, restorative justice, and nature would effectively disrupt the colonial model and offer a path to human rights and justice for all.

Kinship

Western society, in its religion, law, and cultural norms prioritizes the individual and his/her needs and efforts over the collective or communal (Champagne 2016). This is particularly true in the United States, and this value is mirrored in the US Constitution and its Bill of Rights, which focus on the individual and his/her relationship to the government. Yet many (perhaps most) indigenous societies are rooted in kinship and community (Champagne 2016). For the *Diné*[1] (Navajo) "all creation shares an equality that is foundational for Navajo conceptions of justice" (Wall 2001: 532) through *k'é* kinship, friendship, good relations, and equality of all the members of the community, and *hózhó*, relationships of harmony with the entire cosmos (Wall 2001). The clans define kinship among the Diné people, with a structure that has expanded to accommodate people they have contact with, such as the Utes, Zunis, and Paiutes (Iverson 2002).

Deloria and Lytle (1983) note the importance of clans and family in the leadership structure of the *Haudenosaunee*[2] and the Creek nations. It was the clan system that allowed the Creek nations to escape a thick fog safely by holding hands with people and animals as they wandered (Deloria and Lytle 1983). The Hopi Constitution codifies roles for the *Kikmongwi*, traditional clan leaders. The Cherokee nation also valued clan and family, citing this as their second social postulate: "the matrilineal clan is the primary social unit, whose purity of blood must be safeguarded at all times" (Strickland 1975: 22). The actions of a clan brother may impact a person's afterlife (Strickland 1975), meaning if your clan brother commits murder he may risk your chance to pass to Nightland (the afterworld). In the land of the Protestant ethic, where one's efforts ensure entrance to heaven in the afterlife, it is quite radical to think that the actions of another might alter my afterlife! While individualism is the assumption adopted by the US Constitution and embraced in US life, indigenous peoples instead center kinship and relationships. It is the basis of who they are as individuals and as nations.

Leadership Traits

Offering an indigenous perspective on leadership in the Cheyenne nation, Killsback (2011) notes the importance of leaders displaying courage, discipline, compassion, selflessness, generosity, respect, kindness, is someone who values humanity, shows a commitment to service, and acknowledges the sacred virtues of leadership. Cheyenne leaders served their people *unconditionally* (Killsback 2011). Deloria and Lytle (1983) note that important tasks for Cheyenne leaders included caring for widows and orphans, ensuring the wellbeing of all—generosity was an essential trait for a chief, who was required to practice *hetómestôtse* (truth) at all times. Killsback offers an example of Little Wolf to illustrate the ways in which a Cheyenne leader embodied these traits, even in times of challenge and struggle.

Unlike the adherence to a separation of church and state, in the Cheyenne tradition leadership and spirituality were deeply entwined. By the holding of the Chiefs' Medicine Bundle, given by the original prophet, chiefs were "spiritually bound to the ancient virtues of leadership" (Killsback 2011: 90). For the Cherokee (Strickland 1975; Killsback 2011) law was also centered in religion: it was "the earthly representation of a divine spirit order" (11). In the Cherokee nation, law was designed to promote consensus and harmony, not adversarial relationships. Social harmony was valued and popular consensus was required for tribal effectiveness—and could be withheld to stop action (Strickland 1975).

The ability to promote peace is an important skill for tribal leaders. Indeed, some indigenous nations (e.g., the Cherokee, Creek, Cheyenne, and Pacific Northwest villages) had different leaders for war and peace, indicating the recognition that different skills and practices would be required to lead the community in war or peace (Strickland 1975; Deloria and Lytle 1983). The Great Law of Peace, the Haudenosaunee Constitution which informed the writing of the US Constitution, asserts that "The first principle is peace…the process of discussion, putting aside warfare as a method of reaching decisions" (Lyons, as quoted in Dunbar-Ortiz 2014: 26).

Both Cheyenne and Choctaw leaders were called upon to act as mediators, sometimes making sacrifices themselves for the good of the community (Deloria and Lytle 1983). "Performing the function of a chief, therefore, was hardly the enriching experience that modern politicians enjoy when assuming their office" (Deloria and Lytle 1983: 84). Within the Haudenosaunee Confederacy the chief largely served as a mediator when private settlements could not be reached among community members. Thus traditional government is judicial rather than legislative: through mediation, the chief "provided the cement that held the tribe together peacefully" (Deloria and Lytle 1983: 89). The mediation model was applied at the village level and across the Haudenosaunee Confederacy, where a sophisticated system of representation and communal discussion of topics led to a consensus outcome and the use of reason to reach a solution (Dunbar-Ortiz 2014). The value of consensus is also found in the Constitution of the Yurok Tribe: "In accordance with Tribal tradition, the Yurok Tribal Council shall attempt to conduct business by consensus whenever possible" (Article 5, Section 6). This statement not only shows the importance of consensus but also the role of tradition in decision making.

Honorable leaders willing to make sacrifices, utilizing the community's spiritual values, promoting peace within and between communities can accomplish amazing things. While it is common among US citizens to doubt or distrust their political leaders, to actively vote against potential leaders rather than for them, the leadership models presented here offer a revolutionary shift towards a new model of governance and leadership.

Equality

One of the ways that indigenous peoples of the Pacific Northwest expressed communal living was via the potlatch. A potlatch is a community gathering, often occurring to commemorate an event (e.g., a wedding or birth). Potlatches might last for several days, with food, drink, songs, dancing, stick game, and more. The potlatch ended with the host giving away everything he owned to the guests who had come to witness the event. By attending the potlatch, members of the community sanctioned the event, and they were thanked with an informal system of redistribution of resources. Law does not compel this sharing of resources, it is not mandated; rather it is an expression of gratitude for the honor given by guests.

Sharing and equality are valued among indigenous nations beyond the Pacific Northwest. The Hopi Bill of Rights includes two sections: one dedicated to freedom of religion and one granting resident members of the Tribe "equal opportunities to *share* in the economic resources and activities of the jurisdiction" (emphasis added). The US Constitution protects religious expression, yet it is silent about sharing and equality. In the Cherokee nation, natural resources are free and commonly held. While food, wealth, and property may be privately owned, they are to be shared (Strickland 1975). Valuing competition is foreign to Diné philosophy and ethics (Wall 2001). Rather than competing with each other, Diné people seek to form connections with each other to create and restore harmony both within the person and between people (Wall 2001). Equality is thus a key component of Diné cosmology (Wall 2001).

The *Haudenosaunee* enshrined the importance of equality in their constitution, which supported equal suffrage (Deloria and Lytle 1983). The Cherokee assert the value of equality of men and women, and all classes—all people are useful to Cherokee society (Strickland 1975). While the US Constitution was amended to allow voting regardless of gender or race, it does not grant equality to all men and women, or all classes beyond the right to suffrage. These examples illustrate how among indigenous nations, sharing of resources and treating community members equally are valued deeply, sometimes codified in law and at other times so entrenched that codification would be irrelevant.

Restorative Justice

In the pre-colonial era, one of the worst punishments given by many indigenous communities was banishment (Richland and Deer 2010). Living outside of one's community meant living without the protection of living in a group, without the resources and skills shared among community members, without the knowledge and access to places to gather, hunt, or fish for much needed supplies. When a person survived banishment, his/her return to the tribe was made possible by the sacrifice of others (Richland and Deer 2010).

It is the value of community and the role of individuals *in* communities that restorative justice emphasizes. Lauderdale and Oliverio (2012) note that restorative justice among indigenous nations tends to involve interconnected structures that bring together practices and duties with spiritual obligations. Using Haudenosaunee traditional teachings as their exemplars, Lauderdale and Oliverio (2012) note the importance of kinship, duty, reciprocity, and harmony. Here peace is not the absence of war—rather it is the prevention of injustice (Lauderdale and Oliverio 2012). Cherokee law also used restorative justice, expressed in an annual communal offering of forgiveness before a divine fire. Cherokee people could only attend this ceremonial reading of the law if they were willing to forgive others (Strickland 1975). By attending and forgiving, people were spared the burden of carrying grudges, allowing them to live peacefully as a community (Strickland 1975). For both the Haudenosaunee and the Cherokee, restorative justice was applied, either through communal norms that promoted harmony or through forgiveness.

For the Diné people, it was quarreling and conflict that forced their migrations to this world (Iverson 2002). Wall's (2001) study of peacemaking demonstrates that through peacemaking it is possible to restore right relations, *hózhó*, both within a person and between people. In the Peacemaker Court all participants are equal and the court is thus viewed as a horizontal justice system (Wall 2001), unlike the hierarchical structure found in the United States justice system. The Peacemaker Court follows a series of steps that merge spirituality, Diné cosmology, and philosophy, relying upon the willingness of all to seek resolution (Wall 2001). The importance of *k'é* (kinship) and *hózhó* (harmony in the universe) are reaffirmed through the peacemaking process, allowing Diné people to live in accordance with their spiritual traditions even as they face modern challenges (Wall 2001). Thus, among indigenous nations many models exist to practice justice through community based restorative practices. They demonstrate the holistic nature of life and the importance of good relationships.

Nature

From a Western perspective, nature is a God-given resource to be utilized. It is only fears of scarcity and climate change that have shifted the paradigm to "sustainable development." Some of the rhetoric in support of sustainable development is rooted in indigenous ideologies. For instance, the practice of reserving enough resources to last the community for seven generations is in accordance with *Haudenosaunee* law. The Hopi Constitution acknowledges the importance of the right to farm, protection of range land, and it discusses the use of occupied and unoccupied land (Hopi Constitution, Article VII). Rights to water are also protected under Article VII, Section 3, "no individual or group of individuals shall be allowed to prevent the reasonable use of any spring by members of the tribe generally." In this way both *Haudenosaunee* Great Laws and the Hopi Constitution identify the importance of land and resources.

The Diné people seek to live a good life by embodying *hózhó*. Focusing on the prefix *hó*, Wall (2001: 537) underscores that *hózhó* "includes a kind of cosmic, abstract, infinite, and invisible whole...literally implies a relationship to the entire cosmos." When a person lives according to *hózhó*, she lives in harmony with the universe both within and beyond herself. In this way our relationship to nature is a part of who we are as individuals and as a society; it is the duty of humans to honor that relationship. For some indigenous nations nature assists in ensuring compliance with community norms. Features in nature become reminders of how to follow norms or represent cautionary tales of what happens if one violates norms. For example, some Pacific Northwest tribes use stories about Mount Saint Helens to discourage vanity. It is because Mount Saint Helens was too vain, looking in the mirror all the time (Spirit Lake), that one of her sisters knocked her top off. Thus for some indigenous nations it is the entire cosmos that we are seeking to be in a harmonious relationship with—and for other indigenous nations it is through nature that we can learn how to practice harmony.

In Contrast

Looking at the Bill of Rights, the first ten amendments of the US Constitution, reveals a legal structure that assumes conflict between the government and citizens. Rather than prioritizing kinship, equality, restoration, leadership, or interrelatedness, amendments to the US Constitution reveal an undercurrent of antagonism.[3] To read the full text of the Bill of Rights and further amendments to the US Constitution see Appendix 1. The discussion below categorizes the amendments, identifying the type or relationship implied by the language and subject of the amendment.

Collaborative or Adversarial

Only two amendments to the US Constitution can either be viewed as collaborative *or* adversarial. The text of the 1st Amendment demonstrates a society whereby it is congress that may overstep its bounds and inhibit individual freedoms and some rights to collective groups (assembly and "the press"). Citizens are permitted to petition the government. The text of the 2nd Amendment establishes a well-regulated militia that might either serve to protect the government and citizenry or allow the citizenry some degree of power in opposition to the government (as in the case of the revolutionary Americans-to-be during the colonial era).

Adversarial

The majority of the amendments to the US Constitution either imply or overtly assert an antagonistic relationship between citizens and the government. Under the 3rd Amendment rather than allowing citizens to be vulnerable to an overbearing government that houses its military anywhere, the constitution mandates that the owner must consent to the housing of soldiers in both peace and war. The 4th Amendment describes the circumstances under which the security of citizens in their "persons, houses, papers, and effects against unreasonable searches and seizures" may be violated—only with "probable cause." It is the government that determines whether or not probable cause exists, which may be a conflict of interest. The provisions in the 5th Amendment assume that citizens may be at risk of aggressive prosecution. As the state and its agents perform the prosecution, the 5th Amendment positions citizens in opposition to the government. The fifth Amendment also offers protection of a citizen's right to hold property and be compensated if it is taken for public use also creates an adversarial relationship between citizens and the government.

The protections of citizens when they are on criminal trial are considered further in the 6th Amendment. While many of these conditions are meant to empower citizens to defend themselves against prosecution (e.g., obtaining witnesses, an attorney), they also protect the citizen/defendant against questionable conditions during prosecution (speedy, public trial, impartial jury, witnesses for prosecution will be present). This amendment thus seeks both to protect citizens by empowering them and by establishing the conditions for prosecution. It is largely establishing an adversarial relationship between citizen/defendants and their government/prosecutor.

Under the provisions of the 7th Amendment, citizens gain the right to a jury of peers rather than decision making by an officer of the court (the judge). All three prohibitions in the 8th Amendment (no excessive bail, no excessive fines, no cruel and unusual punishment) are designed to protect citizens from an overbearing government. According to the 9th Amendment, the constitution itself shall not overstep the bounds of rights retained by people, protecting citizens from one that may violate their rights. Powers not delegated to the US Government by the constitution remain in the hands of the state or the people, in accordance with the 10th Amendment. This protects people from a government that may wish to expand its powers beyond the legal limits—primarily at the federal level. However, it seems that there is still provision for both states and persons to have rights that they have not reserved from the other powers.

Following the Bill of Rights, the recent Amendments perpetuate an adversarial relationship between the government and its citizens. There are prohibitions on the extension of judicial power (11th Amendment) and strict rules for the electoral process (12th Amendment). Through the 13th Amendment, the prohibition of slavery protects citizens from other citizens, but it also reveals the role of the government in permitting enslavement prior to this amendment. Other amendments limit the state's power to make laws and protect life, liberty, and property (14th Amendment) and create provisions for taxation (16th Amendment). Several amendments establish rules for the federal government, regarding: the electing senators (17th Amendment), when the president and vice-president will take office (20th Amendment), the number of terms a person may serve as president (22nd Amendment), succession rules if a president is removed from office, dies, or resigns (25th Amendment), and regarding wage changes for senators and representatives (27th Amendment). Under prohibition (18th Amendment), the powers of the government are extended to policing the consumption of alcohol.

In some cases, the practice of the amendments expands rights for US citizens, but the language frames the expanded right as a negative provision, a freedom from intrusion, rather than as a positive right. Under the 15th Amendment, rights "*shall not be denied* due to race, color, or previous condition of servitude" (emphasis added). With the 24th Amendment, the citizen's right to vote "*shall not be denied* or abridged by reason of failure to pay any poll tax or other tax" (emphasis added). Finally, in the 26th Amendment, the right to vote is extended to citizens over eighteen—"their right shall not be denied." These three amendments protect citizens from the denial of rights, rather than offering provisions to practice their rights.

Only the 19th Amendment, expanding suffrage to women, the 21st Amendment repealing prohibition, and the 23rd Amendment creating provisions for the District of Columbia to participate in the Electoral College expand the rights of US Citizens.

This close look at the US Bill of Rights reveals a domination of negative rights, expressing a fear of the overreach of government and individuals within the government, especially on behalf of the president, vice-president, members of congress, prosecutors, and judges. This is representative of a political culture that fears, rather than a political culture that embraces. Fearing power and its misuse presumes that members of the community and government do not seek "to form a more perfect union, establish justice, insure domestic tranquility, provide for the common defense, promote the general welfare, and secure the blessings of liberty to ourselves and our posterity" (US Constitution, Preamble). Instead, it promotes a climate of fear and distrust, anticipating the abuse of power, and establishing the citizens and government as opposing parties.

Models for a Decolonized Constitution

To achieve a decolonized US Constitution, it is essential both to reject the vertical authority structure established within the current amendments *and* to reject the antagonism they create and reinforce between citizen and government. The best model of a decolonized constitution can be found in Bolivia's Constitution (2009), which is notable for its acknowledgement of colonial history and efforts to integrate indigenous knowledge and tradition in all aspects of governance.

The US might also look *again* at indigenous governance models. While it was common for early observers to see no government and no law in indigenous nations, they observed only the absence of structures like European and Anglo-American legal systems. There was not an individual who had the power to make others do what they may not otherwise do (Richland and Deer 2010). But as Richland and Deer question:

> Is this kind of coercive force a necessary element of all governments? What about those societies where respected individuals lead by example and instruction rather than force? What about those where the main form of coercion is public opinion—where acting contrary to social expectation is avoided because doing so will result in people (such as family relatives) not wanting to cooperate with you at times when such cooperation is crucial to your survival? Is it fair to say that societies like these have no governments? (Richland and Deer 2010: 59–60).

Deloria and Lytle (1983) also note the absence of written law, but indicate the importance of stories and anecdotes among indigenous communities, along with social pressure, to encourage appropriate behavior.

While many tribal constitutions today were written to comply with the 1934 Indian Reorganization Act (IRA), a few constitutions exist which are not the "boilerplate" models approved by the Bureau of Indian Affairs under the IRA. The Constitution of the Yurok Tribe (1993) includes an elaborate preamble describing the Yurok people, where they live, the importance of village headmen in resolving problems, the importance of the river, ceremonies, and the effects of colonialism. It ends with seven reasons why the Yurok tribe adopts this constitution, including to "provide for the health, education, economy, and social wellbeing of our members and future members" and to "insure peace, harmony, and protection of individual *human rights* among our members and among others who may come within the jurisdiction of our tribal government" (emphasis added). While the constitution of the Yurok Tribe was only authored one year after the US Constitution was last amended, its assertion of the importance of protecting human rights, wellbeing, peace, and harmony is light years ahead.

As we rewrite the US Constitution we can look to tribal nations and the essential structures to maintaining those communities: kinship, leadership traits, equality, restorative justice, and the role of nature. Cheyenne leadership and law have changed, with new standards added in response to new political problems (Killsback 2011). Cheyenne leadership and people thus recognized the value of evolving legal structures to respond to changing life conditions—something that the current US Constitution fails to either recognize or embody. Yet by adopting this Cheyenne concept, the US can improve the lives and wellbeing of all its citizens.

How Can We Proceed?

Reading the US Constitution as it is today reveals a document designed to keep government from overstepping boundaries, becoming too controlling and inhibiting the freedoms of citizens. This is the basis of the three-branch government—each branch represents a way to block the power of the other, designed to ensure that power cannot be concentrated in the hands of too few. This was thought to be for the good of the masses, or at least for the good of the landholding men. Even the Bill of Rights sets up an opposition between the citizens and the state. The state becomes the adversary of the citizens, out to seize their civil and political rights if they are not vigilant in protecting them. Each citizen is thus in opposition to the state. The implication of "Congress shall make no law…" implies a congress that may seek to make laws even though it ought not. Each citizen is thus in opposition to the state. Rather than mandating that rights and protections are only for those who can pay for a lawsuit, only for those who can manage to frame their problems as due to threats from the state, it is time for US citizens to control and possess their rights.

When the US Constitution was written, voting rights extended to only white male landholders. Today most US citizens are not white landholding males—even when the constitution was written, most people living with the US were not white landholding males. The US Constitution remains largely unchanged, in spite of the great shift in how we live our lives and who we regard as citizens. Dunbar-Ortiz notes that "in other modern constitutional states, constitutions come and go, and they are never considered sacred in the manner patriotic US citizens venerate theirs" (Dunbar-Ortiz 2014: 50). Rather than proving fidelity to this document (Dunbar-Ortiz 2014), it is time to decolonize the US Constitution in the name of our fidelity for each other. In a decolonized constitution we will acknowledge our humanity and what we need to express ourselves as human. Being rooted in our contemporary conception of community, rather than the narrow one defined by the founding fathers, a decolonized US Constitution will be *of* the people. Reflecting the myriad voices within the US, a decolonized constitution will be *by* the people. Finally, rather than perpetuating a government that serves its own interests at the expense of its citizens, a decolonized constitution will create a government that is *for* the people.

In a decolonized society, I am not afraid of my neighbor or my government. A decolonized society cares for rather than harms its citizenry, it is a society that offers provisions for needed health care, a society that facilitates mental health rather than threatening it, a society that manages resources for the good of all rather than the good of one percent (1%), a society that acknowledges the humanity of all—men, women, children, the elderly, people like us and people not like us. Even non-human life is sacred and demands dignity, justice, and peace. A society of people who speak many languages, facilitating cultural and economic exchanges. A society that learns from the wisdom of all life. A society that fights its wars at a safe distance…not with drones, but rather with implements that only inflict superficial, symbolic harm. Rather than living in the shadow of fear, this United States lives in the sun and the rain, under the shelter of shared interests and our interconnectedness. For the good of all rather than the good of the few. It is utopia and it is ours to behold.

Notes

1 Note that although most authors that I cite use the word Navajo, I have elected to use the preferred term, *Diné*. *Diné* is what Navajo people call themselves in their native language and increasingly what they are asking others to call them, rather than Navajo.
2 Note that although most authors that I cite use the word Iroquois, I have elected to use the preferred term *Haudenosaunee*. *Haudenosaunee* is what the people formerly known as Iroquois now prefer to be called—it is the term they use to refer to themselves in their native language.
3 To read the full text of the Bill of Rights and further amendments to the US Constitution, please see Appendix 1.

References

Bolivia (Plurinational State of). 2009. *Constitution*. Translated by Max Planck Institute. www.constituteproject.org/constitution/Bolivia_2009?lang=en (last accessed May 2, 2016).

Champagne, Duane. 2016. "Traditional Kinship Versus Christian Individualism." *Indian Country Today Media Network*. http://indiancountrytodaymedianetwork.com/2016/04/09/traditional-kinship-versus-christian-individualism-163836 (last accessed October 11, 2016).

Corntassel, Jeff. 2012. "Re-envisioning Resurgence: Indigenous Pathways to Decolonization and Sustainable Self-determination." *Decolonization: Indigeneity, Education & Society* 1(1): 86–101.

Deloria, Jr., Vine and Clifford M. Lytle. 1983. *American Indians, American Justice*. Austin, TX: University of Texas Press.

Dunbar-Ortiz, Roxanne. 2014. *An Indigenous Peoples' History of the United States*. Boston, MA: Beacon Press.

Fox, Jr., William F. 1983. "Amending the Constitution to Accomplish Social Goals." *Social Thought* 9(3): 3–14.

Hopi Tribe. 1936. *Constitution and By-laws: The Hopi Tribe*. http://thorpe.ou.edu/IRA/hopicons.html (last accessed May 2, 2016).

Iverson, Peter. 2002. *Diné: A History of the Navajos.* Albuquerque, NM: University of New Mexico Press.

Killsback, Leo. 2011. "The Legacy of Little Wolf." *Wicazo Sa Review* 26(1): 85–111.

Lauderdale, Pat and Annamarie Oliverio. 2012. "Traditional Indigenous Restorative Practices and Perspectives on Current Frameworks of Justice and Human Rights," in *Rights and Restoration within Youth Justice*, Theo Gavrielides (ed.): 19–37. Whitby, Ontario: de Sitter Publications.

Lee, Lloyd L. 2013. "The Fundamental Laws: Codification for Decolonization?" *Decolonization: Indigeneity, Education & Society* 2(2): 117–131.

Marshall, Rain Archambeau. "The Evolution of Tribal Governments and Constitutions: A Look at Ten Modern Tribal Governments and their Constitutions or Codes." www2. humboldt.edu/itepp/crc/cicd%20publications/constitution.pdf (last accessed May 2, 2016).

Richland, Justin B. and Sarah Deer. 2010. *Introduction to Tribal Legal Studies: Second Edition.* Lanham, MD: AltaMira Press.

Strickland, Rennard. 1975. *Fire and the Spirits: Cherokee Law from Clan to Court.* Norman, OK: University of Oklahoma Press.

Vizenor, Gerald and Jill Doerfler. 2012. *The White Earth Nation: Ratification of a Native Democratic Constitution.* Lincoln, NE: University of Nebraska Press.

Wall, Barbara E. 2001. "Navajo Conceptions of Justice in the Peacemaker Court." *Journal of Social Philosophy* 32(4): 532–546.

Yurok Tribe. 1993. *Constitution.* www.yuroktribe.org/government/councilsupport/documents/Constitution.pdf (last accessed May 2, 2016).

14

THE UNIVERSAL DECLARATION OF HUMAN RIGHTS AS A CONSTITUTIONAL MODEL

Zachary Elkins, Tom Ginsburg, and James Melton[1]

One might think, on first encounter, that international human rights is a subject on which all agree. After all, who could oppose norms against torture, genocide, and or other abuses? No one, anywhere, regardless of the presiding government, ought to be denied certain basic freedoms. This simple intuition gave rise to the Universal Declaration of Human Rights (UDHR), adopted in the aftermath of World War II.

Yet the idea of international human rights has become a subject of intense controversy among scholars. Critics claim the movement has ignored empirical evidence and been too ideological (Posner 2014). A major empirical literature turns on whether international instruments are effective at all, and if so under what conditions (Neumayer 2005; Simmons 2009; Powell and Staton 2009; Hill 2010; Fariss 2014; Lupu 2015). The historiography of human rights, too, has become a subject of intense controversy (Roberts 2014). The traditional view is that the movement emerged during World War II and spread rapidly thereafter (Henkin 1990), but the revisionist historian Samuel Moyn (2010: 6) has recently argued that the movement really emerged several decades later. These various critics in different disciplines imply that the Universal Declaration is of only peripheral importance.

Our own view is that documents like the UDHR are indeed central in helping to crystallize ideas and in inspiring action. Like other classic rights documents that represent major junctures in the history of human rights—such as the Magna Carta, the US Bill of Rights, the French Declaration of the Rights of Man— the Universal Declaration of Human Rights (UDHR) is an iconic statement of claims by which a community articulates its fundamental values. These kinds of documents seem to consolidate ideas and shape subsequent thinking. Of course, none of the documents mentioned above was written on a blank slate; each drew from prior attempts at higher law. And each, we think, played an important role as a menu for subsequent documents.

A vexing analytical problem looms over this last assertion. If the major documents simply enshrine conventional wisdom at the time, then how influential were they, really? In this more skeptical reading, these documents seem merely epiphenomenal: reflections of the era rather than exogenous influences on what would come. We conceptualize this distinction as one of *reflective* versus *formative* events. We have worked on this problem recently (e.g., Elkins, Ginsburg, and Simmons, 2013), and are convinced that the UDHR—at *minimum* —reflected leading ideas in mid-century constitutional thought. We are also persuaded that post-war constitutions share many ideas with the UDHR. We are less certain about the UDHR's independent role in *shaping* future constitutions. Our modest goal in this is to assemble evidence to distinguish the UDHR from the ideas in which it marinated. We use this evidence to reach for the less modest goal of assessing the formative effects of the UDHR. Was it simply a reflection of existing ideas or did it shape the future? Ultimately, we are interested in estimating the content and practice of human rights conditional upon the counterfactual absence of the UDHR.

Drafting the UDHR

The Universal Declaration was one of the first projects that the then-fledgling United Nations established after World War II. It was steered by the Commission of Human Rights set up under the UN's Economic and Social Council, and drafted initially under the charge of an eight-member Drafting Committee chaired by Eleanor Roosevelt. The initial draft was produced by a Canadian Professor, John P. Humphrey, who headed the UN Secretariat's Division of Human Rights. He and his staff combed a wide array of sources. National constitutions were part of the formative material, as some fifty of them were included in the background materials, along with national government proposals and one from the American Federation of Labor (Schabas 2013: lxxxix).[2] This material was then integrated by Rene Cassin into a working document which formed the basis of further discussion. The document proceeded through the Commission to the United Nations General Assembly, which adopted it on December 10, 1948. The final vote was forty-eight in favor, none opposed and there were eight abstentions (the Soviet bloc, South Africa, and Saudi Arabia each abstained for their own reasons).

The significance of the UDHR lay in its universality. Its articles were addressed not just to citizens of a particular country or region, but to "everyone" by virtue of their humanity. The UDHR consisted of thirty articles, drafted in simple language for all to understand. It marked a major statement in the aftermath of the Holocaust, expressing the commitment of the new United Nations to the project of advancing human rights for all. It was, however, unenforceable as a legal document. As is well known, the normative consensus embodied in the Universal Declaration took legal form only later through the two International Covenants promulgated in 1966, the International Covenant on Civil and Political Rights (ICCPR) and the International Covenant on Economic, Social and Cultural Rights (ICESCR).

There has been a substantial amount of work on the drafting of the Universal Declaration of Human Rights (Morsink 2000; Ishay 2004; Schabas 2013; Waltz 2001; Waltz 2002). Despite some suspicions that the UDHR was a kind of Western imposition, a more accurate characterization is that it reflected the culmination of a long-standing international political movement (Waltz 2002: 439). Simmons (2009) recounts the important role played by Lebanon's Charles Malik and China's Peng Chun in the formation of the text of the UDHR, though the two were sometimes in disagreement. Articles 22–27, which address socio-economic rights, were promoted not just by the Soviet bloc but also Latin American, Asian and Middle Eastern countries (Waltz 2002: 444).[3]

Our sense from both the highly inclusionary and open process of its drafting, as well as our analysis of its content, is that the UDHR represented an expansive view of constitutional rights that had become popular in constitutions written in the interwar era and immediately after World War II. That is to say, many of the ideas were already "in the air."

In our previous analysis, we compared the content of the UDHR to that of a large sample of constitutions written since 1789 (Elkins, Ginsburg, and Simmons 2013). We tested hypotheses that the constitutions of larger, wealthier, and politically important countries had served as models for the UDHR's drafters. We found no support for any of these hypotheses, which corroborated the characterization of the process as an inclusive one. The only robust predictor of dyadic similarity was the age of the referenced constitution: more recent constitutions were considerably more similar to the UDHR than were those drafted in earlier eras. We found, for example, that the constitutions of Haiti (1946) and Iceland (1944) were most similar to the UDHR of all those in our sample. The UDHR, we concluded, was very much a product of its time.

Reflective versus Formative Events

We can characterize our earlier findings as being consistent with a view of the UDHR as both *reflective* and *formative*. Our approach was a macro-constitutional one, which leveraged original data resources (see below). In that analysis, the UDHR seemed *reflective* to the extent that its rights matched those of then-recently-drafted constitutions, such as the French charter of 1946. It seemed *formative* to the extent that its rights matched those of subsequent constitutions. These findings conformed to our (and probably most others') theoretical intuitions.[4] Our very strong hunch is that the UDHR, and its follow-up covenants, have served as an important coordinating mechanism for future constitution makers who have multiple instrumental and functional reasons for harmonizing their document with something as legitimate and authoritative as the UDHR (see Elkins 2009).

However, a very reasonable source of skepticism remains, one that was central to a recent and astute consideration of our conclusions (Roberts 2013). Simply stated, we cannot fully refute the idea that the creation of the UDHR, and its subsequent legal covenants, was merely the articulation of prevailing trends in the post-World War II era—trends that also happen to be taken up in post-World War II constitutions. "Merely" in the prior sentence suggests that a reflective event *can* also be formative. Indeed, one might think that mirrors of conventional wisdom can be especially influential *because* they represent conventional wisdom. What we are saying, to be precise, is that we cannot determine in that analysis whether the UDHR happens only to *share* the ideas of subsequent constitutions or whether it has helped to inspire such ideas. Reflective events can also be formative events, but they are not necessarily so. Our ongoing research task is to untangle these two phenomena.

Conceptual Challenges to Analyzing Rights (A Short Digression)

The analysis below is based on a set of 116 rights found in a nearly complete set of national constitutions and human rights documents written since 1789. We digress briefly here to clarify several details of our empirical approach. Our focuses on written constitutional texts, for reasons that we elaborate in our earlier work (e.g., Ginsburg, et al. 2009). Our conceptualization of "constitutions" distinguishes between what we call the constitution-as-function and the constitution-as-form. Constitutions are assumed to play certain functions, such as defining government institutions, limiting government, or expressing the fundamental values of a people (Breslin 2009). No doubt there are many others we could list, but however we define the functions of constitutions, we must recognize that other things can play identical roles, including unwritten norms, legal decisions, statutes, government statements, international treaties, and popular understandings. The formal constitution is only a part of the broader constitutional order.

Our definition of a formal constitution is fairly straightforward. For the vast majority of states, we use the formal or nominal constitution in place; for the small number of states that do *not* have a formal constitution in a single document, we use statutes that create a branch of government, or articulate a bill of rights. Thus we would include, in the present exercise, the Human Rights Act of the United Kingdom in 1998 or the New Zealand Bill of Rights Act, because these countries do not have single codified constitutions. We do not, however, include statutory rights. Our intention is to limit analysis to the "highest" (most foundational and most entrenched) set of norms in the land.

This draws on the authors' data regarding the content of the world's constitutions—as thus conceptualized—a project that involves some observational and interpretive challenges. We have described our process of data collection in various places and various ways. Here follows another summary. At the root of our project is a conceptual inventory of constitutional topics and provisions. Using this inventory, in the form of survey questions, two trained coders code each constitution and their answers are then compared and reconciled. In the event of any disagreement, a third person reviews the answers. One of the methodological challenges that we face is that constitutional texts are not self-interpreting. Judgment is required to ensure that two constitutions are, in fact, talking about the same thing. Consider, for example, the right to silence. Brazil's Constitution of 1988 (Art. 63) provides that the accused has a right to remain silent, as well as many other criminal procedure protections. But what about the 1858 Constitution of Nicaragua, which liberally provides that the accused "may not be compelled to answer if he refuses to do so; but his silence is presumptive evidence against him"? Is there a right to silence or not? The Brazilian language says nothing about the effect of remaining silent; the Nicaraguan language provides a right, but then disincentivizes its invocation. These are not equivalent though both can be considered a species of the same right. Also, rights are often nested in others. For example, a right to personal autonomy might be seen as prohibiting torture and censorship. The right to dignity is one of the most encompassing constitutional protections, and could imply any number of more specific rights.

Our effort has proceeded on the assumption that a rigorous coding protocol can minimize the measurement error introduced through interpretive ambiguity, but we have certainly not resolved every ambiguous case. There are challenges inherent in any ontology that structures data for interpretation (Noy and McGuinness 2001). At a certain level of abstraction, things may look very similar; move the microscope a bit closer and differences become apparent. The level of generality problem is, alas, a general one in philosophy, science, and law (Samaha 2013). We have been self-conscious about the comparability/equivalence of our measures and concepts (Melton, et al. 2013; Elkins 2013), but there is no doubt that our view of an equivalence class will not always be the same as that of another.

In many ways, our own effort has sensitized us to the challenges faced by constitutional courts when they are called on to interpret constitutional texts. Texts are difficult to interpret and meanings can change over time. In other cases, constitutional interpreters may bootstrap new meanings into old rights. This will obviate the felt need for textual updating. We lack comprehensive local knowledge for the more than 800 constitutional systems[5] in our database, and so are, by necessity, forced to adopt what would be called a "textual" theory of constitutional interpretation: we rely on the plain language of the text. It is surely true that the same textual language is understood locally in quite different ways in different countries, so at some level there is no "plain" language comparable across context. We recognize that rights might simply replicate a general feature of communities of discourse, which is that they can be "rhetorical achievements," in which different actors use similar expressions without actually meaning similar things (Bomhoff 2008). But similar expressions are, for our pragmatic and limited purposes, good enough to categorize different texts similarly. Two communities can express themselves similarly and mean two different things, but we believe that it is meaningful that they have expressed themselves similarly. Surely a lesser level of abstraction or generality would be appropriate for different scholarly purposes.

The Growth and Spread of Rights: UDHR in Historical Perspective

As an initial matter, it is worth noting that there has been a general expansion in the number and type of rights claims over the past two centuries. Law and Versteeg (2011) call this "rights creep" and in other writing we used the concept of a "one-way ratchet" (Elkins, Ginsburg, and Simmons 2013), to suggest the additional idea of the trend's seeming irreversibility. We view this proliferation, in part, as a process of disaggregation, whereby a relatively small number of core interests (beginning with the iconic life, liberty, and estate) are gradually distinguished through a political process of claiming and evolution. The proliferation is captured, in part, by the mean number of rights from our list of 116 found in national constitutions over time (Figure 14.1).

We can think of this disaggregation and proliferation of rights as the narrowing of the "intension" (meaning) of rights claims and the expansion in the "extension" (application) of "root rights" to disparate domains of human activity. One sees some of this disaggregation and proliferation in recent innovations, such as the right to food,[6] the right to form political parties based on indigenous status,[7] and a proposed right of internet usage.[8] The Constitution of Ecuador (2008) gained international attention for extending rights to nature herself. These rights may also be evolving with respect to exactly how they are expressed (i.e, the particular turn-of-phrase), but we leave that aside for the moment.

As we show elsewhere, the emergence of new rights-claims is part of a staggered process in which particular periods are associated with greater innovation.[9] The post-World War II period, one would expect, would be just such a moment of innovation. It also seems likely that it would be a moment of norm crystallization. Consider each of these ideas.

Norm Crystallization (Rights Concentration)

Norm crystallization has to do with the degree to which countries converge on the set of rights that are at the core. Mathematically, it has to do with the distribution of each of these rights across constitutions: whether they are concentrated or dispersed. We might consider a right "mainstreamed" in the international

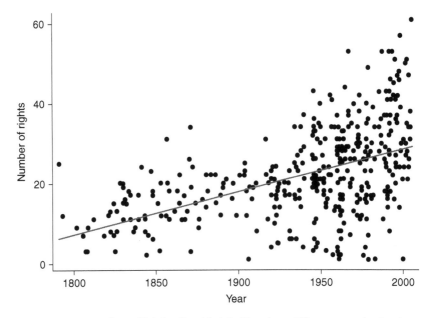

FIGURE 14.1   Number of Rights Provided, by Year (n = 680 new constitutions)

community if it is constitutionalized by at least half of the constitutions in force in a given year.[10] In our writing, we refer to these rights, variously, as "mainstream," "consensual," or "core" rights and the hypothetical constitution that contains all of them (and only them) as the "vanilla" or "median" constitution, an important reference point that we identify in each year under analysis. The number of rights in the vanilla constitution changes dramatically between 1800 and 2010. The only core right in 1810 is freedom of press, but by 2010, forty-six rights had made it over the majority threshold.

Innovation (Rights Proliferation)

Tracking the number of core rights tells us something about the number of "must-have" elements: namely, we learn that there is a growing consensus about a growing number of rights. But this accounting of core rights does not tell us much about the overall population of rights. For example, mathematically, it is possible for the number of core rights to increase while the overall population of rights remains constant. But of course, as we suggest above, there has been considerable innovation and corresponding growth in the overall population of rights. One indicator of this growth is the average number of rights in the world's constitutions, by year. Like the number of core rights, the average number of rights has dramatically increased over the last 200 years, from roughly ten in 1800 to about forty-eight in 2010.

The UDHR and the Concentration and Proliferation of Rights

These trends correspond to our general intuition about the historical proliferation of, and convergence on, rights. How, exactly, do these trends relate to the UDHR? In particular, we wonder whether the UDHR is coincident with a shift in these two trends. We therefore fit a change-point model over the trend lines in concentration and proliferation. A non-parametric change model, like the one we use here, usefully identifies structural breaks, or shifts, in a time series (see Western and Kleykamp 2004). Scholars of human rights often periodize rights evolution in terms of rights "generations." Our data confirms four distinct generations of rights, at least in terms of their concentration and creation. With respect to rights concentration, the first generation spans 1800 to 1867 and is associated with consensus on about eight rights. The second occurred between 1868 and 1962 and is associated with consensus on about fifteen rights. The third occurred between 1963 and 1989 and is associated with consensus on about nineteen rights. The fourth occurred between 1990 and 2010 and is associated with consensus on about thirty-eight rights. In terms of rights proliferation, the periodization is similar. One difference is that the third generation begins slightly earlier—in the years immediately following World War II. The UDHR (introduced in December 1948), is therefore in the "neighborhood" of dramatic shifts in the concentration and proliferation of rights in constitutions. We see this as further evidence of the coincidence of the UDHR with a changing rights landscape. Whether the UDHR was primarily responsible for this new landscape is another question.

Projection of the UDHR onto Subsequent Constitutions

What do we know about the degree to which the UDHR shares content with subsequent constitutions? One bit of evidence for the *projection* effect is simply to look at constitutional references to the Universal Declaration. Of constitutions in force in independent states today, forty (more than 20%) mention the UDHR in the text. Some of these references are symbolic and appear in the preamble (n=23): for example, Afghanistan's Constitution refers to it as "Observing the United Nations Charter as well as the Universal Declaration of Human Rights." Others bind the state to observing the Universal Declaration, essentially turning a non-legal document into a legal one (Constitution of Andorra 1993, Art. 5).

A recent paper (Elkins, Ginsburg, and Simmons 2013) analyzed the projection of the UDHR on the content of subsequent constitutions. In that analysis, we also trace these effects all the way to the enforcement of rights on the ground, through some presumed legal channels: i.e., from Declaration, to Covenant, to Constitution, and to the respect (or non-respect) for rights in a given country.

The data we analyzed in that article suggested some very strong projection effects. We found that the number of rights increased dramatically following 1948, as did the similarity of constitutions' rights choices to the set included in the

UDHR. Our analysis found that a right's inclusion in the UDHR increased the probability of its inclusion in a subsequent constitution by 50 percent. The analysis controlled for the baseline popularity of the right, as measured by its inclusion in constitutions in force in 1948 as well as the age of the right.

However, we could not tie these effects *directly* to the UDHR, or at least directly *enough*. The theory supporting a UDHR role is compelling. Does anyone really dispute the *idea* that the UDHR could serve as an important coordinating device for drafters struggling to produce—under a deadline—universal principles that would endure for generations? Indeed, in some cases of constitutional design, the use of the UDHR by drafters can probably be documented easily enough. Nevertheless, as important as the Declaration was (and is), the post-war era was a dynamic and interesting era. Conversations about human rights abounded in universities, legislatures, radio shows, and dining rooms all over the world. New, modern rights could just as easily have come from any number of sources as well as the UDHR. We also know that these new rights were enshrined in contemporary constitutions (e.g., France 1946), which may have been just as important in disseminating ideas as was the UDHR.

Still, we suspect that the document is not *just* a reflection of contemporary ideas about rights. The drafting of constitutional documents—like any collective writing project—is a sprawling, chaotic, and sometimes idiosyncratic process. The UDHR was no exception. Indeed, one could not imagine a broader and more diverse constituency than that of the world's recognized states. Collectively written documents, as any co-author knows, can often amount to more than the aggregated opinion of its authors. The analyst's research agenda, then, should be to find elements of the process that were unique to the crafting of the UDHR and that led to particular, identifiable outcomes. These could be elements of the process that suggested a discretionary, contingent affair. Ideally, these would be simple twists of fate that tipped the balance towards a particular right, or a particular expression of a right. These twists are our instruments—the accidental moments—with which we intend to trace the signature effect of the UDHR. If we can follow the effect of these accidents on the UDHR and through to subsequent constitutions, then we can be more confident of the document's effect.

Conclusion: What Would Constitutions Look Like Today Without the UDHR?

The Universal Declaration was an inspired project, understandably embraced by many in the wake of a war fought and won for human rights. The document was not inevitable, though it may seem that way now precisely because it has been so successful. The agenda of international organizations is littered with big (and small) ideas that have never materialized. The agreement upon a set of "universal" rights by a set of countries with vastly different cultural and economic endowments, not to mention competing political and ideological programs, seems almost heroic from this perspective. Indeed, the UDHR had its skeptics at the time. Morsink opens his book with a letter from the American Anthropology Association, most of whose members apparently saw the task as both ill advised and fraught with epistemological challenges (AAA 1947). Presumably, there were others who were equally unenthusiastic about the idea. Clearly, some member countries were wary. We can draw again from Morsink (2000: 2), who reminds us that the Soviets had only supported the UN itself after Stalin and western powers had brokered a deal in which two constituent republics were admitted as UN members. If mixed feelings hadn't doomed the project, then procedural constraints might have done so. The United Nations is an organization that moves only with deliberate and consensual steps. Serious objections from a member of the Security Council on a bill of rights would have meant an uphill battle, if not a wall. So, how would the world's constitutions look if the UDHR had not, in fact, been declared?

Our sense is that subsequent national constitutions—the principle legal device for enforcing rights—would be different. They might have fewer rights, a smaller core of consensual rights, and—outside the core—a different cast of elective rights. Whether or not it would be possible to estimate differences in societal outcomes—something perhaps more meaningful than the effect on text—is unclear. But for those of us that are persuaded that written constitutions can serve as important devices for constraining and inducing state action, effects on the written word may be enough.

We close with a reflection on the Constitution of the United States. We are not surprised by its lack of congruence with the Universal Declaration, since the US Constitution was drafted in an earlier era in which the emphasis was on negative rights rather than positive governmental obligations. It is also the case that the US Government has traditionally been skeptical about promoting economic and social rights at the international level. Yet it would not be accurate to say that positive rights are lacking in the United States. As Emily Zackin (2013) has pointed out in an important recent contribution, American state constitutions are often full of positive social and economic rights, and these are sometimes adjudicated before state courts. State constitutions are frequently redrafted and so are likely to be younger than that of the country as a whole (Ginsburg and Posner 2010). Perhaps, in line with our analysis, these constitutions reflect the dominant ideas of their era—including the ideas enshrined in the Universal Declaration.

Notes

1 The authors gratefully acknowledge Christopher Roberts, Fabrizio Gilardi, Judith Blau, Louis Esparza, and Keri Iyall Smith, and participants at conferences in Austin, TX, Iowa City, IA, and Belo Horizonte, Brazil. We thank the National Science Foundation, the Cline Center for Democracy, the University of Texas, and the University of Chicago for their early and continued investment.

2 The initial proposals from national governments included those from Chile, Cuba, Panama, India, and the US. The Constitutions considered were largely from Europe and Latin America. Four socialist constitutions were included (Byelorussia, Ukraine, USSR, and Yugoslavia). Only five from Asia were included (Afghanistan, China, India,

Philippines, and Siam (Thailand)), five from the Mideast (Iran, Iraq, Lebanon, Saudi Arabia, and Syria) and four from Africa (Egypt, Ethiopia, Liberia, and South Africa). See Schabas 2013: lxxxix. Morsink (2000:10) lists several other governments that made later proposals, and notes that the nongovernmental input also had an influence.

3 Note that some the "second generation" rights, such as a right to education, had been instantiated in national constitutions since the latter part of the nineteenth century, and are associated with the rise of the welfare state.

4 The evolution of human rights is, of course, more nuanced than this, as Samuel Moyn's (2012) work shows. We view any effect of the UDHR on written constitutions as consistent with Moyn's ideas.

5 "Systems" refer to constitutions and their amendments. Replacements of a constitution, defined as a revision that does not use the instituted amendment procedure, inaugurate a new system. So, the US Constitution, and its amendments, constitute one system, which replaced the Articles of Confederation system.

6 Found, in part, in Bolivia, Brazil, Ecuador, Guyana, Haiti, Kenya, and South Africa.

7 Bolivia 2009.

8 Iceland's failed 2012 draft.

9 Innovation and Diffusion in Constitutional Rights, manuscript.

10 A majority is a somewhat arbitrary threshold, though it has a certain democratic resonance. Still we would see the same basic trend (a steady increase) if we adopt more or less consensual thresholds.

References

American Anthropological Association. 1947. "Statement on Human Rights." *American Anthropologist* 49(4): 539–543.

Bomhoff, Jacco. 2008. "Balancing the Global and the Local: Judicial Balancing as a Problematic Topic in Comparative (Constitutional) Law." *Hastings International and Comparative Law Review* 31(2): 555–588.

Breslin, Beau. 2009. *From Words to Worlds: Exploring Constitutional Functionality*. Baltimore, MD: Johns Hopkins University Press.

Elkins, Zachary. 2009. "Constitutional Networks," in *Networked Politics: Agency, Power, and Governance*, Miles Kahler (ed.): 43–63. Ithaca, NY: Cornell University Press.

Elkins, Zachary. 2013. "Comparability and the Analysis of National Constitutions." *APSA-CP Newsletter* 23(1): 7–9.

Elkins, Zachary, Tom Ginsburg, and Beth Simmons. 2013. "Getting to Rights: Treaty Ratification, Constitutional Convergence, and Human Rights Practice." *Harvard International Law Journal* 54(1): 61–95.

Elkins, Zachary, James Melton, Tom Ginsburg, and Kalev Leetaru. 2012. "On the Interpretability of Law: Lessons from the Decoding of National Constitutions." *British Journal of Political Science* 43(2): 399–423.

Fariss, Christopher J. 2014. "Respect for Human Rights Has Improved Over Time: Modeling the Changing Standard of Accountability." *American Political Science Review* 108(2): 297–314.

Ginsburg, Tom and Eric Posner. 2010. "Subconstitutionalism." *Stanford Law Review* 58: 1583–1631.

Ginsburg, Tom, Zachary Elkins, and Justin Blount. 2009. "Does the Process of Constitution-Making Matter?" *Annual Review of Law and Social Science* 5: 201–223.

Henkin, Louis. 1990. *The Age of Rights*. New York: Columbia University Press.

Hill, Daniel W. 2010. "Estimating the Effects of Human Rights Treaties on State Behavior." *Journal of Politics* 72: 1161–1174.

Ishay, Michelle. 2004. *The History of Human Rights*. Berkeley: University of California Press.

Law, David S. and Mila Versteeg. 2011. "The Evolution and Ideology of Global Constitutionalism." *California Law Review* 99(5): 1163–1258. http://scholarship.law.berkeley.edu/californialawreview/vol99/iss5/1 (last accessed October 11, 2016).

Lupu, Yonathan. 2015. "Legislative Veto Players and the Effects of International Human Rights Agreements." *American Journal of Political Science* 59(3): 578–594.

Melton, James, Zachary Elkins, Tom Ginsburg, and Kalev Leetaru. 2013. "On the Interpretability of Law: Lessons from the Decoding of National Constitutions." *British Journal of Political Science* 43(2): 399–423.

Morsink, Johannes. 2000. *The Universal Declaration of Human Rights: Origins, Drafting and Intent*. Philadelphia, PA: University of Pennsylvania Press.

Moyn, Samuel. 2010. *The Last Utopia*. Cambridge: Harvard University Press.

Moyn, Samuel. 2012. "Substance, Scale, and Salience: The Recent Historiography of Human Rights." *Annual Review of Law and Social Science* 8: 123–140.

Neumayer, Eric. 2005. "Do International Human Rights Treaties Improve Respect for Human Rights?" *Journal of Conflict Resolution* 49(6): 925–953.

Noy, Natalya F. and Deborah L. McGuinness. 2001. "Ontology Development 101: A Guide To Creating Your First Ontology." Technical report, KSL-01-05, Stanford Knowledge Systems Laboratory. http://protege.stanford.edu/publications/ontology_development/ontology101.pdf (last accessed October 11, 2016).

Posner, Eric. 2014. *The Twilight of Human Rights Law*. Oxford: Oxford University Press.

Powell, Emilia Justyna and Jeffrey K. Staton. 2009. "Domestic Judicial Institutions and Human Rights Treaty Violation." *International Studies Quarterly* 53(1): 149–174.

Roberts, Christopher. 2013. "Convergence, Reaction, and Translation: Human Rights in History." *Harvard International Law Journal: Volume 54(1) Symposium*.

Roberts, Christopher. 2014. *The Contentious History of the International Bill of Rights*. New York: Cambridge University Press.

Samaha, Adam M. 2013. "Levels of Generality, Constitutional Comedy, and Legal Design." *University of Illinois Law Review* 5: 1733–1774.

Schabas, William A. 2013. *The Universal Declaration of Human Rights: The Travaux Préparatoires*, 3rd ed. Cambridge, UK: Cambridge University Press.

Simmons, Beth A. 2009. *Mobilizing for Human Rights: International Law in Domestic Politics*. New York, NY: Cambridge University Press.

Waltz, Susan. 2001. "Universalizing Human Rights: The Role of Small States in the Construction of the Universal Declaration of Human Rights." *Human Rights Quarterly* 23(1): 44–72.

Waltz, Susan. 2002. "Reclaiming and Rebuilding the History of the Universal Declaration of Human Rights." *Third World Quarterly* 23(3): 437–448.

Western, Bruce and Meredith Kleykamp. 2004. "A Bayesian Change Point Model for Historical Time Series Analysis." *Political Analysis* 12(4): 354–374.

Zackin, Emily. 2013. *Looking for Rights in All the Wrong Places: Why State Constitutions Contain America's Positive Rights*. Princeton: Princeton University Press.

15

REWRITE FOR RIGHTS

Creating a Modern Constitution

Judith R. Blau

The year 2016 was calamitous. Just halfway into the year, the UN Refugee Agency announced that the number of people displaced by war, conflict or persecution had reached an all-time record high. On average 42,500 people fled their homes *each day* to seek protection in their own or another country. Besides that, despite the optimism at the beginning of the year, there was no sign by June or July that ISIS (Daesh) was in retreat. Oxfam International reported in 2016 that world inequality had never been so extreme and specifically that sixty-two people owned the same as half the world's population. Economists and the World Economic Forum made similar estimates. Conflict between Palestine and the Gaza Strip, on the one hand, and Israel, on the other, worsened, and instability in the entire Middle East grew worse. Yet as horrific as all of these were, and continue to be, global warming poses the most serious long-term threat to the entire world. According to predictions, icecaps will melt, small island states will become submerged, many species will become extinct, and deserts will be too hot to be habitable.

One needs to ask, how will the US fare through the rest of this century and beyond? Is its founding legal and political framework—very specifically, the Bill of Rights—robust enough to ensure the kind of solidarity—among Americans and between the US and other countries—that is necessary to adapt to these conditions and to shape the best future possible? What consequences might we face without institutional support and social solidarity?

Two things need to be stressed in this regard. First, the articles of the Bill of Rights only pertain to individual rights *vis-à-vis* the state. That is to say, it protects "my right to speech;" "my right to own a gun;" "my right to vote;" and so forth. Each American has the same rights, but each of us enjoys these rights independently of other Americans. For this reason, the 1791 Bill of Rights has long been regarded as a document that sets standards for individual freedom and liberty (not security, society or nationhood, and not solidarity). It addresses key political issues laid out after the war of independence against Britain, and by highlighting individual rights, lays down the basic building block of capitalism.

Second, much later, in 1948, a new paradigm emerged with the recognition of the rights of security. The Universal Declaration of Human Rights (UDHR) encompasses civil and political rights in the first twenty articles and addresses rights of security (that are essential for society or nationhood and solidarity) in Articles 21 through 30. With independence, in the later decades of the twentieth century, most new nations incorporated much or all of the UDHR's provisions into their constitutions, and older countries revised their constitutions to include human rights. Besides, human rights are incorporated into the charters of the European Union, the African Union, the Organization of American States, and international human rights treaties. The United States does not unconditionally ratify any human rights treaty (either the ones of the Organization of American States, of which it is a member, or international ones).

One can only speculate why the US does not ratify human rights treaties since this has been the case over many administrations, and both when Democrats and Republicans were in power. Our best guess is that we, as a nation, have been wedded to the idea that we are "exceptional" because of our belief in the supremacy of individual freedom and liberty. This paradigm began to unravel in World War II when cooperation among allies was imperative, and further so with globalization, which leaves so many people vulnerable. Most country constitutions highlight the importance of security and solidarity, which are the two prominent themes of the UDHR. It is important to stress that practically every article of the UDHR begins with the pronoun, *everyone*.

We strongly advocate that the US join the rest of the world and recognize the great importance of human security and solidarity. Of course these are aspirational but so was freedom and liberty.

Appendix 1
BILL OF RIGHTS AND SUBSEQUENT AMENDMENTS (ABBREVIATED)

Amendments I through X, ratified in 1791

Amendment I

Congress shall make no law respecting an establishment of religion, or prohibiting the free exercise thereof; or abridging the freedom of speech, or of the press; or the right of the people peaceably to assemble, and to petition the Government for a redress of grievances.

Amendment II

A well-regulated Militia, being necessary to the security of a free State, the right of the people to keep and bear Arms, shall not be infringed.

Amendment III

No Soldier shall, in time of peace be quartered in any house, without the consent of the Owner, nor in time of war, but in a manner to be prescribed by law.

Amendment IV

The right of the people to be secure in their persons, houses, papers, and effects, against unreasonable searches and seizures, shall not be violated, and no Warrants shall issue, but upon probable cause, supported by Oath or affirmation, and particularly describing the place to be searched, and the persons or things to be seized.

Amendment V

No person shall be held to answer for a capital, or otherwise infamous crime, unless on a presentment or indictment of a Grand Jury, except in cases arising in the land or naval forces, or in the Militia, when in actual service in time of War or public danger; nor shall any person be subject for the same offence to be twice put in jeopardy of life or limb; nor shall be compelled in any criminal case to be a witness against himself, nor be deprived of life, liberty, or property, without due process of law; nor shall private property be taken for public use, without just compensation.

Amendment VI

In all criminal prosecutions, the accused shall enjoy the right to a speedy and public trial, by an impartial jury of the State and district wherein the crime shall have been committed, which district shall have been previously ascertained by law, and to be informed of the nature and cause of the accusation; to be confronted with the witnesses against him; to have compulsory process for obtaining witnesses in his favor, and to have the Assistance of Counsel for his defense.

Amendment VII

In suits at common law, where the value in controversy shall exceed twenty dollars, the right of trial by jury shall be preserved, and no fact tried by a jury, shall be otherwise reexamined in any Court of the United States, than according to the rules of the common law.

Amendment VIII

Excessive bail shall not be required, nor excessive fines imposed, nor cruel and unusual punishments inflicted.

Amendment IX

The enumeration in the Constitution, of certain rights, shall not be construed to deny or disparage others retained by the people.

Amendment X

The powers not delegated to the United States by the Constitution, nor prohibited by it to the States, are reserved to the States respectively, or to the people.

Changes and Additions

Amendment XI (1795)

The Judicial power of the United States shall not be construed to extend to any suit in law or equity, commenced or prosecuted against one of the United States by Citizens of another State, or by Citizens or Subjects of any Foreign State.

Amendment XII (1804)

The Electors shall meet in their respective states and vote by ballot for President and Vice-President, one of whom, at least, shall not be an inhabitant of the same state with themselves.

Amendment XIII (1865)

SECTION. 1. Neither slavery nor involuntary servitude, except as a punishment for crime whereof the party shall have been duly convicted, shall exist within the United States, or any place subject to their jurisdiction.

Amendment XIV (1868)

SECTION. 1. All persons born or naturalized in the United States, and subject to the jurisdiction thereof, are citizens of the United States and of the State wherein they reside. No State shall make or enforce any law which shall abridge the privileges or immunities of citizens of the United States; nor shall any State deprive any person of life, liberty, or property, without due process of law; nor deny to any person within its jurisdiction the equal protection of the laws.

Amendment XV (1870)

SECTION. 1. The right of citizens of the United States to vote shall not be denied or abridged by the United States or by any State on account of race, color, or previous condition of servitude.

Amendment XVI (1913)

The Congress shall have power to lay and collect taxes on incomes, from whatever source derived, without apportionment among the several States, and without regard to any census or enumeration.

Amendment XVII (1913)

The Senate of the United States shall be composed of two Senators from each State, elected by the people thereof, for six years; and each Senator shall have one vote. The electors in each State shall have the qualifications requisite for electors of the most numerous branch of the State legislatures.

Amendment XVIII (1919)

SECTION. 1. After one year from the ratification of this article the manufacture, sale, or transportation of intoxicating liquors within, the importation thereof into, or the exportation thereof from the United States and all territory subject to the jurisdiction thereof for beverage purposes is hereby prohibited.

Amendment XIX (1920)

The right of citizens of the United States to vote shall not be denied or abridged by the United States or by any State on account of sex.

Amendment XX (1933)

SECTION. 1. The terms of the President and the Vice President shall end at noon on the 20th day of January, and the terms of Senators and Representatives at noon on the 3rd day of January, of the years in which such terms would have ended if this article had not been ratified; and the terms of their successors shall then begin.

Amendment XXI (1933)

SECTION. 1. The eighteenth article of amendment to the Constitution of the United States is hereby repealed.

Amendment XXII (1951)

SECTION. 1. No person shall be elected to the office of the President more than twice, and no person who has held the office of President, or acted as President, for more than two years of a term to which some other person was elected President shall be elected to the office of President more than once.

Amendment XXIII (1961)

SECTION. 1. The District constituting the seat of Government of the United States shall appoint in such manner as Congress may direct:

A number of electors of President and Vice President equal to the whole number of Senators and Representatives in Congress to which the District would be entitled if it were a State.

Amendment XXIV (1964)

SECTION. 1. The right of citizens of the United States to vote in any primary or other election for President or Vice President, for electors for President or Vice President, or for Senator or Representative in Congress, shall not be denied or abridged by the United States or any State by reason of failure to pay poll tax or other tax.

Amendment XXV (1967)

SECTION. 1. In case of the removal of the President from office or of his death or resignation, the Vice President shall become President.

Amendment XXVI (1971)

SECTION. 1. The right of citizens of the United States, who are eighteen years of age or older, to vote shall not be denied or abridged by the United States or by any State on account of age.

Amendment XXVII (1992)

No law, varying the compensation for the services of the Senators and Representatives, shall take effect, until an election of representatives shall have intervened.

Source: National Constitution Center: http://constitutioncenter.org/constitution/the-amendments

Appendix 2

UNIVERSAL DECLARATION OF HUMAN RIGHTS: ADOPTED AND PROCLAIMED BY GENERAL ASSEMBLY RESOLUTION 217 A (III) OF 10 DECEMBER 1948 (EXTRACTS)

Preamble

Whereas recognition of the inherent dignity and of the equal and inalienable rights of all members of the human family is the foundation of freedom, justice and peace in the world,

Whereas disregard and contempt for human rights have resulted in barbarous acts which have outraged the conscience of mankind, and the advent of a world in which human beings shall enjoy freedom of speech and belief and freedom from fear and want has been proclaimed as the highest aspiration of the common people,

Whereas it is essential, if man is not to be compelled to have recourse, as a last resort, to rebellion against tyranny and oppression, that human rights should be protected by the rule of law,

Whereas it is essential to promote the development of friendly relations between nations,

THE GENERAL ASSEMBLY proclaims THIS UNIVERSAL DECLARATION OF HUMAN RIGHTS as a common standard of achievement for all peoples and all nations.

Article 1. All human beings are born free and equal in dignity and rights. They are endowed with reason and conscience and should act towards one another in a spirit of brotherhood.

Article 2. Everyone is entitled to all the rights and freedoms set forth in this Declaration, without distinction of any kind, such as race, colour, sex, language, religion, political or other opinion, national or social origin, property, birth or other status.

Article 3. Everyone has the right to life, liberty and security of person.

Article 4. No one shall be held in slavery or servitude; slavery and the slave trade shall be prohibited in all their forms.

Article 5. No one shall be subjected to torture or to cruel, inhuman or degrading treatment or punishment.

Article 6. Everyone has the right to recognition everywhere as a person before the law.

Article 7. All are equal before the law and are entitled without any discrimination to equal protection of the law.

Article 8. Everyone has the right to an effective remedy by the competent national tribunals for acts violating the fundamental rights granted him by the constitution or by law.

Article 9. No one shall be subjected to arbitrary arrest, detention or exile.

Article 10. Everyone is entitled in full equality to a fair and public hearing by an independent and impartial tribunal, in the determination of his rights and obligations and of any criminal charge against him.

Article 11. (1) Everyone charged with a penal offence has the right to be presumed innocent until proved guilty; (2) No one shall be held guilty of any penal offence on account of any act or omission which did not constitute a penal offence, under national or international law, at the time when it was committed.

Article 12. No one shall be subjected to arbitrary interference with his privacy, family, home or correspondence, nor to attacks upon his honour and reputation.

Article 13. (1) Everyone has the right to freedom of movement and residence within the borders of each state; (2) Everyone has the right to leave any country, including his own, and to return to his country.

Article 14. Everyone has the right to seek and to enjoy in other countries asylum from persecution.

Article 15. Everyone has the right to a nationality.

Article 16. (1) Men and women of full age, without any limitation due to race, nationality or religion, have the right to marry and to found a family. They are entitled to equal rights as to marriage, during marriage and at its dissolution; (2) Marriage shall be entered into only with the free and full consent of the intending spouses; (3) The family is the natural and fundamental group unit of society and is entitled to protection by society and the State.

Article 17. Everyone has the right to own property alone as well as in association with others.

Article 18. Everyone has the right to freedom of thought, conscience and religion; this right includes freedom to change his religion or belief, and freedom, either alone or in community with others and in public or private, to manifest his religion or belief in teaching, practice, worship and observance.

Article 19. Everyone has the right to freedom of opinion and expression; this right includes freedom to hold opinions without interference and to seek, receive and impart information and ideas through any media and regardless of frontiers.

Article 20. Everyone has the right to freedom of peaceful assembly and association.

Article 21. (1) Everyone has the right to take part in the government of his country, directly or through freely chosen representatives; (2) Everyone has the right of equal access to public service in his country; (3) The will of the people shall be the basis of the authority of government; this will shall be expressed in periodic and genuine elections which shall be by universal and equal suffrage.

Article 22. Everyone, as a member of society, has the right to social security and is entitled to realization, through national effort and international co-operation and in accordance with the organization and resources of each State.

Article 23. (1) Everyone has the right to work, to free choice of employment, to just and favourable conditions of work and to protection against unemployment; (2) Everyone, without any discrimination, has the right to equal pay for equal work; (3) Everyone who works has the right to just and favourable remuneration ensuring for himself and his family an existence worthy of human dignity, and supplemented, if necessary, by other means of social protection; (4) Everyone has the right to form and to join trade unions for the protection of his interests.

Article 24. Everyone has the right to rest and leisure, including reasonable limitation of working hours and periodic holidays with pay.

Article 25. (1) Everyone has the right to a standard of living adequate for the health and well-being of himself and of his family, including food, clothing, housing and medical care and necessary social services, and the right to security in the event of unemployment, sickness, disability, widowhood, old age or other lack of livelihood in circumstances beyond his control; (2) Motherhood and childhood are entitled to special care and assistance. All children, whether born in or out of wedlock, shall enjoy the same social protection.

Article 26. (1) Everyone has the right to education. Education shall be free, at least in the elementary and fundamental stages. Elementary education shall be compulsory. Technical and professional education shall be made generally available, and higher education shall be equally accessible to all on the basis of merit; (2) Education shall be directed to the full development of the human personality.

Article 27. (1) Everyone has the right freely to participate in the cultural life of the community, to enjoy the arts and to share in scientific advancement and its benefits.

Article 28. Everyone is entitled to a social and international order in which the rights and freedoms set forth in this Declaration can be fully realized.

Article 29. (1) Everyone has duties to the community in which alone the free and full development of his personality is possible; (2) In the exercise of his rights and freedoms, everyone shall be subject only to such limitations as are determined by law solely for the purpose of securing due recognition and respect for the rights and freedoms of others and of meeting the just requirements of morality, public order and the general welfare in a democratic society.

Source: United Nations: www.unhchr.ch/udhr/lang/eng.htm

INDEX

Printed in Great Britain
by Amazon

84480966R00124